The Generation of Crisis

An Examination of the Last Days, Perilous Times, and the Converging Crises of the Twenty-First Century

By Jerry R. Duke

The Generation of Crisis
An Examination of the Last Days, Perilous Times,
and the Converging Crises of the Twenty-First Century
by Jerry R. Duke

Printed in the United States of America

ISBN 978-1-60791-479-2

www.xulonpress.com

ACKNOWLEDGEMENTS

Thank you, first to God, without whom I would never have been able to accomplish such a formidable task as that which was set before me. Secondly, to my wife Lisa whose love and support continually supplied me with the motivation needed to persevere.

CONTENTS

INTRODUCTION

A prudent man foreseeth the evil, and hideth himself: but the simple pass on, and are punished. (Proverbs 22:3)

Prophecy is one the most exciting studies of the Bible. The scripture from the book of Genesis to the ending pages of the Revelation are full of prophetic promises. In Genesis we find fundamental prophecies concerning the coming and purpose of Jesus Christ, to the more specific prophetic revelation to Abraham of the coming destruction of Sodom. Noah's revelation of the flood was prophetic just as was Enoch's message of coming judgment. The interpretation of Pharaoh's dream concerning a period of abundance which was to be followed by a time of severe famine was prophetic. A study of Genesis would show that it is filled with numerous examples of prophetic revelation and promises. A comprehensive study of prophecy would show that throughout the Bible this same pattern of revelation and promise is revealed. The Bible is a book of prophecies, and prophecy is the cornerstone of biblical authority. God chose prophecy not only to inform and enlighten concerning impending significant events, but also to establish the fact that his word is true and that he is in control of all events past, present, and future.

Other than salvation and the redemptive plan, no other study of the Bible is as important. In fact prophecy is so fundamental that no scriptural subject (including redemption) can be considered in depth without involving prophecy in some manner. The reason of course is that the eternal God cannot be limited by time. Time is a creative act of God who exists in eternity and is not limited by man's concept of time. When God speaks, he speaks of those things that are not as though they already were. When God thinks, he thinks in the realm of eternity with a complete knowledge of all things past, present, and future. I realize that this becomes pretty overwhelming to the human mind, but when one considers prophecy one must realize we are dealing with a spiritual realm that encompasses all eternity and cannot be limited by the physical element of time.

Prophecy is the instrument through which God informs people of events which are to occur in the future. We usually envision prophecy as the message of an Elijah or Jeremiah warning the wicked of impending judgment and encouraging them to repent. While this is truly one reason for prophetic revelation, this by no means is the only reason that prophecy is given. Prophecy has been used not only as a warning, but also to foretell magnificent and miraculous events such as the birth of Christ. Additionally, it has also specifically been used to provide insight into all manner of future events so that appropriate preparation for the coming event could be made.

All of these reasons provide the primary motivation for this book. I believe that this generation has more reason than any before it to believe that we are living in the last days. This of course is definitely a warning for those who are not prepared to meet God. But it is also a promise concerning the greatest and most magnificent revelation the world has ever seen. That is the second coming of Jesus Christ. While this coming brings thoughts of judgment to many, it is an event which signals the fulfillment of the redemption plan of God for Christians. But more than this, the warnings of the approach of the prophetic events associated with the second coming are meant to provide insight or a road map into the future so those that understand and believe might be prepared for those coming events.

Jesus told us in Luke chapter twenty-one that in the last days, as the end approached, men's hearts would fail them "for fear, and for looking after those things which are coming on the earth" (Luke 21:26). On the other hand, he told his followers that "when these things begin to come to pass, then look up, and lift up your heads; for your redemption draweth nigh" (Luke 21:28). In other words, the fulfillment of prophetic events will catch some completely unaware and their hearts will be filled with fear. But to those who have been forewarned of these coming events, they are to be prepared with the understanding that these signs are simply the precursor of the greatest redemptive event in history – the second coming of Jesus Christ. This is exactly how God intended his prophetic word to be used. It was to be not only a confirmation of his divine authority but also a means by which to prepare people for coming events. Preparation, watching, and readiness, have always been key factors in prophetic utterances.

In the book of Genesis we find that Noah was warned of the impending flood in order that he might prepare an ark for the saving of himself and his family. Abraham was informed beforehand of the coming judgment on Sodom and Gomorrah so that intercession could be made. Joseph was given the interpretation of Pharaoh's divinely inspired dreams of seven years of abundance and seven years of famine so that preparation could be made for the salvation of not only Egypt, but most importantly, his family.

This pattern of insight and preparation continues throughout the Bible. God warned the captive Israelites of his coming visitation on the night of the Passover so that they could be prepared by insuring that the blood of a sacrificial lamb had been placed on the doorposts. Moses the prophet told the Israelites in Exodus 12:23 that "when he seeth the blood upon the lintel, and upon the two side posts, the Lord will pass over the door, and will not suffer the destroyer to come in unto your houses to smite you." It was incumbent upon the Israelites to believe the prophetic message and make the appropriate preparations.

Prophetic insight is provided to the people of God so that they might prepare for those things that are to come. Preparation is an act of faith. Noah would not have built an ark in preparation for the flood if he had not believed what God had told him concerning the flood. Joseph and the King of Egypt would not have prepared for the famine if they had not believed what God had revealed to Joseph concerning Pharaoh's prophetic dream. Israel would not have prepared for the Passover if they had not believed the message delivered by Moses from God.

After Jesus' initial message concerning the signs of his coming and the end of the age in Matthew twenty-four, Jesus devoted the rest of the chapter and all of chapter twenty-five providing solemn warnings in which the fundamental message was to "watch" and be prepared. His warnings were continually filled with examples of the lack of preparation for those things which were to come. With an abundance of scriptural evidence supporting this fact, I cannot help but believe that prophetic revelation is provided so that people should not be caught unaware when momentous and prophetically significant events occur. This is one of the most important reasons for a thorough knowledge and understanding of prophecy. It is provided so that we may be prepared for events which will occur as the ultimate plan of God is fulfilled.

As we see the fulfillment of end-time prophecy being accomplished in our lifetime, I cannot help but believe that God intends for his church to be in tune with him as these events occur. The revelation of end-time events should not catch us unaware. The Church should be on the same mental frequency as God when significant end-time events unfold. While the world may be surprised and even filled with uncertainty and fear, the Church should neither be surprised nor fearful when these events occur. But more than simply having an insight and foreknowledge of future events, the Church should understand the context in which these events are taking place. Christ is the head of the Church and we are the body. The body cannot be separated from the head and should work in concert with the head. Prophecy is the means by which the head (Christ) communicates his eternal will and plan to the body. Through prophecy God reveals his plan of action prior to its execution. The body responds by doing what the head has instructed as far as preparation and action is concerned. They work in continuity and coordination.

I cannot help but believe that if the most significant event in prophetic history is about to occur on Planet Earth (the second coming of Jesus), then preparation for this event should have preeminence in what the Spirit is saying to the Church in this hour. If the events which precede the second coming of Jesus Christ are soon to manifest themselves on Planet Earth, I cannot help but believe that the Spirit is urgently attempting to prepare the body of Christ (and the world) for these occurrences. Not simply in some abstract manner but both physically and spiritually by the unification of our faith and our actions. I believe that Jesus is coming soon. Because I believe that Jesus is coming soon I realize that certain things must occur in this world in preparation for this great event. These things should not catch the Church unaware. We should have a special insight into these events and be anticipating their occurrence. This is essentially is the message which the Apostle Paul delivered to the church at Thessalonica:

> But of the times and the seasons, brethren, ye have no need that I write unto you. For yourselves know perfectly that the day of the Lord so cometh as a thief in the night. For when they shall say, Peace and safety; then sudden destruction cometh upon them, as travail upon a woman with child; and they shall not escape. But **ye, brethren, are not in darkness, that that day should overtake you as a thief.** Ye are all the children of light, and the children of the day: we are not of the night, nor of darkness. Therefore **let us not sleep, as do others; but let us watch** and be sober. For they that sleep, sleep in the night; and they that be drunken are drunken in the night. But let us, who are of the day, be sober, putting on the breastplate of faith and love; and for an helmet, the hope of salvation. For God hath not appointed us to wrath, but to obtain salvation by our Lord Jesus Christ. (I Thessalonians 5:1-9)

This special insight and foreknowledge, which God has provided us through his Word and Spirit, is given to us so that we might prepare. The prophetic events which are unfolding before our eyes should not come as a surprise. We are the children of the day and not of the night. These end-time events should not "overtake" us "as a thief." We should be well aware of the signs of the times and those things which are to occur in the very near future. This is the essence of the message of this book. Truly, it is meant to awaken those that are asleep to the nearness of the coming of Jesus Christ, but it is also written as a guide to help those that believe to prepare both physically and spiritually. I trust that it will be enlightening to the skeptic and an encouragement to the believer.

Chapter 1

A WORLD ON THE THRESHOLD

Human beings and the natural world are on a collision course with destiny. Biblical prophecy along with evidence from all disciplines of science indicates that the decline and end of civilization as we know it is in sight. The words of Jesus Christ and the prophets are even now being echoed not by doomsday extremists but by secular men of science and specialists in all fields. These experts intimate that there are numerous emerging and converging crises which will climax in the next few decades. Their research indicates that each one of these crises has the potential of ending civilization as we know it. One such writer notes that "in historical memory, the world has never faced such dangerous circumstances as it does early in the twenty-first century."[1]

Although every generation has had its share of end-time prognosticators, the fact remains that there is something significantly unusual occurring at this time. Throughout recorded history religious zealots and students of prophecy have continually pointed at specific events and unusual occurrences and attempted to attach some prophetic significance to them. But there is a unique difference taking place at this particular time. It is not only ministers and the so-called prophets of doom that are sounding the apocalyptic alarm, but now a significant number of secular men of science and experts in non-religious fields have taken up the warning cry. Countless articles, journals, and books written by authorities in various fields of science and research have documented evidence which warns of approaching catastrophes and crises which threaten human civilization. Although these specialists, writers, and men of science are secular in persuasion – and do not approach their respective subjects from a spiritual perspective – their message clearly echoes (albeit unintentionally) the end-time apocalyptic message of Jesus and the prophets.

The evidence presented by these experts indicates that our world is approaching a unique time in human history. Although their subjects are diverse, they all agree that our modern civilization is now confronting circumstances with which man has had little or no previous experience. They all unite in one common theme by vigorously emphasizing that unless some drastic measures are taken, these unique and converging crises could spell the end of civilization as we know it.

We have heard the message before – and often. The end of the age (or civilization) is coming. But the difference in today's message is that we have never heard it with such intensity, from so many fields, and from so many experts at the same time. The signs which are currently manifesting themselves are so significantly apparent that not only can the spiritually aware see them, but anyone who will open their eyes and look about them should be able to see the "signs of the times."

But strange as it may seem, as these potentially civilization ending crises loom on the horizon, most people are completely unaware of their approach. Perhaps it is because we have heard similar warnings so often – and for so long – that we now have difficulty recognizing them. Maybe we have heard the apocalyptic warnings so often that we have simply become desensitized. Now, when the warnings are being sounded once again, we have difficulty separating fiction from reality. The message sounds so familiar and seems to be just like the ones we have heard a thousand times before. But this message is not the same. There is a distinct difference between what we are hearing today and what we have heard in times past. The warnings we are hearing today are coming from a myriad of nonreligious sources. They are all united in the essence of their message which eerily reflects the warnings of ancient prophets. The evidence now being presented by these established secular sources is frighteningly obvious and overwhelming.

It is the presentation of this evidence that is the focus of this book. Throughout the pages of this book you are going to see evidence presented that will demonstrate that this is truly a generation unique in time and history. But we will see that not only is our time in history unique, but we are a generation that is entering into uncharted waters. We are a generation that is even now confronting crises of unprecedented magnitude with which we have little or no experience. These unprecedented crises potentially carry such enormous consequences that each has the potential of ending civilization as we know it. Dr. Jared Diamond exhaustively examined many forms of these crises in his work *Collapse*. He wrote that the "problems facing us today… will become globally critical within the next few decades." Dr. Diamond continued by describing how these "problems" were of such magnitude that they could precipitate a global societal collapse. He emphatically indicated that "they are like time bombs with fuses of less than fifty years."[2]

These "problems" presented by Dr. Diamond along with many others will be examined thoroughly in later chapters. The evidence presented is such that it should give cause for consideration by the most critical of skeptics. The evidence that is presented is from so many varied sources and is so overwhelming that it is almost unbelievable that society and humankind can continue its daily existence completely oblivious to what lies ahead. Yet, as Planet Earth enters the most perilous and uncharted waters of its history, most of its inhabitants are not even aware of the perils that await them. Author James Kunslter states in his book, *The Long Emergency*, that mankind is literally "sleepwalking into the future."[3] In spite of all the evidence and signs, he indicates that people are generally indifferent to the ramifications of what is happening around them.

But actually this should not come as a surprise. This complacent business as usual attitude is the very attitude which Jesus said would be prevalent in the days just prior to the "end." After his momentous message concerning the unmistakable signs that would herald the end of the age, Jesus compared the attitude of that generation to that of Noah's day just prior to the flood. He said, "as in the days that were before the flood, they were eating and drinking, marrying and giving in marriage, until the day that Noah entered into the ark; and they knew not until the flood came, and took them all away..." (Matthew 24: 38 and 39).

The Bible specifically teaches that although the world will enter into a period of crises such as it has never known – there will be a prevalent spirit of unconcern, apathy, and disbelief. In spite of unmistakable signs and warnings, a sin-intoxicated world will sleep on in spiritual stupor as it speeds toward eternity just as it did in the days of Noah. There will be a spirit of spiritual intoxication that will dull spiritual perception and foster a belief that "all things (will) continue as they were..." and tomorrow will be much the same as today (II Peter 3:4). It will be a business as usual attitude that will prevail.

But along with all the experts of today, the Holy Scriptures plainly declare that there is a day swiftly approaching when tomorrow will not be anywhere near the same as it is today. There is a day dawning in which every life, every plan, and every future will be interrupted by a divine appointment. We are entering into an era of time such as we have never seen before! The evidence is undeniable and over-whelming – yet the world sleeps on!

We have arrived at the prophetic point in time when everything that can be shaken will be shaken, so "that those things which cannot be shaken may remain." Putting it plainly, God is saying that the time has come that those things that are not established upon his word or by his authority will be shaken and removed, so that only those things that are established upon his word and by his authority will remain.

Whose voice then shook the earth: but now the hath promised, saying, Yet once more I shake not only the earth only,
but also heaven. And this word, yet once more, signifieth the
removing of those things that are shaken, as of those things
that are made, that those things which cannot be shaken may
remain. Wherefore we receiving a kingdom which cannot be
moved, let us have grace whereby we may serve God accept-
ably with reverence and godly fear. (Hebrews 12:26-28)

Mankind has marched through history building their kingdoms and civilizations. They have attained unbelievable accomplishments through technology, industry, and science. Modern man has achieved accomplishments that are so amazing that it staggers the imagination. Man has gone to the moon and returned. He has traveled through the air faster than the speed of sound. He has invented electronic communications that travel at the speed of light. Medical science has triumphed over diseases of past centuries. Modern engineering has erected vast cities with modern conveyances and conveniences that could not have been imagined two hundred years ago. Man's wisdom and technology have increased to the point that it appears nothing is unattainable or beyond man's power. We have built great earthly kingdoms. Human wisdom, wealth, and technology have become our gods. During this quest for an earthly Nirvana, the Creator has become archaic and outdated. He has been ridiculed, blasphemed, and banished. During this historical journey of progress and accomplishment, God has been replaced by manmade ideas and inventions. The Apostle Paul said it in this manner:

Because that when they knew God, they glorified him not as God, neither were thankful; but became vain in their imaginations, and their foolish hearts were darkened. Professing themselves to be wise, they became fools... (and) changed the truth of God into a lie, and worshiped and served the creature (man) more than the Creator, who is blessed forever... (Romans 1:21, 22 and 25)

Although some enlightened inhabitants on Planet Earth are clearly aware of the nature of some of the impending crises, they apparently are not aware of the spiritual implications. Somehow, intoxicated with human wisdom, they blindly trust that man will discover a solution to these unprecedented problems. Biblical warnings, along with any consideration that these problems may be the precursors to an impending divine judgment are not even considered. All crises are regarded from a natural perspective with no spiritual implication. God, the sovereign lord of all creation is not even considered in the equation. While they continue to trust in some as yet undiscovered technological miracle to save mankind, they cannot conceive that "all these things" may be the fulfillment of biblical prophecy and the repercussions of a world that has rejected God.

But we have now arrived at a point when the world and civilization man has created are being confronted by numerous earth shaking crises. These crises will shake and try the very foundations of our civilization. The storms we are to encounter will test the very limits of man's wisdom and technology. It will be a time when every individual will have to make a choice as to whom, or in what they will trust. They will have to decide if man's wisdom will suffice to find the answers and solutions to the impending crises which threaten civilization, or will they put their trust in the God of the Bible. It will be a day of great and eternal decisions. The prophet Joel described the day like this:

> Multitudes, multitudes in the valley of decision: for the day of the Lord is near in the valley of decision. The sun and moon shall be darkened, and the stars shall withdraw their shining. The Lord also shall roar out of Zion, and utter his voice from Jerusalem; and the heavens and the earth shall shake: but the Lord will be the hope of his people, and the strength of the children of Israel. (Joel 3:14-16)

When all is said and done, all of man's wisdom, wealth, power, and technology will prove ineffectual. Every natural, earthly, and manmade thing will be shaken to its foundation. This will truly be an era which will try men's souls. All that has been built upon the sand of this world will crumble and fall. Only that which has been built upon the solid rock of the word of God will stand. When all is finished, the last man standing will be the one who has put his trust in God – and God alone.

The unfolding of these crises will undoubtedly bring gloom and despair to many as they see the foundations of civilization begin to crumble. It will truly be a day of "darkness" for the kingdoms of this world. But as the darkness begins to cover the earth, the glory of God will begin to manifest itself. God will reveal himself during this time as has never been witnessed by this generation. This generation will see the fulfillment of the plan of God that has been kept secret since the foundations of the world (Romans 16:25 and Revelation 10:7). I truly believe the evidence indicates this generation will witness the second coming of Jesus Christ. To some it will be a time of despair and fear, but to those "who love his appearing" it will be a time of anticipation and redemption.

This time of world-wide crises will be a time of great revival for the church. It will be a time when the church will return to the basics of Christianity and the fundamentals of trusting and living for God. When this happens – God will reveal himself through his church in a manner never witnessed before by this generation. Even the prophet Daniel bore witness to this manifestation of God during his vision of the end-times. He stated emphatically that "the people that do know their God shall be strong and do exploits" (Daniel 11:32). Isaiah also confirmed that in the midst of this time of darkness God's glory would shine upon his people:

> For, behold, the darkness shall cover the earth, and gross darkness the people: but the Lord shall arise upon thee, and his glory shall be seen upon thee. (Isaiah 60:2)

The great revival that the church has awaited with anticipation will very likely occur during this time. For the world it will be a day of shaking and despair. For the church it will be a day of revival, miracles, and revelation. Values, priorities, and ideas will be changed. For some, their hopes, dreams and ambitions will be dashed and destroyed. For others, it will be the dawning of a new day. It will be the day when spiritual and eternal things will replace the natural and temporal.

Chapter 2

FIRST DAYS AND LAST DAYS

Before we plunge into an examination of the crises which are even now materializing, we need to analyze the prophetic evidence pertaining to our generation. I believe there is more evidence indicating that we are living in the last days than ever before. But we must begin with the scriptural foundation. We should honestly and fairly ask ourselves if there is any scriptural basis for believing that we are living in the last days. Are there any prophetic time tables that indicate we are nearing the end of the age? These are honest and fair questions and we would be remiss if we did not address them.

When one enters into a study of the Bible, one quickly discovers that everything God did was to reveal something to mankind. God wants us to know who he is and what his plan is. Everything God did or said was designed for a specific purpose and to reveal something to man. In fact the Bible teaches that from the very beginning God revealed things concerning the end, and those things that were not yet done:

> **Remember the former things of old:** for I am God, and there is none else; I am God, and there is none like me, <u>declaring the end from the beginning,</u> and <u>from ancient times the things that are not yet done,</u> saying, my counsel shall stand, and I will do all my pleasure. (Isaiah 46:9-10)

Now taking this counsel from God, let us examine the "former things of old." In fact let's examine things right from the beginning. In Genesis 1:1 the scripture states that "In the beginning God created the heaven and the earth…" In Exodus Moses summed up the creative acts of God in this manner. "For in six days the Lord made heaven and earth, the sea and all that in them is, and rested on the seventh day…" (Exodus 20:11).

We know that God is all powerful and that there is nothing impossible with him (Matthew 19:26; Luke 1:37; and Genesis 18:14). We also understand that the "worlds" and all "things which are seen" were brought into being by "the word of God" (Hebrews 11:3). God simply spoke and all that we see and know came into existence. He did not physically labor or work during his creative acts in the sense that we human beings would work at something. He spoke, and worlds came into existence. This was illustrated time and time again during his fleshly incarnation. Through the simple utterance of a command, the wind would stop, the dead would come to life, and all manner of sickness and disease would be healed. God simply has to speak his word, and whatever is commanded is immediately done.

With this knowledge we can easily see that God did not actually need six days in order to create the world and all that is therein. He could have simply spoken the word and all of creation would have come into existence with complete perfection. But for the sake of temporal man the eternal God specifically worked his creative majesty out over six consecutive days and rested on the seventh. By doing this, he established the twenty-four hour day, the seven day week, and ultimately the calendar of time and the separation of seasons with which we are familiar today. In essence God established the "times and seasons" in order to guide and regulate human activity:

While the earth remaineth, seedtime and harvest, and cold and heat, and summer and winter, and day and night shall not cease. (Genesis 8:22)

To understand this concept is very important. God established the days of creation as a guide to regulate human activity and thereby created a calendar, or schedule which would govern man's measurement of time. The eternal God cannot be limited by time – but man is. God does not need a calendar to determine times and season – but man does. God created the seven day week so that man would have a measured concept of time.

It is very important to understand that God created man's concept of "times and seasons" for a specific purpose. By establishing regulated "times and seasons," man would have an idea of what lay ahead. He would understand that night followed evening, and morning followed the night. He would understand summer followed spring, and winter followed fall, and so on and so forth. Man would have a concept of certain established patterns by this calendar.

When God created heaven and earth, he used seven days and nights to manifest his ultimate plan for creation. It was his desire to reveal through his creative acts exactly what his plan for the future was. He wanted man to understand not only the natural times and season, but to also be aware of the spiritual times and seasons. Just as summer should follow spring in the natural realm, so also would certain conditions follow after others in the spiritual or prophetic realm. Once again, God said that he would make known "the end from the beginning, and from ancient times" those things that were yet to come (Isaiah 46:10). This was the purpose for the six creative days and the final day of rest.

As in the creation of this natural world, God's greater and ultimate plan for man will be worked out over seven *biblical* or *spiritual* days. God will work out his purpose for man in "six days," and then on the "seventh day," the Sabbath, he will complete his work by restoring all creation and enter into his rest. With an understanding of the seven-day creation pattern, we will have a greater understanding of what the Bible means when it refers to the "last days." But first we must know how long a biblical day is.

Both the Old Testament and the New Testament are very clear in this. In Psalm 90:4, we are told that "a thousand years in thy sight are but as yesterday when it is past, and as a watch in the night." In other words, according to the Psalmist, one watch or day, is as a thousand years with the Lord. Now in the mouth of two or three witnesses let everything be established, so the Apostle Peter affirms this point by specifically stating that "one day is with the Lord as a thousand years, and a thousand years as one day" (II Peter 3:8).

God, the eternal being who is not limited by "times or seasons," is communicating his timetable to mankind who lives within the restraints of time. He has clearly revealed through his word that when men who are temporal, attempt to relate their restricted concept of time to God who is eternal, "one day is with the Lord as a thousand years" is to us. This comparison between a day as understood by humanity, and a day as understood by God is repeated twice in the Bible for emphasis.

Using the guide of seven creative days as found in Genesis, and the biblical revelation concerning 1,000 years as a day with God, we should find that there are a total of seven days, or 7,000 years, in which God's ultimate plan for creation and mankind will be worked out. If one traces the genealogies as recorded in Genesis and throughout the Bible, we find that the creation occurred approximately 4,000 years B.C., or approximately 6,000 years ago. This would mean that nearly six prophetic days have passed in the fulfillment of God's ultimate plan for man. We are about to enter into the seventh day, or the millennial Sabbath of day of rest. Using this scriptural guideline, we can envision the biblical calendar for God's ultimate plan for humanity in this manner.

Day 1	Day 2	Day 3	Day 4	Day 5	Day 6	Day 7
1,000 years	1,000 years	1,000 years	1,000 years	1,000 years	1,000 years	1,000 years
Creation	Flood	Abraham	David	Jesus' Birth	Church-age	Millennium

Looking now at Day 7, we can see that the last day (1,000 years) is the millennial reign of Christ. This of course corresponds with Revelation 20:4-6 where the first resurrection of the dead (righteous) occurs at the start of the 1,000 year reign, and the second resurrection (the unrighteous) occurs at the end. This is important, as it was understood by Jewish scholars that the resurrection of the dead was to occur at the "last day." This is the reason for the discussion between Jesus and Martha at the tomb of Lazarus. Jesus had told Martha that Lazarus would "rise again." Martha had responded by saying, "I know that he shall rise again in the resurrection **at the last day**" (John 11:23-24).

The "last day" is the day of resurrection. That day is the last day of the biblical week. It is the day of the millennial reign of Christ, and the first resurrection is to occur at the beginning of that reign. This is when Martha understood and believed that Lazarus would "rise again."

We should be able to see from this that the first days of the biblical week include days 1, 2, and 3. Day 4 is the middle of the week. Days 5, 6, and 7 are the last days, with day 7 being the last day. This is why the New Testament writers understood themselves to be in the "last days." The coming of the Messiah, or Jesus Christ, was to usher in the "last days" of prophetic time. This understanding would be confirmed by the Apostle Paul in the opening verses of Hebrews chapter one:

> God, who at sundry times and in divers manners spake <u>in times past</u> unto the fathers by the prophets, hath **in these last days** spoken unto us by his Son, whom he hath appointed heir of all things, by whom also he made the worlds. (Hebrews 1:1-2)

The Apostle Peter also confirmed this marking of time in his message as recorded in Acts chapter two. The Apostle opens his message to the unbelieving Jews gathered in Jerusalem on the day of Pentecost by explaining the outpouring of the Spirit of God in this manner:

> But **this is that** which was spoken by the prophet Joel; And it shall come to pass **in the last days,** saith God, I will pour out of my Spirit upon all flesh: and your sons and daughters shall prophesy, and your young men shall see visions, and your old men shall dream dreams: And on my servants and on my handmaidens I will pour out **in those days** of my Spirit; and they shall prophesy. (Acts 2:16-18)

Peter's message was emphatic. This event to which they were a witness was an event that was prophesied to happen "in the last days." He specifically stated that "this is that" of which the prophet Joel prophesied. Joel prophesied, and Peter confirmed that this event was to occur in the prophetic "last days." The birth and ministry of Jesus ushered in the last days, and the outpouring of his Spirit was a prophetic event which was to occur "in the last days."

Jesus Christ's first coming (as the child Messiah), was the beginning of the fifth day, and this was to be the beginning of the "last days." As to the exact date, I will not be dogmatic. Some scholars use the year of Jesus' birth which was calculated to be around 4 B.C. Others use the date of his triumphal entry into Jerusalem just prior to his crucifixion. This has been dated at 32 A.D. (see Matthew 21:1-9 and Zechariah 9:9). Either way, the first coming of Jesus included his birth, life, death, and resurrection. It has been almost 2,000 years since this memorable event. It is easy to see we are living near the end of the sixth prophetic day as our current date places us exactly 2,000 years after Jesus birth, and a few years short of 2,000 years of his death. In other words, we are living 2,000 years from the time that Jesus lived. If Jesus was crucified, was buried, resurrected, and ascended into heaven in 32 A.D., as calculated by historians, then by the year 2032 Jesus will have been gone for about 2,000 years, or two days.

It is interesting to note in this context, that when the Pharisees brought Jesus word that Herod would seek to kill him, Jesus answered that they were to tell him that he would "do cures <u>today</u> and <u>tomorrow</u>," but that on "**<u>the third day</u>**" he would be "perfected" (Luke 13:32). The word "perfected" comes from the Greek word *teleioo*, which means to complete, to finish, or to reach a goal.[1] According to God's ultimate plan, the mission of Jesus Christ is the redemption of mankind and the institution of the Kingdom of God on this world. The redemption work will not be completed until the second coming of Jesus, the resurrection, and the final victory when all things are subdued unto him (I Corinthians 15:24-25 and Revelation 11:15-18). Jesus said this would be accomplished on the "**third day**." If Jesus lived during the fifth day, then the "third day" from the time he made this statement corresponds with the seventh and final day of God's redemptive plan. *Jesus Christ must return <u>at the beginning of Day Seven</u>*!

In this context the prophet Hosea prophesied concerning the nation of Israel. It is interesting to note the time standard he used when speaking of Israel's "reviving" or resurrection:

> Come, and let us return unto the Lord: for he hath torn, and he will heal us; he hath smitten, and he will bind us up. <u>After two days will he revive us:</u> **in the third day he will raise us up,** and we shall live in his sight. (Hosea 6:12)

Hosea prophesied from approximately 755 B.C. until 710 B.C. He prophesied concerning Israel and Judah's continued idolatry and warned them of an impending judgment. This judgment of course fell in 586 B.C. when Nebuchadnezzar, king of Babylon, came and destroyed Jerusalem and the temple. Israel at this time ceased to be a nation, and the Jews were dispersed over all the then known world. As we are aware (and will examine in detail later), God had promised to revive Israel and bring them back to their land once again. Hosea at this time adds his prophesy to the long list of prophets that foretold this great event. The interesting context of Hosea's prophecy is the timetable he uses. He indicates that from the date of Israel's judgment, or as he describes being "smitten" by the Lord, that God would raise them up in two days. He states specifically, "<u>after two days</u> will he revive us: <u>in the third day he will raise us up</u>..."

Jerusalem and the temple were sacked and burned by Nebuchadnezzar in 586 B.C. One thousand years (or one day) from that date would be – 586 A.D. Another one thousand years (or the second day) would be somewhere near 1589 A.D. Anything after this date up until 2586 A.D. would be in the third prophetic day from their destruction and dispersion. According to Hosea's timetable, Israel would be resurrected after two days, or after 1586 A.D. They would become a nation again sometime after 1586 A.D. and sometime before 2586 B.C. This is exactly what happened when Israel became an independent nation in 1948. For the first time since 586 B.C., after 2,500 years, Israel was revived and became a nation just as Hosea had prophesied.

LEARN THE PARABLE OF THE FIG TREE

Of course any discussion of a prophetic time-line must include the significance of Israel's becoming a nation in 1948. This is one of the most prominent signposts along the prophetic time-line. The fact that this occurrence was foretold by numerous prophets of the Old Testament over two thousand years before it happened stands testament to the reliability of God's word. Israel has always been and always will be one of the primary focal points of God's word. It has been said that Israel is God's time-clock. If you want to know where we are prophetically on God's timepiece, just look at Israel. This subject of course brings us to one of the most important prophetic discussions found in the Bible.

In Matthew chapter 24 we find that Jesus was alone with his disciples on the Mount of Olives. During this private time they asked him two very important questions which pertain to our current subject. They asked Jesus, "What shall be the sign of thy coming and of the end of the world (age)?" (Matthew 24:3) Since this question was answered by our Lord himself, we should give the utmost attention to what he had to say.

Jesus introduced his answer by warning the disciples not to be deceived. He indicated that there would be many false Christs and false messages prior to the actual manifestation of the real event. He began speaking of many signs including wars, famines, pestilence, and natural disasters of which we will speak later. He continued his discourse by enumerating certain events which were to transpire as the age came to a close. He indicated clearly that these events were to culminate with his second coming:

> <u>Immediately after the tribulation of those days</u> shall the sun be darkened, and the moon shall not give her light, and the stars shall fall from heaven, and the powers of the heavens shall be shaken: And then shall appear the sign of the Son of man in heaven: and **then** shall all the tribes of the earth mourn, and **they shall see the Son of man coming in the clouds of heaven with power and great glory.** (Matthew 24:29-30)

This was the climactic finish of Jesus' response to the disciple's question as to what would be the sign of his coming and the end of the age. He had enumerated crisis after crisis which would come upon the inhabitants of the earth, and then explained that these crises would climax with his second coming which would bring this age to a close.

Immediately after this description of his second coming, Jesus told his disciples to "learn" the parable of "the fig tree." In most instances when Jesus introduced a parable he had simply told his audience to "hear" the parable. In this case Jesus specifically called his disciples attention to the importance of what he was about to say. He did this by indicating that they were to "learn," or understand what it was he was about to say.

We should take a moment at this point to explain why Jesus spoke in parables. He explained this to his disciples in Matthew chapter 13 when they had directly asked him why he taught the people in parables (Matthew 13:10). Jesus' answer is of the utmost importance to our present discussion:

> And his disciples came, and said unto him, Why speakest thou unto them in parables? He answered and said unto them, because it is given unto you to know the mysteries of the kingdom of heaven, but to them it is not given... Therefore I speak to them in parables: because they seeing see not: and hearing they hear not, neither do they understand... But blessed are your eyes, for they see: and your ears, for they hear. (Matthew 13:10-16)

His explanation is clear. The mysteries of the kingdom were delivered in parable form so that only those who were sincere of heart and believed in his words would understand. Those whose minds were clouded by doubt and refused to believe in the validity of his teachings would not understand what was being said. Faith has always been the key to the kingdom of God and the understanding of its mysteries. There are those today who still doubt the words and teaching of Jesus Christ. There are those who contend that it is not relevant and that Christ's coming again is a fairy tale. Those are the ones that will not understand the parable of the fig tree. But to those who believe in the authority of the words of Jesus, to you it is given to understand, "learn," and know the parable of the fig tree.

So what was Jesus talking about when he introduced the parable of the fig tree? Most biblical scholars agree that the fig tree depicts the nation of Israel in scriptural symbolism. Israel has always been the cornerstone of understanding biblical chronology and time. We understand that historically the ancient nation of Israel had been overthrown by Nebuchadnezzar in 586 B.C. This of course had been the final result of their idolatry and wickedness as they rejected God and the word of his prophets. The prophets had foretold this, and had warned Israel of the dire consequences of their rejection of God and his commandments. But we also understand that the prophets had prophesied that in the "last days" God would gather Israel out of all nations to which they had been scattered "and bring you (them) into the land of Israel" (Ezekiel 37:1-14 and Ezekiel 39:26-29).

But Ezekiel had not been the only prophet to talk about Israel's desolation and restoration. Joel had addressed this subject in the first chapter of his small but powerful book. He had provided this unique description of Israel's desolation:

> For a nation is come up upon my land, strong, and without number, whose teeth are the teeth of a lion, and he hath the cheek teeth of a great lion. <u>He hath laid my vine waste, and</u> **<u>barked my fig tree</u>**: he hath made it clean bare, and cast it away; <u>the branches thereof are made white</u>. (Joel 1:6-4)

Joel in describing the desolation of Israel used the analogy of the vine, and more specifically, the fig tree. Notice his description. He states that the fig tree was "barked" and made "clean bare." It was cast away and the "branches thereof are made white." Anyone that has worked on a farm or in an orchard understands this description. To "bark" a tree is to skin the bark away in a circle around the girth of the tree. This will cause a tree to slowly die and wither away. This is why Joel would say in verse twelve, "the fig tree languisheth... even all the trees of the field are withered." His prophetic analogy is that a great army has come against Israel and laid her waste. They have barked her as a "fig tree" and made her bare. She has withered and died. As a nation Joel prophesied that Israel was going to perish and die. Her "branches" would be "made white" and "languish" and would whither away.

At the time of Jesus' ministry, Israel had been a conquered nation for nearly 600 years. They had endured domination by the Babylonians, the Persians, the Greeks, and now the Romans. They had waited for the coming of the Messiah and the restoration of their nation for 600 years. Now when Jesus opened this parable by saying, "learn a parable of the fig tree," there was no doubt that he understood the correlation between his analogy and that of Joel. He would also understand that his Jewish disciples would immediately recognize the significance of this analogy.

Jesus began by saying, "when his branch is yet tender, and putteth forth leaves, ye know that summer is nigh." The message is short and to the point. This tree that had endured the harshness of a long spiritual winter, and had been dead for many years, was going to live again. When the branches that had been dead began to manifest signs of life, then they would "know that summer is nigh" (Matthew 24:32). To the disciples, with the understanding that Israel has been described by the prophets as a fig tree, and more specifically a fig tree that has been barked and left for dead, this would carry the utmost significance. Israel as a nation was a people who were dried up, whose hope was lost, and who was cut off from their parts (Ezekiel 37:11). Now Jesus was telling them that this fig tree (Israel) was going to live again. He stated that when they saw the branches on the fig tree (Israel) begin to come to life, then "know that it is near, even at the door" (Matthew 24:33).

The fact that Israel was going to be resurrected as a nation would have been no great surprise to the disciples. They undoubtedly would have been aware of many of the prophecies concerning this event; including Joel's which we have just addressed. But even more specifically, they would have known of Ezekiel's prophecy of the valley of dry bones. Here God had described the dry bones as "the whole house (or nation) of Israel." He continued in this manner:

Then he said unto me, Son of man, these bones are the whole house of Israel: behold, they say, our bones are dried, and hour hope is lost: we are cut of for our parts. Therefore prophesy and say unto them, thus saith the Lord God; Behold, O my people, <u>I will open your graves, and cause you to come up out of your graves, and bring you into the land of Israel</u>. And ye shall know that I am the Lord, when I have opened your graves, O my people, and brought you up out of your graves, and shall put my spirit in you, and ye shall live, and **<u>I shall place you in your own land: then shall ye know that I the Lord have spoken it, and preformed it saith the Lord.</u>** (Ezekiel 37:11-14)

That Israel was going to be visited by God and resurrected as a nation was not news to the disciples. They would have known of this great and anticipated event from the time that they could understand the teaching of the Law and the Prophets. What would have been unknown to the disciples, and of extreme interest to them, was the time that this event was going to occur. Now Jesus was confirming that it was in fact going to occur, and was connecting it with his coming and the end of the age. In fact Jesus plainly declared that when they saw this great prophetic event take place they were to know that Jesus' second coming and the end of the age was "near, even at the doors."

Jesus did not stop with just saying his coming was near. He continued with one of the most important prophetic announcements that has ever been uttered. He said, "<u>Verily I say unto you, **This generation shall not pass, till all these things be fulfilled**</u>" (Matthew 24:34). The importance of this statement cannot be over-emphasized. It provides one of the most significant time markers along God's prophetic time line. Here is a physical and historical event that can be marked and noted. Jesus Christ himself has prophesied that when Israel is resurrected and becomes a nation once again, the generation that is alive and sees that event "shall not pass, till all these things be fulfilled."

The significance of this prophetic statement is enormous. First – never at any time in the history of civilization has a people ever retained their national identity after being conquered and scattered abroad for such a period of time. (It has been over 2,500 years since the nation of Israel was conquered.) Secondly – never has a nation or people been reestablished after this manner or after such an extended period of time. But thirdly – and most importantly – no less prophet than Jesus Christ himself has prophesied that "when you see these things" we would know that "this generation shall not pass, till all these things be fulfilled." That is – when Israel returns to their homeland and is established as a nation (along with all the other signs indicated in Matthew 24 and Luke 21), we will know that the generation which is alive at that time shall not pass away until all the things which were prophesied have come to pass. Keep in mind that Jesus was speaking of the end of the age and civilization as we know it. He was speaking concerning the signs of his coming, the tribulation, his return to earth, and the end of the age. All this would be fulfilled within the life span of the generation that saw the resurrection of the nation of Israel.

While it is impossible to predict how long any one person from the generation that was alive in 1948 will live, it would seem reasonable to assume that this generation could very possibly consist of the next one hundred years. It is not unusual for people to live to the age of one hundred years. Both my grandmother and great grandmother lived to the age of ninety-seven, so one hundred years easily seems to be within the realm of possibility. But even as we consider this figure, we need to keep in mind that Jesus had simply stated, "this generation shall not pass..." The scriptural fulfillment of this prophecy could easily occur at any point after the budding of the fig tree, or Israel returning to the land of promise. With this in mind, I believe it shall become apparent that the years between 1948 and 2050 will be recognized as significant both naturally and spiritually.

The fact that Israel became a nation once again after more than 2,500 years is a matter of record. On May 14, 1948, as the British mandate over Palestine came to an end, Israel was declared a free and independent nation for the first time since 586 B.C. The seed of Abraham were once again in sole control of the very land that God had promised Abraham he would give to his seed forever. With one declaration, God fulfilled his promise to Abraham, Isaac, and Jacob. He fulfilled the words of the Old Testament prophets and his own prophetic words which he had uttered as he stood on the Mount of Olives approximately 2,000 years ago.[2]

Beyond question, May 14, 1948, was the greatest prophetic fulfillment of the twentieth century. This was one of the most significant markers on God's prophetic timepiece. This date would mark the beginning of the Generation of Crisis. I believe there is overwhelming evidence that indicates that the generation that began around 1948 will see the fulfillment of all the signs spoken of by Jesus on the Mount of Olives. I believe the evidence will show that all the signs that Jesus spoke of in Matthew chapter 24 are emerging to crisis proportions even as you read this book.

THE TIMES OF THE GENTILES

As significant as the birth of the nation of Israel was prophetically, there is yet another significant time marker that we need to address. Jesus specifically addressed this time period and correlated its importance with the other signs that heralded his second coming and the end of the age. He referred to his period as "the times of the Gentiles" (Luke 21:24).

Luke provides us with the parallel account to Matthew's version of Jesus' message concerning the signs of his coming and the end of the age. In Luke's narrative we find more detail in reference to Jesus' prophecy concerning the siege and destruction of the city of Jerusalem.

There is no doubt that Jesus was referring to the destruction which Titus and the Roman army was to inflict upon Jerusalem in 70 A.D. This would have been an appropriate response to the statement the disciples had made to Jesus concerning the stones of the temple. The dialogue had begun when the disciples had observed the beauty of the Temple and voiced their admiration of its beauty and the size of the stones with which it was built. Jesus had apparently looked at the Temple and then remarked that "the days will come in which there shall not be left one stone upon another, that shall not be thrown down" (Luke 21:5-6).

It was this cryptic remark that had led to the disciples' questions concerning when "these things" would be, and what would be the sign of the end of the age. Jesus had then begun his discourse in reference to the signs which were to precede his coming and the end of the age. As he enumerated the signs which would occur prior to his coming, he moved right into the prophecy concerning the destruction of the temple.

Many scholars have struggled with the sequence of events as unfolded by Jesus in these verses. They seem to have trouble with the fact that Jesus was articulating signs which apparently have their fulfillment just before his coming and the end of the age, and then almost inexplicably, he reverts back in time and speaks of things that were to occur in 70 A.D. What they fail to recognize is the fact that Jesus was intentionally making a direct connection between the destruction of Jerusalem in 70 A.D., and the signs which would presage his coming. The destruction of Jerusalem is so significant as a prophetic marker that it cannot be overlooked. It was a critical event which would mark the beginning of a period of time which would have its consummation just prior to Jesus' second coming. It was an event that had to be included in the signs of the end-time.

After describing the horrible desolation which was to come upon Jerusalem and its inhabitants just thirty-eight short years in the future, Jesus then revealed what connection these things were to have with the end of the age. He stated that "they (the inhabitants of Jerusalem) shall fall by the sword, and shall be led away captive into all nations: **and Jerusalem shall be trodden down of the Gentiles until the times of the Gentiles be fulfilled**" (Luke 21:24).

Jesus provided a prophetic time marker that is of the utmost importance in its connection to his second coming. As Jesus concluded this statement concerning the "times of the Gentiles," he immediately began speaking of signs in the sun, moon, and stars. He continued by describing the great fear that will come upon mankind, and then he declared that: "**then shall they see the Son of man coming in a cloud with power and glory**" (Luke 21:27).

The important fact concerning the destruction of Jerusalem <u>was not so much when it occurred in 70 A.D., but the period of time it inaugurated that was to be consummated just prior to Jesus' second</u>

<u>coming</u>. The connection between the destruction of Jerusalem, the times of the Gentiles, and the resurrection of Israel as a nation are inexorably bound together and cannot be broken. Israel or Jerusalem is God's prophetic timepiece. This timepiece is inescapably marked by God's working out his plan for the seed of Abraham and the house of David. The Apostle Paul would address this marvelous plan and its relationship to the Gentiles in Romans chapter 11. In Romans 11:25 he referred to this plan as a "mystery" that would remain shrouded "<u>until the fullness of the Gentiles be come in</u>." In other words, <u>this plan of God with Israel would have its fulfillment at the conclusion of the "times of the Gentiles.</u>" This is why this date is so very important. It cannot be ignored or overlooked. To do so would be a mistake of monumental importance. Jesus could not fail to address the destruction of Jerusalem as it initiates one of the most significant prophetic time periods in the Bible.

A brief overview of Jewish history is necessary for a basic understanding of the "times of the Gentiles." As we recall, Babylon had descended upon Jerusalem in 586 B.C. and taken the city and carried the Hebrews away into captivity. Yet as we know, Cyrus the king of Persia had allowed the Hebrews to return 70 years later just as God had told the prophets that he would do. The Jews had returned to Jerusalem and restored the city and rebuilt the temple under the leadership of Zerubbebel, Nehemiah, and Ezra. After this period many Jews had been allowed to remain in Israel and the city of Jerusalem. The kingdom of Persia had been succeeded by Greece, and then the Greeks had been succeeded by the mighty Roman Empire. The Roman Empire had remained in power during and after the life of Christ. During this time the Jewish people had been allowed a certain amount of autonomy. The Romans had allowed them to maintain a provincial government which consisted of a king and their own legal and religious system (the Sanhedrin).

Although the Jews were a conquered nation, and were ultimately ruled by Gentile authorities, Jerusalem and the land of Israel were inhabited by Jews. This was the condition at the time of Christ. As Jesus entered the picture, the land was one of political turmoil. For years many groups of Jews had sought to overthrow the Roman rulers and had contrived numerous failed rebellions. Those Jews who sought independence were known as Zealots, one of whom was converted and became a disciple of Jesus. The desire of the Jews to escape Roman authority had continually seethed and brewed throughout the land of Israel for years. This burning desire would continually climax and break into open rebellion when a charismatic leader would step to the forefront. This was the atmosphere that Jesus was born into at approximately 4 B.C.

In 6 A.D. the land of Judea (or Israel) was formally annexed into the Roman Empire and Jewish resistance movements began in earnest. This resistance caused an increase in Roman oppression and only strengthened their resolve to bring the Jews into submission. The Jewish religion was viewed to be one of the major causes of rebellion as its practice was tied to ethnic separation and an extreme spirit of nationalism. In 37 A. D. Emperor Caligula, who viewed himself to be a god, demanded that his statue be erected in the Temple. Caligula died before his orders could be carried out. But Rome's local procurators (governors) became more abusive in their attempts to control a fermenting nationalistic movement. Beginning with Pontius Pilate in 26 A.D. this trend continued until it climaxed with the appointment of Gessius Florus in 64 A. D. Florus' oppressive policies provoked an open Jewish rebellion.

The Great Revolt of the Jews against Roman rule began in 66 A.D. It broke out under the rule of Roman Emperor Nero and lasted until 73 A.D. At the outbreak, Nero dispatched his trusted general Vespasian to Galilee to crush the rebellion. Upon arrival he immediately went on the offensive and enacted a scorched-earth policy. Entire Jewish towns in Galilee were completely destroyed during this brutal offensive as well as the fortress of Gamla in the Golan Heights. Over 5,000 Jews took their own life at this fortress rather than surrender. During this campaign, Nero committed suicide and Vespasian returned to Rome where he was made emperor. Vespasian's son, Titus, assumed command of the campaign and led the final Roman assault against Jerusalem.

In the spring of 70 A.D. Titus lay siege to the city of Jerusalem. The Jewish historian, Josephus, records the suffering of the inhabitants during this time. He describes the famine within the city as being so horrible with so many people dying that the bodies lay unburied and putrefying in the street. Josephus indicated that the starving inhabitants of the city who had attempted to sneak out of the walls were captured by the Romans and crucified. He wrote that so many were crucified and "their multitude was so great, that room was wanting for the crosses and crosses wanting for the bodies."[3]

In May the Romans broke through Jerusalem's outer wall, and on August 28, 70 A.D. they broke through the inner courts on the Temple Mount and destroyed the Temple. Emperor Vespasian had given orders that the entire city and the Temple were to be destroyed. The account is recorded by Josephus:

> Caesar gave orders that they (the Romans) should now demolish the entire city and temple... it was so thoroughly laid even with the ground by those that dug it up to the foundation, that there was left nothing to make those that came thither believe it had ever been inhabited.[4]

Josephus recorded that over one million Jews perished during the seven years of war in Judea,[5] including "thousands of Jewish survivors" who were crucified after the fall of Jerusalem.[6] The suffering experienced by the Jews was appalling. The prophetic warning of Christ concerning the Temple and the "great distress in the land" was fulfilled far beyond the imagination of those that heard it. The only positive note during this horrible time was the fact that the Christians who had resided in and around Jerusalem had fled the area prior to the siege. They had recalled the warning of Christ, and when they recognized the significance of the approaching Roman army they had fled to other cities in Transjordan.[7]

The revolt of the Jews continued simmering for decades after Titus' destruction of Jerusalem. Finally in 135 A.D., Emperor Hadrian wearied with the constant Jewish resistance to Roman rule finally issued a series of laws "designed to crush any lingering national spirit of Jews." He banned Jewish religious ceremonies, renamed Judea *Palestina,* and ordered all of Judea to be "depopulated of its Jewish population."[8] The Roman armies completed their desolation of Judea by razing 985 villages to the ground and making nearly the whole of Judea desolate. Dio Cassius estimated that more than a half million Jews were killed and thousands were enslaved or driven from the country. Jews were completely banned from Jerusalem and Judea.

With this historical background of desolation of the Jews and the destruction of Jerusalem, we can see the shocking reality of the fulfillment of Jesus' words. The only ones who had escaped were those of the Jewish Christian community who had remembered his words and fled. **Divine warning had been given and those that chose to ignore it had suffered horribly**.

But as we recall, Jesus had not only prophesied concerning the destruction of Jerusalem, but more importantly, he had connected this devastation to a significant prophetic marker:

> ...for there shall be great distress in the land, and wrath upon this people. And they shall fall by the sword, and shall be led away captive into all nations: <u>and Jerusalem shall be trodden down of the Gentiles, **until the times of the Gentiles be fulfilled.**</u> (Luke 21:23-24)

Jesus placed the emphasis of his discourse on the fact that this desolation of Jerusalem marked the beginning of a prophetic era. This era known as the "times of the Gentiles" is the period of time in which Gentile nations have controlled and dominated Jerusalem beginning with the destruction of that city and the Temple in 70 A.D. Jesus was calling attention to the fact that the "times of the Gentiles" would be fulfilled, and that event would be one of the precursors to his coming just as all the other signs were. In fact he was delivering a chronological unfolding of events that would precede his coming. The destruction of Jerusalem and the temple was not the end-time event in and of itself, but it had to be addressed as it marked the beginning of the era that would have its fulfillment just prior to the second coming of Christ. This is why "the times of the Gentiles" are of such prophetic significance. This prophetic significance is based upon the fact that Jesus had indicated that when the Gentiles were no longer in control of Jerusalem, the end of the age and his second coming was near, "even at the doors."

In June of 1967, during the Six Days War, the Israeli army pushed back the Jordanian and Syrian forces and took the city of Jerusalem. Jewish soldiers ran to the Wailing Wall and began praying and offering thanksgiving to the God of Abraham. He had restored the holy city to them after nearly 2,000 years. In fact for the first time since 586 B.C., Jerusalem was once again under the sovereign authority of an independent Jewish nation. The seed of Abraham were once again in control of their most holy site. The "times of the Gentiles" are almost over. Anyone should be able to see that we are living in the sunset of a prophetic era. Just as Jesus' prophecies concerning the destruction and captivity of Jerusalem have been fulfilled, so also are the prophecies concerning its deliverance and restoration being fulfilled. June of 1967 marked the beginning of the end of a prophetic era. "The times of the Gentiles" are swiftly coming to a close and the second coming of Christ is at hand, "even at the doors."[9]

Notice Jesus' listing of events that he said was to precede his coming. A great escalation of wars, natural disasters, plagues, and persecution will occur. These are not static events, but events which will increasingly become more severe and intense as time progresses. But even while these things are increasing in intensity the "times of the Gentiles" will be fulfilled or come to completion. He then continues describing signs in the heavens and great distress or trouble on the earth. He states that there shall be "great tribulation," or trouble on a scale never experienced in the history of mankind. He then states that "Immediately after the tribulation of those days... shall appear the sign of the Son of man in heaven."

This is the unfolding of events as recorded by Jesus in Matthew 24 and Luke 21. But immediately after providing this chronology, Jesus stated, "learn the parable of the fig tree." He then gave the prophetic message concerning the resurrection of the nation of Israel. He concluded this prophetic analogy by saying, "When ye see ALL these things, (all the signs previously enumerated including Israel's resurrection as a nation) know that it is near, (his coming and the end of the age) even at the doors." Then he provided the most significant historical marker. "Verily I say unto you, this generation (the generation that sees these signs) shall not pass away until all these things be fulfilled." I believe we are the generation of crisis. I believe that the evidence will show that during this generation we will see the fulfillment of "all these things." I believe our generation has more reason to believe that we will see the coming of Jesus Christ and the end of the age than any other before it.

PROPHETIC TRANSITION PERIODS

There is one thing we as humans must understand about the unfolding of prophetic time. It does not occur in neat little measured increments. We human beings love things to be neat, measured, and physically consistent. This is not always the case with prophetic fulfillment. It occurs in God's time and not ours. God exists in eternity and is not bound by the human limitations of time. His time marches according to his word and a plan predestined before the foundations of the world (or time) Ephesians 1:3-11.

For example, as we have seen, one day with the Lord is a thousand years to us. Is this exactly one thousand years to the day? We cannot tell. Is it calculated by 360 day years based upon the lunar calendar, or is it based upon the solar calendar of 365 day years? I am not sure. We simply know that God's measurement of time is not the same as man's. Also, dispensations have a nasty habit of overlapping, or perhaps a better description is that they go through a transition period. Once again for example, we know the scripture says that the dispensation of "the Law of the Prophets were until John" (the Baptist). Just exactly when did the Law end and Grace begin? At Jesus' birth? During his ministry? Before he was crucified there was no atoning blood. The sacrifice had not yet been made nor had the Holy Spirit been given. He had not yet ascended to heaven to be glorified as he indicated to Martha the morning after his resurrection. So just when did the Law end and Grace begin? We cannot tell with perfect certainty. It defies our human need for clear-cut time lines. There seems to have been a transition period which covered the life span of Jesus. During his life the dispensation of the Law was passing and the dispensation of Grace was being ushered in.

Even before Jesus was crucified he was forgiving sin. Before he died on the cross he told the thief that he would be with him in Paradise. How can this be if the sacrifice which makes Grace possible had not yet been offered? We understand that it was by faith of course, but my point is that it defies our human inclination to have neat little lines that mark when the Law ended and when Grace began. All we can say is that the Law was until John, and began passing away during the life of Jesus, and was ultimately fulfilled by his death and resurrection. Grace began with Jesus' birth and was manifest throughout his ministry, but came to complete fruition with the shedding of the blood and resurrection of Jesus. (After all, if Jesus had not died and resurrected, there would be no salvation or Grace.) Prophetic and theological fulfillment works on God's time line and not ours. We recognize God's plan as being fulfilled and observe a change in prophetic seasons by the occurrence of certain events, but the exact timing is in God's hand.

I say this to illustrate that there can be no mathematical formula which will designate exactly when Jesus will return. No man knoweth the day nor the hour. We may know the season. We may see signs and indicators that a theological or prophetic transition is occurring, but we cannot tell the exact date or time. Right now we can see significant prophetic markers being fulfilled. We can recognize that there are significant signs indicating that a change in the prophetic season is occurring. We can see the budding of the fig tree, and by this we know that spring is quickly fading away and summer is almost here.

Contrary to our calendar, summer does not start on a specific day. It occurs as a gradual change in time and season. Spring slowly turns into summer as the days get warmer and longer. Summer then slowly turns to fall as the days get shorter and cooler, and so on and so forth. This is how nature works. Day turns into night by the slow gradual setting of the sun. We go from broad daylight into dusk, then into twilight, and finally darkness arrives. We do not go from bright sunlight one minute, to pitch darkness the next. This is how man would do it. Like flipping a light switch, we like our definitive lines, but that is not God's way. He has a dusky twilight time. There is always a transition time. There is always a short period of time during which times and seasons change.

I believe that we are now in a prophetic period of transition. I believe we have witnessed prophetic markers which indicate that the season is changing. Notice how Jesus said that we would recognize the approach of the time of his coming and the end of the age. He said that when we see the fig tree "putteth forth leaves, ye know that summer is nigh." When we see the prophetic signs being fulfilled we will know the season is changing. We will know that winter is gone, spring is passing, and summer is almost here. We have witnessed Israel become a nation. We have seen Jerusalem return to Jewish possession for the first time in over 2,500 years. These signs alone indicate that times-are-a-changin. The church-age is coming to a close. The times of the Gentiles are passing away. A new day, a new dispensation is almost upon us. The end of the age is almost here and it will be heralded in by the second coming of Jesus Christ. As Jesus said, "when ye see all these things, know it is near, even at the doors."

The following chapters are going to present evidence that will show that the years between 1948 and 2050 are immensely significant. We are going to see that these years — especially the years from 2000 to 2050 will be described repeatedly by scientists as being critical years of crisis for mankind. In fact, all authorities will generally agree that in every crisis we examine, all will be consummated for the better or for the worse by the year 2050. There is compelling spiritual and natural evidence that suggests that our generation has more reason that any before it to believe that we are living at the end of the age. There are numerous signs that point to the nearness of the end and the second coming of Christ. But even at that, we will not (and cannot) set a time or date for the return of Jesus Christ. But — we will very emphatically submit that the end is near, and "even at the doors."

Chapter 3

THE GROWING POPULATION CRISIS

Nations, and even entire civilizations can perish and come to an end in many ways. They can be conquered and overthrown by invading armies. They can succumb to the depletion of natural resources necessary for survival. They can be overwhelmed by natural disasters, food shortages, disease, and climatic changes from which they cannot adapt. Societies have even collapsed as the result of economic failures and internal upheaval. History is replete with instances in which cities, nations, and even empires have been devastated by any number of these catastrophes. Civilizations have come and gone throughout history, but the world has never before seen the foreboding potential of all these catastrophes being consummated on a global scale during the same period of time.

Scientists, legislators, and government rulers have become aware that our world is facing enormous problems that will impact the future of humanity itself. The problems we now face are not isolated to any certain geographical location. All nations on Planet Earth, through modern technology and population growth, have become irretrievably dependant one upon another. For better or for worse, what affects one nation and culture will affect us all in one crucial way or another. People can no longer live in one isolated part of the globe and ignore a crisis in another land. The shock waves of any political, environmental, or economic crisis in any part of the world will shortly be felt throughout the world with devastating results.

Dr. William Haviland, an established authority in human cultures and history, and the author of a college level text on *Cultural Anthropology*, concludes his book with this ominous summary:

> If humanity is to have a future, human cultures will have to find solutions to problems posed by population decline in some areas and rapid growth in others, food and other resource shortages, pollution, and a growing culture of discontent. Unless humanity has a more realistic understanding of the "global society" than presently exists, it cannot solve the problems whose solutions are crucial for its future.[1]

Dr. Haviland continued by asserting with even more foreboding certainty:

> ...the problems of human existence seem to be outstripping any culture's ability to find solutions.[2]

Dr. Haviland does not stand alone when he catalogs the list of impending problems facing our world. It now seems to be the common consensus among authorities at all levels that world hunger, stemming from resource depletion, pollution, population growth and migration, economic disparity, and cultural discontent, lead the list of obstacles to human survival. The 2005 September issue of *Scientific American* devoted an entire issue to addressing these imminent crises. The issue was appropriately entitled, *Crossroads for Planet Earth*. Within its pages were articles examining problematic population growth, energy deficits, water shortages and conservation, and evolving diseases, to name a few. The introductory article entitled "The Climax of Humanity," by George Musser stated, "as humanity grows in size and wealth...it increasingly presses against the limits of the planet." He continued by indicating there were "three concurrent, intertwined transitions" in the area of demographics, economy, and environment which pose problems on a scale that humans have little experience with."[3]

Many authorities are clearly aware of the impending crises and the extraordinary potential of their devastating consequences for human civilization. But while they are aware of the natural implications of these approaching calamites they cannot make the spiritual connection. With an unfounded trust in human wisdom and technology they desperately search for natural solutions to these unprecedented problems. They continually hope that man will find a solution to problems for which there is no precedence and are emerging on a scale never seen before. Jesus said that there would be "great tribulation such as was not since the beginning of the world to this time…" (Matthew 24:21). The prophet Daniel confirmed this distressing portrayal in this manner; "…and there shall be a time of trouble, such as never was since there was a nation…" (Daniel 12:1):

The crises confronting our generation are so devastatingly immense, and the results of these approaching contingencies so dire in their consequences, that one can literally sense the anxiety and consternation of the writers as you read their articles and books. As one reads the words of these authorities you cannot help but sense the urgency with which they write and recall the words of Jesus as he described the reaction of mankind to these coming crises. He said, "Men's hearts (would) fail them for fear, and for looking after those things which are coming on the earth: for the powers of heaven shall be shaken" (Luke 21:26).

The undeniable fact remains that we are a generation in crisis. The gravity of the situation is multiplied exponentially because it is not just one isolated problem. The crises are numerous and appear to be converging upon humanity all at this precise juncture in history. Dr. Ron Nielsen, a member of the New York Academy of Sciences, explains that **"for the first time in human history, we have a series of events that threaten not just the survival of one group of people or one country, but the survival of all the people in the world."**[4]

We will examine a few of these approaching crises in the following chapters, but they all essentially rise from one basic and fundamental problem of immense proportions – unprecedented population growth. All sources, even though they address many different subjects, agree that the number one underlying problem confronting the human race is the overall growth of world population. For countless generations from the time of Adam the world's population remained below 100 million.[5] It was not until sometime near Christ's death in 32 A.D. that the world population approached the 300 million mark. The world did not even reach the one billion mark until around 1800. From that point the rise in human population would become almost breathtaking.

Approximately one hundred and thirty years after 1800, the world reached the two billion mark – in 1930 – in just one hundred and thirty short years the population had doubled to two billion people. By 1960, world population had climbed to an impressive three billion people. By the year 2000 the world's population doubled itself again reaching over six billion people. Just think for a moment, the world population has doubled itself three times since 1930. Never before in human history has mankind seen such an explosive growth in human population. Over six and one half billion people reside on planet earth at the time of this writing. By the year 2050 the prognosis is that the world population will increase to somewhere between 9 and 12 billion people.[6]

WORLD POPULATION GROWTH

Population	Year
250,000,000	32
500,000,000	1650
1 billion	1850
2 billion	1930
3 billion	1960
4 billion	1975
6 billion	2000
8-9 billion	2025
10-12 billion	2050

Source: Geoscience News and United Nations Data

The problems generated by this phenomenal growth and expansion of world population are enormous. Most importantly – where will the natural resources come from to feed and supply the needs for so many people? Earth is a closed system with finite resources.

Farmers and ranchers are all familiar with what is known as "carrying capacity." This simply means that a certain amount of land can only support so many livestock depending on the resources available. Planet Earth is the same. Eventually human population will reach a point where there are not enough resources to support it. This critical situation is called "overshoot and collapse." Places such as India and Africa are already suffering from the distresses of famine and resource depletion. Can a limited supply of finite resources continue to support modern society and this massive population explosion? How long will our resources last? The questions generated by population growth are numerous and complex.

When considering all the problems that confront mankind, Dr. Dott, a Professor of Geology at the University of Wisconsin, and President of the History of Earth Sciences (1990), and his associate Dr. Prothero, Chairman and Associate Professor of Geology at Occidental College, describe the problem in this manner:

> Clearly, the fundamental problem behind all other dilemmas…is the human population growth. As long as population continues to explode, no miraculous breakthroughs in energy production or agricultural yields will be able to keep pace with it. Exploding population is the fundamental cause behind the grinding poverty of the less developed countries, which in turn leads to greater overpopulation.[7]

Dr. Dott and Dr. Prothero continue with their examination of the complex problems generated by population growth. They consider the ability of the Planet Earth to provide enough food to feed a world populated with over 6 billion people. They examine energy sources and other resources needed to sustain human societies, and then provide this dismal summary:

> Ultimately, the question boils down to the limits of growth on this planet. How many people can it sustain? Considering how impoverished most of the world is at present with only 5 to 6 billion people, most environmentalist doubt that we can support 10 billion people on earth… Yet unless current

trends are reversed soon, world population will reach 10 billion people early in the 21st century...[8]

Keeping in mind the prophetic significance attached to the generation which began in 1948, we can see that the massive rise and doubling of the human population began in the middle of the 20th century. No person who died before 1930 had ever lived through a doubling of human population. In contrast, everyone 45 years old or older today has seen more than a doubling of human numbers from 3 billion in 1960 to 6.5 billion in 2005. Human numbers currently increase by 74 million to 76 million people annually, the equivalent of adding another United Sates to the world every four years.[9] Human population has never grown with such speed as before the middle of the twentieth century. There has been more growth in world population since 1950 than during all of human history![10] Now, with over 6 billion people on earth, and projections that skyrocket beyond belief, questions pertaining to human survival have become critical issues for this generation. Edward Goldsmith, cofounder of the International Honors Program Global Ecology Course, warned that:

> The biosphere is incapable of sustaining all six billion of us at the consumption levels of the North (developed nations). Indeed, the destruction that the global environment has suffered in the last fifty years (since 1950), since global economic development has actually gotten under way, is certainly greater than all the destruction we have caused since the beginning of our tenancy on this planet. Our planet cannot possibly sustain a repetition of the last fifty years, let alone a similar period of still greater environmental destruction, without becoming incapable of sustaining complex forms of life (human life).[11]

It is clear from numerous studies from various experts and universities that the world is now pushing against its limits. Overshoot and collapse have become foreseeable consequences of population growth. Three professors from the Massachusetts Institute of

Technology (MIT) conducted extensive research compiling an enormous amount of statistical data essentially confirming that Planet Earth has even now pushed beyond its sustainable limits. Their data indicates that the rapid growth of human population has reached the point that there is a realistic "potential for catastrophic overshoot." They summed their conclusions in this manner:

> ...since the 1980's earth's peoples have been using more of the planet's resource production each year than could be regenerated in that year. In other words, the ecological footprint of the global society has overshot the earth's capacity to provide... The potential consequences of this overshoot are profoundly dangerous. The situation is unique; it confronts humanity with a variety of issues never before experienced by our species on a global scale... a crash of some sort is certain. And it will occur within the lifetimes of many who are alive today.[12]

Dr. Tim Flannery, professor at the University of Adelaide in Australia, confirmed this analysis. By his calculations 1986 was the "watershed" year. He records that "1986 marked the year that humans reached earth's carrying capacity, and ever since we have been running the environmental equivalent of a deficit budget..." Dr. Flannery continues by indicating that "by 2050, when the population approaches or surpasses 9 billion people, the burden of human existence will be such that we will be using...nearly two planets worth of resources."[13] Evidence and reason both indicate that man and modern civilization cannot long continue their unrestricted exponential growth. There simply are not enough resources on a finite planet for infinite growth.

Other studies have shown the same discouraging findings. Human population cannot continue at its present pace without reaching some sort of natural limitations. Even now it appears that we have passed many of these sustainable limits and are nearing a "collapse" that may very well manifest itself not only as an economic breakdown, but with shortages of basic resources that are vital for human survival. Dr. Ron Nielsen adds his consensus to the others by succinctly stating that "global population is shooting towards infinity, and as we cannot have an infinite number of people on planet earth, a breakdown in one form or another will have to occur – and soon."[14]

The problems of human population growth are abundant and diverse. Cities are growing faster than their sustaining infrastructure creating problems with congestion, housing, and pollution. In under-developed countries power and water shortages are common occurrences. Streets are choked with people, animals, and cars. Squatter settlements and slums are ubiquitous and contain one-fourth to two-thirds of the population. Urban areas are increasing in all countries and continually encroach on vital arable land needed for farming and food supplies. Political unrest, environmentally destructive pollution, and famine are just a few of the collateral problems caused by over population. These problems are presently growing at an alarming rate and increasing exponentially in an already troubled world.

The crisis is growing steadily. The United Nations Food and Agriculture Organization estimates that 64 of 117 third world countries will be unable to feed their projected populations in the first decade of the 21st century.[15] Though we have yet to feel its presence in the United States, famine is a specter that is even now manifesting itself on Planet Earth and is growing larger with each passing day. Jesus' words of Matthew 24 cannot be ignored. He spoke of political unrest as ethnic groups turned against ethnic groups, and famines such as the world had never seen before begin to make their appearance – but "all these are the beginning of sorrows" (Matthew 24:7-8).

Population growth and the expansion of population to other areas through immigration have created massive cultural and political instabilities. Cultural and philosophical beliefs that were once isolated and had little effect upon one another are now brought into confrontation by being thrust into the same geographical location. Internal dissensions within established nations have become commonplace. The politics of scarcity have become driving forces as nations find themselves competing for natural resources in order to sustain their burgeoning societies. Nations are finding themselves at odds with other nations as the "best interests" of their particular societies come into conflict. And to our dismay, we have learned that any political disruption in any part of the globe has the potential to affect every nation on earth in some way.

The tremendous growth in human population during the last 100 years has placed great strains on the agricultural resources of the planet. As human numbers grow, its demands have increased exceeding many of the planet's natural capacities. The bottom line is that our shrinking forests, eroding soils, falling water tables, more frequent crop-withering heat waves, collapsing fisheries, expanding deserts, and deteriorating rangelands are all evidence that we have entered the "collapse - and - overshoot" mode. Human demands on the natural environment have exceeded the sustainable yield of natural systems. Dr. Lester Brown of the Earth Policy Institute warned that if humanity continues on its current path, "the question is not whether environmental deterioration will lead to economic decline, but when. No economy, however technologically advanced, can survive the collapse of its environmental support systems."[16]

THE AGRICULTURAL CRISIS

A study published by the National Academy of Sciences in 2002 concluded that the year 1980 was when the collective demands of the human population on Planet Earth first exceeded the natural sustainable limits. This study indicated that global demands in 1999 exceeded the sustainable capacity by 20 percent. This overshoot gap has increased by at least 1 percent a year and is still growning.[17] The natural carrying capacity for the resources of Planet Earth has been exceeded by an exploding population. If it had not been for the intervention of modern technology which launched the Green Revolution we may have already seen the effects of famine on an even greater scale than has been manifest.

Dr. David Pimentel, along with numerous other scientists from Cornel University's College of Agriculture and Life Sciences, calculates that Planet Earth's natural carrying capacity is somewhere between 2 to 3 billion people.[18] Without modern technology, and especially petroleum based agricultural technologies, Planet Earth could not sustain 6 billion people, much less the additional 3 to 4 billon expected before mid-century. According to the calculations of these experts, Planet Earth would already be experiencing an unprecedented famine without these innovations. James Kunstler, the author of *The Long Emergency,* confirms this assessment by indicating that "the so called Green Revolution of the late twentieth century increased world grain production by 250 percent." He continued by explaining that this "increase was almost entirely attributable to fossil fuel inputs: fertilizers made out of natural gas, pesticides made from oil, and irrigation powered by hydrocarbons..."[19] Dr. Pimentel summarizes the situation in this manner; "if fertilizers, partial irrigation, and pesticides were withdrawn, corn yields would drop from 130 bushels per acre to about 30 bushels."[20]

The advent of petroleum based fertilizers, pesticides, mechanized farm machinery, and genetically modified seeds and plants undoubtedly delayed an impending era of scarcity by greatly improving world-wide agricultural yields. Statistics from numerous sources confirm that the world-wide yields increased dramatically from 1950 through 1996. Between those years the world grain harvest nearly tripled in overall production. After 1996 the production leveled off for seven straight years through 2003 showing no increase at all. However, an examination of the last four years of that period (1999-2003) shows the consumption level of earth's human population had exceeded production. The shortfalls were nearly 100 million tons of grain in 2002, and then once again in 2003. These were the largest shortfalls in recorded history.[21]

Although the natural carrying capacity of the planet has been exceeded, through technology and petroleum based machinery, fertilizers, and pesticides, and other synthetic means, an impending crisis of food scarcity had been averted. But it appears that we have squeezed all the increase possible from innovation and technology. Genetically modified seeds have yielded all they can. Synthetic fertilizers, pesticides, and increased irrigation have not produced any further increases. The crisis that was averted late in the twentieth century seems to be awaiting us early in the twenty-first century. Dr. L. Grant, another agricultural expert, insists that nations should even now be finding ways to decrease their demand for agricultural products.

> The 50-year rise of yields is slowing or ending, and the world is paying a high and rising price for the effort to keep raising yields. Countries that have become dependent on high yields should be seeking to escape the squirrel cage of rising demand. Countries that are not yet hooked on commercial fertilizers should recognize their potential limits and costs, and look to controlling demand – population growth – rather than hopefully relying on higher food yields to solve their problems.[22]

Since 2003, world-wide grain production has been in decline.[23] Reserves have been depleted and global demand has increased. If this was not enough bad news in itself, we have learned that the technologically mechanized farming methods employed during the Green Revolution have caused severe environmental and ecological damage to the arable farmlands which we depend upon for survival. The synthetic fertilizers have depleted the soil of its natural nutrients and mechanized farming, whose focus has been yield and profit margins, have eroded the fragile topsoil.[24] The land has degraded to the point where its yields are now decreasing instead of increasing in spite of (or perhaps because of) synthetic additives and mechanized farming methods.

The remarkable increases in yield from the middle of the twentieth century were not due to land increases, but to the advent of artificial nutrients, genetic engineering, chemical fertilizers, and petroleum based mechanized farming methods. Modern technology and industrialization transformed agricultural practices and miraculously increased food production. Dr. Walter Youngquist explains in his article entitled "The Post-Petroleum Paradigm – and Population," that it was mechanization, petrochemicals, and genetic engineering which powered the "Green Revolution." He summarizes his assessment in this manner:

The "green revolution," which has enabled the Earth to support so many more people now than in the past, is a combination of genetic engineering in plants, mechanization, and petrochemicals provided by oil and natural gas.[25]

Modern technology provided the means by which man could artificially increase food production and distribute it over large distances. The natural agricultural capacity of Planet Earth was increased by human innovation, but at a grievous cost to our arable land and invaluable topsoil. However, this dangerous innovation was vitally necessary as the human population increased from 2.5 billion in 1950 to over 6 billion people by the year 2000. This was an increase of over 3 billion people. This is twice the number of people that had ever existed at one time on this planet prior to this century. All of this in just fifty short years.

But now numerous experts agree that technology seems to have reached its limits. Production has leveled and is no longer meeting the ever increasing demands of the growing population. For the past five years grain production has been in decline and demand keeps rising. The food shortages that threatened humanity in middle of the 20th century are once again posing an ominous threat. A world-wide famine of unimaginable proportions is looming upon the horizon. If the world has truly passed its sustainable limits in the 1980's as experts insist, how will the earth supply the needs of the 7 to 9 billion people that will inhabit the planet in a few short years?

DIMINISHING WATER RESOURCES

Fresh clean water is fundamental to agricultural production and life itself. This resource is taken for granted in most parts of the world because it seems so abundant. It is only when water runs out, or becomes extremely scarce does society realize its fundamental importance. In most parts of the United States water is as close as any faucet in the house. Turn the tap and let it run. It is readily available and there seems to be an infinite supply.

What most people do not realize is that our fresh water supply is a finite resource. The total amount of water on Planet Earth is estimated to be approximately 1386 million cubic kilometers, of which only 35.029 million cubic kilometers is fresh water. Only 2.5 percent of the total amount of water on Planet Earth is fresh water, and 68 percent of that amount is locked up in glaciers and snow cover.[26] The rest of the water is saltwater that is found in our enormous oceans and seas. The fresh water we use for human consumption, agricultural, and industrial needs is found in our rivers, streams, and groundwater sources. These sources are swiftly being depleted and polluted. Dr. Sandra Postel, Director of the Global Water Policy Project of the World Watch Institute, noted that "there is only so much water that is available in any given location. Therefore, as the human population continues to increase there will be a decline in the amount of water available per person."[27]

The pressure that Earth's freshwater reserves are receiving from an expanding population is substantial. More people demand more food which demands more irrigation and fresh water. More people also demand more consumer products which are produced by industrial plants and factories. These factories and plants use enormous amounts of fresh water and generate massive amounts of chemical pollutants. These chemical pollutants, either directly or indirectly, find their way back into our fresh water reservoirs. More people also use more water in everyday life. Showers have to be taken. Dishes must be washed. Lawns need to be irrigated and cars washed. The list could go on almost endlessly. Water seems to be so abundant that most people do not even notice how much we human beings use.

This is a crisis that has crept upon us almost unnoticed. Dr. Brown explains that "the world is incurring a vast water deficit – one that is largely invisible, historically recent, and growing fast." Because much of the deficit comes from aquifer over pumping, it is often not apparent. Unlike burning forests or invading sand dunes, falling water tables are often discovered only when wells go dry."[28]

The wells that have supplied millions of people with fresh water for centuries have started to go dry. The spread of water shortages has been documented by scientists the world over. Dr. Nielsen describes the world-wide decline and spread of water shortages in detail in his book:

The rapid decline in the availability of fresh water began about 1950. In the 1950's only some countries in the northern parts of Africa suffered from a very low level of water availability, but no region of the world had yet reached the catastrophically low level.

By 1995, water availability in the northern part of Africa had fallen to the catastrophically low level. The Middle East and most parts of Central and South Asia fell to a very low level, and parts of Asia and Europe, and some countries of East Africa slid to a low level.

By 2025, the whole Middle East, as well as other parts of Central and South Africa, will join North Africa and experience the catastrophically low level of water availability. The rest of Asia, almost all of Africa, and Central America will become dryer than in 1995. Water availability in various countries of these regions will be between low and very low.[29]

Currently the water shortages in many regions are so severe that thousands of infants are dying due to a lack of clean water and sanitation facilities. It is estimated that 500,000 infants a year perish in South Asia due to the lack of clean water and sanitation facilities. The World Business Council for Sustainable Development reports that "1.8 million people die every year from diarrheal diseases (including cholera)" as a result of polluted water and unsanitary conditions.[30] Dr. Nielsen relates that "water pollution is high, and fresh water availability is decreasing, and the withdrawal of groundwater is excessive."[31] This scenario is repeated time and again in places like Africa, the Middle East, and parts of Central America. The fresh water shortage that was invisible and insidious in its approach has now become an enormous and highly visible crisis invading all areas of the globe.

The specter of water shortages is not isolated to far and exotic parts of the world. This invisible and insidious calamity is now manifesting itself in the United States. The United States Department of Agriculture has reported that "in parts of Texas, Oklahoma, and Kansas, the underground water table has dropped by more than 100 feet. As a result, many wells have gone dry on thousands of farms in the southern Great Plains."[32] The United States Geological Survey reports that there are problems in Florida with "saltwater intrusion" and "surface-water depletion." They continue the list by describing concerns in "Arkansas, Louisiana, Mississippi, and Tennessee with "significant water level declines." Even places in the Pacific Northwest have experienced "water level declines of more than 100 feet."[33]

The most severe problems, however, are manifesting themselves in the Great Plains states and the American Southwest. The Great Plains states draw most of their water from the giant Ogallala aquifer which lies beneath them. The annual depletion rate is 130 to 160 percent above its ability to replenish itself.[34] In fact the Ogallala is a fossil (non-replenishable) aquifer which will take thousands of years to recover. "If the withdrawal rate continues as they are, this aquifer which is so vital to irrigation and countless communities for their water source is expected to become non-productive by the year 2030."[35]

While falling water tables and aquifer depletion are virtually invisible, rivers and lakes that are being drained are highly visible. The Colorado River that flows through the Southwestern United States is just one such river. The water of this river is vital to the bourgeoning populations of California, Arizona, Utah, Nevada, and Colorado. Even now legal battles are in progress over the limited supply of water from this river. Almost every drop of water from this river is contested and claimed by the surrounding states so that when this river reaches the Gulf of California it is literally drained dry. "The Colorado is both legally and hydrologically one of the most regulated rivers in the world."[36]

A study conducted by the Colorado River Water Users Association revealed that even though the state of Arizona has enormous land area, it has neither the carrying capacity of arable land nor enough water to support its population. The only way Arizona (and Southern California) meet their enormous demand for fresh water is by extracting water resources from the Colorado River that is far beyond their share based on the international standard of fair user per lineal river mile. Nevertheless, in order to meet the needs of their constantly growing cities of Phoenix and Tucson, the Bureau of Reclamation initiated the world's largest and most expensive water delivery project in 1980.

Fred Pierce, in his book *When the Rivers Run Dry*, explains that the Central Arizona Project extracts 1.6 million acre feet of water a year out of the Colorado River and channels it through a 300 mile canal to Phoenix and Tucson. He indicates that "it loses 7 percent of the flow en route due to evaporation. In recent times, the canal has been taking more than a fifth of the entire flow of the Colorado…" It has been this project and the indispensable water from the Colorado River that has sustained the recent explosive growth in these desert communities. But this ever increasing demand on the Colorado cannot continue. As Pearce notes, this canal and the ever growing population of the desert cities "could be the final straw for the beleaguered Colorado, and it could take the American West with it."[37] He succinctly summarizes the crisis concerning the waters of the Colorado River in this manner:

> The 1450 – mile Colorado, which drains a twelfth of the continental United States, is the lifeblood of seven states, delivering water to burgeoning cities, feeding irrigation projects, and generating hydroelectricity… But now the river itself is faltering. And from the snow-covered mountains of Wyoming and Colorado to the desert cities of California and Arizona, the beneficiaries of the Colorado are getting worried.[38]

According to the California Department of Water Resources, residents of Southern California will also face a water shortfall if new supplies are not found soon. The problem is that not only does this desert area have a diminishing supply of water, but the population burden of 18 million people is already enormous, and is expected to continue growing. The thirsty cities of the Los Angeles basin have been diverting water from surrounding lakes and rivers for years. Owens Lake is just one example.

In 1913 the City of Los Angeles began diverting water from this giant lake for its municipal use. By 1926 the lake was dry. Today the dry lake bed produces an enormous amount of wind-blown dust which far exceeds federal air pollution standards and affects more than 40,000 people. Another example is Mono Lake. Mono Lake's fresh water reserves have also been tapped in Los Angeles' never ending search for water. Since its water was first diverted in 1941, the lake has experienced a 35 foot drop in its water level.

The problems concerning diminishing water supplies are inexhaustible and growing each year. The recent ten year drought in the American Southwest has only intensified an already critical problem. Lake Powell and Lake Mead's water levels are falling with no relief in sight.[39] The monsoon rains have decreased considerably in this desert area, and the winter snows that usually create the life sustaining snow pack have diminished, thus increasing the concern. It is this melting snow pack that produces most of the water which flows in the Colorado River. Without sufficient winter snows, this water is not replenished. In his well documented book, *The Weather Makers,* Dr. Tim Flannery bleakly observes that "we are only at the beginning of the West's water crisis."[40]

The historic drought in the Southeastern United States reached critical proportions during the summer of 2007. Cities such as Orme, Tennessee, literally ran out of water. Other cities, large and small also had their water supplies threatened.[41] But the problem is not unique to one area. With headlines warning that "Much of the U.S. Could See a Water Shortage," Brian Skoloff of the Associated Press reports the crisis in this manner:

An epic drought in Georgia threatens the water supply for millions. Florida doesn't have nearly enough water for its expected population boom. The Great Lakes are shrinking. Upstate New York's reservoirs have dropped to record lows. And in the West, the Sierra Nevada snow-pack is melting faster each year. Across America, the picture is critically clear, the nation's fresh water supply can no longer quench its thirst.[42]

Over the planet, fresh water supplies are diminishing. The Aral Sea in the former Soviet Union and Lake Chad in Africa are simply two more examples. Ships that once sailed the waters of the Aral Sea now create a bizarre landscape as they lay stranded in sand of the seabed with no water in sight. In 1963 Lake Chad covered 9,700 square miles. Today it covers less than 485 square miles. It is literally the life source for more than 20 million people who live in the four countries which surround it. The receding waters of Lake Chad have precipitated crop failures, dying livestock, and collapsed fisheries. The hardships that have come as the waters have dried have been unimaginable, but the story is being repeated more and more frequently across the planet. Earth's fresh water supply is being pressed to the limits by a rapidly increasing population and climate change. These two factors are changing the face of Planet Earth almost overnight.

Ron Nielsen predicts that "water shortages will increase everywhere," and these shortages will invariably affect agriculture and industry. He indicates that "it will affect industrial and agricultural production, and will increase the cost of living. Less water in industry will mean lower industrial output and lower availability of industrial goods. Less water for agriculture will mean less food on the market."[43] It is a crisis that has unexpectedly overtaken mankind, but it is very real. Dr. Postel emphasizes that "we are moving into... an unprecedented situation of water stress that we have no historic analogue to understand, and this situation is going to get worse before it gets better, simply because of population growth and an increasing water demand."[44]

What is apparent is that Planet Earth is running out of vital life sustaining resources. Experts foresee inevitable food and water shortages in the very near future. Human population has pushed the resources of Planet Earth to their limits. All of this of course should be no surprise to those who have read the words of Jesus and the prophets. It simply comes down to the fact that when God created man he knew exactly how long that man would inhabit Planet Earth. He created the planet and supplied it with just the right amount of resources needed to sustain the human population until the time of the end. When resources begin to diminish and the earth begins to struggle in her ability to sustain human population – that is a sure sign that we are nearing the end of God's prophetic time. When these signs begin to manifest themselves, it should be apparent that we are approaching the end-time. Even now, if we listen carefully, we can hear the distant drumming of the hoof-beats of the third horseman of the Apocalypse. "And I beheld…a black horse and he that sat upon him had a pair of balances in his hand. And I heard a voice…say, A measure of wheat for a penny (a day's wages), and three measures of barley for a penny (a day's wages)" (Revelation 6:5-6).

Chapter 4

PANDEMICS AND
MUTATING DISEASES

The beginning of the twentieth century brought many changes. Population was beginning its dramatic rise. The Industrial Revolution was shifting into high gear with the invention of the internal combustion engine and the automobile. The great population shift from the rural areas to the cities was well underway, and innovation and technology was increasing at an astonishing pace. Right along with all the other advancements in technology, medical science was experiencing amazing breakthroughs. It was a time of optimism, progress, and success as far as technology and scientific advancement was concerned, and the medical field was not to be left behind.

By the 1950's and 1960's it was thought that the conquest of "infectious" diseases was at hand. There was one medical breakthrough and achievement after another. Antibiotics which were first discovered in the 1940's were growing in number and potency. Doctors and scientists began to discount the impact and effects of bacterial diseases. Scourges such as *Staphylococcus* and *Tuberculosis* had been removed from the "extremely dangerous" list and placed on that of the "easily managed minor infections."[1]

Dr. Jonas Salk's experimental polio vaccination campaign in 1955 was so successful that cases of the disease in Western Europe and North America plummeted from 76,000 in 1955 to less than

1,000 in 1967. This along with numerous other medical successes brought such optimism that the eradication of all infectious diseases was considered to be within reach. Laurie Garrett, in her work entitled *The Coming Plague*, records that "in 1948, U.S. Secretary of State George C. Marshall declared at the Washington, D.C. gathering of the Fourth International Congress on Tropical Medicine and Malaria, that the conquest of all infectious diseases was imminent."[2] Ms. Garrett continued by noting that Marshall had attributed this conquest to "a combination of crop yields to provide adequate food for humanity and scientific breakthroughs in microbe control." He had optimistically proceeded to predict that "all the earth's microscopic scourges would be eliminated"[3] by virtue of these modern technological breakthroughs.

Technological breakthroughs in chemistry had produced "DDT and the class of chemicals known as organochlorines, all of which possessed the remarkable capacity to kill mosquitoes and other insect pests on contact and go on killing for months, perhaps years, all insects which might alight on pesticide-treated surfaces."[4] This discovery was greeted with such enthusiasm and deemed so significant that the World Health Organization reported that "Asian Malaria" could be brought under control to the point that Malaria would "no longer be of major importance."[5]

But instead of a complete and sweeping medical victory, something very strange and ominous occurred. By the latter part of the twentieth century, instead of medical conquest, we were seeing the phenomenal resurgence of old diseases thought to have been eradicated or controlled. Drug resistant microbes and altogether new infectious diseases for which there was no medical answer began to make their appearance. Tuberculosis, which was nearly eradicated from the industrial world by the 1970's began resurgence and now claims 3 million lives annually. Malaria, the disease the World Health Organization felt would "no longer be of major importance," leads to more than 105 million deaths each year. And by 1994 more than 16 million adults and 1 million children had been infected with the AIDS virus – a microbe unknown to humanity prior to 1981. And this is just the beginning.

All around us – in our homes, workplaces, and public areas – bacteria and viruses are evolving at a feverish rate, and our best defenses against them are being overwhelmed. The threat posed by emerging infectious diseases is as formidable as any challenge or crisis the human race has ever faced. SARS (Severe Acute Respiratory Syndrome) erupted out of nowhere. Lyme disease, West Nile Virus, Ebola, AIDS and other disease which had never been seen made their sinister appearance. Older viruses such as the common Streptococcus mutated into the deadly "invasive Group A Streptococcus" which became known as the "flesh eating bacteria." Dr. Elinor Levy, an immunologist and associate professor of microbiology at Boston University, describes the resurgence of these deadly diseases in her book *The New Killer Diseases*:

> The rise of deadly strep (invasive Group A Strep) is just one small part of an alarming escalation of infectious diseases. Scores of other bizarre organisms are springing to life. Since the 1970's – less than a blink in the millions of years that microbes have been evolving – experts have identified twenty old pathogens such as TB and Cholera that have reemerged stronger or spread wider than ever, and thirty newly discovered diseases, including Lyme Disease, West Nile Virus, Ebola, and AIDS, and now SARS.[6]

The problem is complex and diverse. Not only are new diseases emerging and old diseases mutating into stronger and more deadly forms, they are manifesting a strong immunity and resistance to all of our antibiotics and medical technologies. In fact it seems that our discovery of antibiotics and their overuse has played a crucial part in the evolution of these "new killer diseases." Dr. Levy explains the dilemma in this manner:

> More and more bacteria are creating and swapping resistance genes because we are pressuring them into it... Mankind's' sudden, widespread introduction of antibiotics in a few short decades has forced the creation of super bugs we may no longer be able to defeat.[7]

Dr. Levy continues by asserting that "the more researchers investigate the more fast-changing microbes they find."[8] She explains that "one of the most troubling features of this rapid evolution is that many bacteria are learning to resist more and more of the antibiotics" we used to fight them. These "super bugs" have become amazingly resistant to any medical innovation and quickly adapt to any new drugs discovered to combat them. Dr. Levy further illustrates this point:

Penicillin was introduced commercially in 1943, and bacteria that could resist it were discovered only three years later, in 1946. Tetracycline went on the market in 1948 and was being resisted by 1953. Erythromycin and Vancomycin were deployed in 1952 and 1956 respectively, and remained effective until 1988, but bacteria resistant to Methicillin appeared only a year after it was introduced in 1960. Furthermore, once an organism is resistant to one drug, it is likely to resist the whole family of compounds to which that drug belongs.[9]

The evolution and emergence of these new deadly strains of diseases bring with them the potential of precipitating devastating plagues against which man is powerless to defend himself. In fact most experts agree with Dr. Jeremy Farrar, an Oxford University doctor who works at the Hospital for Tropical Diseases in Vietnam's Ho Chi Minh City, when he states that it is not a matter of – if a global pandemic will occur – but when. He states, "It's going to happen, at some point... It's bound to happen. And when it does, the world is going to face a truly horrible pandemic."[10]

This warning is being echoed by expert after expert. Dr. Richard Krause of the United States National Institute of Health has warned that "diseases long thought to be defeated could return to endanger the American people."[11] So critical was the issue that in an address before the United States Congress in 1982 Dr. Krause would say; "Plagues are as certain as death..."[12]

Dr. Krause and Dr. Farrar are not the only authorities who make these dire observations. Numerous periodicals, books, and addresses have been made by a multitude of experts in microbiology. All of them speak of viruses and bacteria that are "mutating at a rapid rate" and becoming "immune" to any known vaccine. Dr. Jonathan Mann, the Professor of Epidemiology and International Health at the Harvard School of Public Health, also joined the chorus of experts with a passionate warning that the newly emerging diseases, and diseases caused by mutating vaccine resistant bacteria along with viruses, will be the source of potential world-wide epidemics:

> The history of our time will be marked by recurrent eruptions of newly discovered diseases, epidemics of diseases migrating to new areas... and diseases which spring from insects and animals to humans, through manmade disruptions in local habitats. To some extent, each of these processes has been occurring throughout history. What is new, however, is the increased potential that at least some of these diseases will generate large-scale, even world-wide epidemics. The global epidemic of human immunodeficiency virus is the most powerful and recent example. Yet AIDS does not stand alone; it may well be just the first of the modern, large-scale epidemics of infectious disease.[13]

The warning is clear. Population growth and human activity have not only precipitated shortages of energy, food, and other natural resources, but has also generated an environment conducive to countless deadly pathogens. We have gone from a world that appeared to be on the verge of the medical conquest of infectious diseases in 1950, to a world in which experts fear we may be overrun by new and mutated pathogens. We have gone from apparent medical security to living under the specter of epidemics on a global scale. The October 2005 issue of the National Geographic documented that in 1957 the Asian flu pandemic caused the death of over 1 million people world-wide. Then in 1968 the Hong Kong flu killed 750,000 people. But now the experts fear that the newly emerging H5N1 bird flu virus may cause the death of anywhere from 180 million to 360 million people. This H5N1 bird flu is very similar to the 1918 Spanish flu epidemic which claimed approximately 100 million lives. The 2005 October issue of National Geographic states that

"public health experts hear the distant rumblings of catastrophe…
experts are urging the world to prepare for the worst." They fear that
with the drastic increase in population and global transportation, this
next avian flu pandemic may reach "apocalyptic" proportions.[14]

Dr. Elinor Levy confirms that the "apocalyptic" pandemic
specter is not only real but has been brought about by man himself.
According to Dr. Levy we have created the global environment
and precipitated the cause of this pathogenic "onslaught." She very
clearly explains how this has happened:

> …we have brought it upon ourselves. Germs are mutating
> faster than ever because we are helping – or forcing – them
> to change. We push economic development into the jungle,
> rousting exotic pathogens. We pump greenhouse gases
> into the atmosphere, altering the planets weather patterns,
> which facilitates the spread of disease-causing organisms.
> In June 2002 scientists reported the first evidence that global
> warming was accelerating outbreaks of new and more viru-
> lent diseases in a range of plant and animal species, and
> that the same warming could trigger similar acceleration of
> diseases in humans.[15]

Dr. Levy continues to explain how our increased population
and modern global progress has increased the potential for a global
pandemic. Chief among the reasons are increased global travel,
the importation of food products from other countries, the over-
prescription of antibiotic drugs, the overuse of anti-microbial soaps,
and most importantly, our underestimation of the microbes themselves. The unpleasant essence is that we humans have created the
circumstances and provided the stimulus which has brought about
the emergence of these deadly new and mutating pathogens. We
have provided the means by which they can travel and spread over
the world in a matter of hours. Our drugs and vaccines have caused
these bacteria and viruses to adapt and mutate until they are imper-
vious. We have created the potential for epidemics and plagues on a
scale which is almost unimaginable. Dr. Levy summarizes the foreboding prospect in this manner:

We are in the midst of an evolutionary war against microbes that have proven more sophisticated and multi-talented than we could ever have expected. We cannot underestimate how serious the struggle is… our bodies alone are unable to outwit many pathogens. Now our drugs are failing as well… The risk is high that there will be widespread suffering as well as social and economic disruption… The threat they pose is as formidable as any that the human race has ever faced, and despite all our brilliant advances in science, pharmaceuticals, and medical technology, these simple organisms could still get the better of us.[16]

The potential for a national or global epidemic of a disease that is entirely resistant to any vaccine is quite possible. The prophetic words of Jesus and the prophets can no longer be dismissed as irrational doomsday ranting. The physical evidence is before us. Men and women of science and medicine are sounding the "apocalyptic" alarm. Yet somehow – in spite of the evidence and warnings our world sleeps on with the false assurance that "it can't happen here." Are we so sure "that all things will continue as they were?" Are we so secure that we cannot see the "signs of the times?" Why is it that we cannot "hear the distant rumblings of catastrophe" as do the public health experts of today?

Chapter 5

CLIMATE CHANGE AND THE ENVIRONMENTAL CRISIS

It seems as if all of nature is in rebellion. Man has plundered, polluted, and exploited this beautiful habitation in which he was placed until it now appears that the planet itself is in revolt. Our arable land has been depleted and its production is falling, our supplies of fresh water are diminishing, new infectious diseases for which there is no cure are emerging, but it does not stop there. In recent years we have seen a marked increase in hurricanes, droughts, floods, and heat waves. We have witnessed the most powerful El Nino ever recorded and the hottest European summer on record. Glaciers all over the globe are in retreat, arctic ice is melting at a record pace, the oceans are warming, and weather patterns are changing. Nature and the environment seem to be in chaos as centuries old patterns are changing and scientists indicate that this is just the beginning.

It appears that the inconsiderate plundering of our planet has resulted in consequences which are now manifesting themselves in various forms of natural catastrophes. Although these catastrophes range from the seemingly insignificant melting of glacier ice, to the more serious increase of major hurricanes and storms, collectively these catastrophes could jeopardize the very existence of modern civilization. When one ponders the potential of numerous devastating disasters such as hurricanes, floods, drought, severe heat waves, not to mention the extinction of countless species, all happening at the same time, the results are horrendous. Yet this very scenario is playing out before our very eyes.

When modern man began to believe that he was as wise as the almighty God, and began his total subjection of earth and her resources in pursuit of material gain, he lost his deep-rooted connection with nature. A civilization arose in the twentieth century totally unlike anything which had ever existed in the history of mankind. Out of the earth, resources in the form of petroleum were harvested which produced energy on a level unimaginable before the twentieth century. By harnessing this new petroleum-based energy, a new civilization arose. Man harvested inordinate amounts of metal, wood, petroleum, and other resources by which he constructed cities and towering institutions of finance. He contrived powerful machines of industry and trade, all of which demanded more and more of earth's resources. A synthetic civilization emerged which was completely disconnected from nature. Nature had become nothing more than an asset to be used and consumed in order to enlarge the foundations of the profit based institutions of this new civilization.

Over the course of a century, the masses abandoned the rural areas where ties to nature and God had reigned supreme. They migrated into those enormous urban citadels of progress where man and technology reigned. Even the rural land itself was transformed into a resource to be cultivated by modern intensive farming instituted and controlled by modern corporate powers. These aggressive farming methods raped the land in order to produce more food for the growing urban populations. The fertile ground deteriorated and precious life supporting water was consumed and polluted. All of this was done in order to sustain the infrastructure of the new synthetic society which had emerged during the twentieth century.

But now nature seems to be revolting against the pillaging and plunder to which she has been subjected. The petroleum based energy used to fuel and construct this civilization has injected billions of tons of carbon dioxide (CO_2) into the atmosphere. This carbon dioxide has warmed the planet's atmosphere to the point where we are now experiencing severe upheavals in the natural system. Apparently the synthetic man-made system and the natural divinely created system do not coalesce well.

Prior to the Industrial Revolution, the atmospheric carbon dioxide level was roughly 280 ppm (parts per million). By 2005 they would register 380 ppm, the highest in recorded history. The Intergovernmental Panel on Climate Change (IPCC) states that the present "atmospheric concentration of carbon dioxide in 2005 exceeds by far the natural range over the last 650,000 years."[1] It is apparent that the amount of carbon dioxide has risen substantially since the Industrial Revolution, with most of the increase coming after 1950. Average concentrations per year have increased from an average of 1.4 ppm in 1960, to an average of more than 2.5 ppm today. By 2025 the concentrations of carbon dioxide in the atmosphere are projected to be at 420-430 ppm, with an increase in the average rise to an average of 3 ppm a year.[2] The unpleasant result of this excessive accumulation of carbon dioxide in the atmosphere is a hazardous warming of the planet.

Under normal conditions, and in the manner in which our planet's atmospheric system was intended to work, the sun's energy filters through the atmosphere and warms the earth. Some of this energy is radiated back into space in the form of infrared rays. A portion of this outgoing energy is trapped by gases in the atmosphere creating a comfortable warm blanket around the earth. These balanced atmospheric gases (greenhouse gases) protect the earth from extremes in temperature. If our planet was stripped of its atmosphere, the earth's near ground temperature would soar by day and plummet at night. As it is, our planet's surface temperature averages a pleasant life sustaining temperature of 57.9 degrees Fahrenheit.

It is this perfect balance of greenhouse gases in our atmosphere that creates our comfortable life sustaining environment on Planet Earth. The greenhouse gases surrounding Venus are comprised of 98 percent carbon dioxide and the surface temperature is 891 degrees Fahrenheit. Conversely, the greenhouse gases surrounding Mars are almost non-existent and the temperatures are far too cold to sustain human life, averaging a negative 62 degrees. It is Earth's unique atmosphere, with her balanced greenhouse gases, that have provided the life sustaining environment which we have enjoyed. But now man is tinkering with the planet's global thermometer. Every year billions of tons of carbon dioxide are released into the atmosphere changing the delicate balance of greenhouse gases which control Earth's climate.

For thousands of years prior to the Industrial Revolution the carbon dioxide level in the atmosphere had virtually remained the same. It has only been in the last 150 years that concentrations of carbon dioxide have risen from about 280 parts per million (ppm) to 380 parts per million, with concentrations now climbing by more than 2.5 parts per million a year. Dr. Joseph Romm, the founder and executive director of the Center for Energy and Climate Solutions, explains this drastic increase in atmospheric carbon dioxide levels:

> ...industrial processes, mainly burning fossil fuels, have released some 1,100 billion tons of carbon dioxide into the atmosphere cumulatively. Fully half these emissions have occurred only since the mid 1970's, which is why the climate has begun to change so dramatically in recent decades. In 2005, emissions of carbon dioxide generated by fossil fuel combustion amounted to more than 26 billion tons.[3]

The modern industrialized civilization that has arisen in the last 150 years has been driven by fossil fuels. It has primarily been petroleum, natural gas, and coal which has fueled the enormous progress which mankind has seen. These seemingly abundant and cheap forms of energy have fueled our transportation, energized our industrial processes, and provided abundant conveniences which are now taken for granted. But what we failed to realize was that the burning of these fossil fuels released enormous amounts of carbon dioxide into the atmosphere. Every time we drive a car, cook a meal, or turn on a light we are creating carbon dioxide. Our homes, industries, factories, and even our modern agricultural machinery are releasing tons of carbon dioxide into the atmosphere. Every facet of our modern civilization is built upon the burning of fossil fuels in some manner either directly or indirectly.

The debate over climate change should be over by this time. The evidence that has been accumulated has become almost insurmountable. Only those who have a financial or political investment in denying its existence are holding out. Even so, many doubters have abdicated in the face of the mounting evidence. The latest report by the Intergovernmental Panel on climate Change (IPCC) was released in May of 2007. The conclusion reached by nearly 1,000 independent scientific researchers from 74 countries was that "warming of the climate system is unequivocal" and that "humankind's reliance on fossil fuels – coal, fuel oil, and natural gas – is to blame for global warming." The report continued by asserting that the "global atmospheric concentrations of carbon dioxide, methane and nitrous oxide have increased markedly as a result of human activities since 1750 and now far exceed pre-industrial values..."[4] The findings of the IPCC were endorsed by over 2,500 independent scientists who supported these findings.

Numerous other independent research foundations including National Oceanic and Atmosphere Administration (NOAA), the National Academy of Sciences, the National Center for Atmospheric Research, the National Sciences Foundation, and many others including the National Aeronautics and Space Administration (NASA), have supplied studies which confirm the validity of global warming. There is no doubt that the planet is warming, and as a result there are climatic changes taking place world-wide. The evidence has also shown that this global warming has been the result of "human activities," primarily our reliance upon the fossil fuels which have powered the industrial progress of our modern civilization. A staggering 32 billion tons of carbon dioxide were released into the atmosphere in 2006, with about 25 percent of that from the United States alone.[5]

As carbon dioxide continues to rise in the atmosphere, so does the thermometer on Planet Earth. A 2004 issue of the National Geographic Magazine noted that "global temperatures are shooting up faster than at any other time in the past thousand years." The magazine continued by citing numerous experts which indicate that "natural forces... can't explain all that warming."[6] While the experts demonstrated that "natural forces" were not to blame, they also unequivocally attributed the climatic changes taking place to human forces. Dr. George Philander, a climate expert at Princeton University, was quoted in the same article as saying, "We're now geological agents (mankind), capable of affecting the processes that determine climate."[7]

The idea that global warming can change our weather has begun to manifest itself with grim reality. As Dr. Romm observed, "our weather is changing, and not for the better." He then cited the World Meteorological Association which stated that "the world's weather is going haywire." They noted that "new record extreme events occur every year somewhere on the globe, but in recent years the number of such extremes has been increasing."[8] The world is experiencing record breaking droughts in many areas, while at the same time record breaking floods are occurring in other areas. In August, of 2003, Europe endured an extended heat wave that caused more than 35,000 deaths. In 2005 Mumbai India recorded the most intense instance of rainfall ever recorded – a full 3 feet of rain in a twenty-four hour period. We have seen an increase in the number and severity of hurricanes and typhoons. The United Sates has experienced an increase in tornados, droughts, floods, and wildfires. And all of this does not even include the melting of glacier and arctic ice, or the rising of the ocean levels and warming of oceanic temperatures which affect global currents and weather. Then of course there has been the dramatic increase in the extinction of animal and plant species. The symptoms now manifesting themselves are indicative of a planet in crisis. Planet Earth has become infected with the toxic unnatural man-made by-products of progress to the point that she is now shivering and shaking with a fever. As a special publication of Time Magazine on *Global Warming* put it – "something has gone grievously wrong... from heat waves to storms to floods to fires to massive glacial melts, the global climate seems to be crashing around us."[9]

THE BIG MELT DOWN – TREADING ON THIN ICE

One of the most obvious places where the planet is manifesting symptoms of a climate in crisis is in the Arctic and glacial regions. It is here that the most visible manifestations of global warming are seen on a consistent basis. In Alaska, winters are now four to five degrees warmer than they were in the 1970's, and at the North Pole the summer ice cap has shrunk more than 25 percent from 1978 to 2005. Dr. Romm notes that the size of this melt down is "a loss of 500,000 square miles of ice, an area twice the size of Texas." He explains that "the Arctic winters were so warm in both 2005 and 2006 that sea ice did not refreeze enough to make up for the unprecedented amount of melting during recent summers."[10]

But the ice is not just contracting horizontally, it is getting thinner as well. Robert Henson, the author of *The Rough Guide to Climate Change*, records that studies from data collected from U.S. submarines traveling under the arctic ice during the Cold War was recently compared to more current data. He indicated that this comparison of data revealed that arctic "sea ice had thinned by up to 40 percent over the intervening forty years." He advised the research had shown that "where the ice in some spots had averaged 3m (10 feet) thick, it now extended down only about 2m (6.6 feet)."[11]

The decrease of sea ice has resulted in an alarming impact on Arctic wildlife. Harp seals and Ringed seals cannot raise their young when there is little or no sea ice. The years of 1967, 1981, 2000, and 2001 were extremely bothersome in this respect, and the years that have opened this century have been even worse. Not enough snow and less ice has resulted in fewer pups and forced seals to migrate to other areas, some as far away as Siberia.[12] The polar bears that depend upon seals suffered greatly. Dr. Tim Flannery described how "those that had enough fat followed the seals on their long journeys, but many that had not fed well enough the previous season could not keep up and simply starved." He noted that "the great bears are slowly starving as each winter becomes warmer than the one before."[13]

Studies of these great carnivores of the Arctic have shown a 15 percent decrease in body fat over the past few decades. There are increasingly fewer cubs and their size is decreasing. Feeding seasons have shortened, diminishing ice has decreased their roaming areas, and their primary food sources are migrating to other areas. As Henson notes, "in the end… it comes down to sea ice. Beyond a certain point, there simply won't be enough of it over a large enough area to sustain polar bears as they now live."[14] The melting arctic ice manifests the truly catastrophic results of a climate in transition and clearly depicts how living creatures can be tragically affected.

What we fail to realize is that these climatic changes that are so drastically affecting the polar bear and other arctic wildlife are also insidiously affecting all life on the planet. The swiftly changing Arctic climate is perhaps the warning signal of changes that are coming to all of us. These powerful climatic forces which control our planet's environment and determine living conditions of all creatures are in upheaval. These powerful forces that are changing the polar bears' age-old home into a hostile and inhospitable environment are also working in our own lives. Modern man cannot recognize these subtle changes because he has become so disconnected to his natural environment. It could be that we will not recognize the warning signals until it is too late and nature strikes not subtly, but with the full force of catastrophic natural disasters.

One of the most alarming things concerning the Arctic is that the effects of climate change are occurring much faster than most scientists and models predicted. Dr. Romm acknowledges this concern by noting that "we appear to be crossing a threshold in the Arctic, one that existing models did not predict would happen so fast." Numerous authorities are now adjusting their findings to the unanticipated acceleration of ice melt and warming. As Dr. Romm notes, the "new research suggests that the summer Arctic could be ice-free far sooner than anyone ever imagined." This unprecedented event would be something that has never occurred in the history of mankind.

In 2002 the world's attention turned to the Antarctic. In a 35 day period early in 2002, a section of the Larsen Ice Shelf covering 1,250 square miles collapsed into the ocean. This momentous event received public notice as it had been recorded by a series of time-lapse satellite images released by the National Snow and Ice Data Center (NSIDC). Researchers determined that this immense shelf, which had been frozen in place for over 12,000 years, had been made unstable by rising temperatures that were causing water to pool on the surface of the shelf. This melted water seeped down through the ice, weakening the shelf's vertical faults and eventually causing it to collapse into the Weddell Sea. Since 2002, another 650 miles has broken away, crumbling into the sea.[15]

But the Arctic icecap and Antarctic ice shelves are not the only areas being affected by this rapid increase in warming. Greenland is also warming much faster than the planet as a whole. This increased rate of warming is having a drastic effect upon the Greenland Ice Sheet which covers more than 650,000 square miles. This ice sheet is nearly two miles thick and contains 750,000 cubic miles of ice.[16] According to Gary Braasch, a remarkable journalist and photographer who traveled to Greenland and spoke to scientists working on site, "vast glaciers streaming off the Greenland Ice Sheet are flowing faster than has ever been measured." He records that "according to the Cooperative Institute for Research in Environmental Sciences, 2005 saw the greatest measured melt of Greenland's ice surface in twenty-seven years of satellite records, with 43 percent of it suffering some thawing. Surveys undertaken since the early 1990's by a low-flying NASA plane showed that many coastal glaciers in Greenland are thinning by up to 40m (130 feet) a year; they are moving so fast that one can see them flow 100 feet a day."[17]

To demonstrate how swiftly the ice in Greenland is melting, Braasch flew with glaciologist Robert Thomas over the Kangerdlugssuaq Gletsjer (Glacier) located on the east coast of Greenland. Thomas had been studying this glacier for some time and confirmed that "it was losing about 33 feet of ice thickness each year and was one of the fastest moving glaciers in Greenland, flowing about 4.4 miles a year." Braasch noted that Thomas has "re-measured the Kangerdlugssuaq twice since 2001, and unbelievably it has thinned by as much as 325 feet more and is racing twice as fast, 8.7 miles per year. That's more than 5 feet per hour."[18] But the Kangerdlugssuaq is not the only glacier reacting in this manner to global warming. Scientists have recorded similar data from the Jakobshavn, Helheim, and others.

Joseph Romm confirmed the northward move of glacial melting through data received from the National Aeronautics and Space Administration (NASA). This data revealed that overall "glacier acceleration was widely found below 66 degrees north latitude between 1996 and 2000, (and) that line had shifted to 70 degrees north by 2005." He indicated that NASA's Jay Zwally had advised that "global warming is rapidly speeding up the disintegration of the entire Greenland Ice Sheet, and if we stay on our current emissions path... the loss of the Greenland's Ice Sheet could become irreversible."[19]

Added to all the other concerns involved in the melting of ice in the Arctic, Antarctic, and Greenland, is the fact that all this melted water goes into the oceans. Most people do not realize the immense amount of frozen water that is contained in the vast ice sheets and glaciers of these areas. The 2001 IPCC report indicated that the West Antarctic ice sheet alone contains enough water that could "raise the sea level by nearly 20 feet" if it were to melt.[20] These ice sheets and glaciers contain hundreds of thousands of cubic miles of water. Their enormous potential for raising the sea level has largely gone unnoticed. Bruce Douglas, a coastal researcher at Florida International University is quoted in the September 2004 issue of National Geographic as indicating that just "3 feet (of sea level rise) – would be an unmitigated disaster."[21]

But the rise of sea levels is just one more concern out of many. The melting fresh water of these ice sheets goes into the ocean changing the salinity of the oceans themselves. As reported in the National Geographic, "changes in water temperature and salinity, depending on how drastic they are, might have considerable effects on the ocean conveyor belt,"[22] which is critical in regulating weather patterns on Earth's terrestrial surfaces. Now, according to NOAA, there is a "declining salinity of the sub-polar seas bordering the North Atlantic."[23] The experts seem to agree that too much change in the temperature and salinity of the ocean's waters could disrupt the ocean's currents and precipitate drastic climatic weather changes in a very short period of time.

Unseen changes are occurring in our oceans that could drastically affect every part of the planet. While the salinity level is declining, the sea level and water temperature are rising. Dr. Flannery notes that prior to 1955 the surface temperature of the tropical Pacific waters commonly dipped below 66.5 degrees, but after 1976 it has rarely been below 77 degrees. In fact, he states that "the waters of the central western pacific have frequently reached 86 degrees and the jet stream current has shifted toward the North Pole."[24]

It has been this temperature and current change that has affected the El Nino and La Nina weather cycles. Prior to 1976, the La Nina phase was the dominant part of the cycle. Now the El Nino, which if extreme enough, can bring droughts, floods, and other extreme weather conditions to over two-thirds of the globe, has been dominant. Climatologist Kevin Trenberth, in Tim Flannery's book, *Hell and High Water,* notes that "ever since 1976 the cycles have been exceptionally long... and there was an imbalance between the phases, with 5 El Ninos and only 2 La Ninas."[25] Scientists have observed that these changes seem to have become permanent about 1998. This change in the El Nino – La Nina weather patterns are now generating more extreme El Ninos which are producing floods and droughts in many areas, including the current 10 year drought in the southwestern United States.

The melting of polar and Greenland ice sheets which contain most of the earth's fresh water has the potential of affecting our climate in ways which have not even been imagined. Only as the ice melts away and these changes begin will we learn to appreciate the delicate balance which has sustained our climate system for so long. But the warming temperatures are not only melting ice at the poles, glacial ice all over the world is being affected by the rise of the global thermometer.

There are more than 160,000 mountain glaciers scattered over the globe. Braasch notes that "except for a few, they are all losing ice mass at an unprecedented rate." He indicates that according to Wilfred Haleberli and Martin Hoelzle of the World Glacier Monitoring Service, this unprecedented melting "represent(s) convincing evidence of fast climatic change at a global scale."[26]

This melting of the earth's freshwater reservoirs presents major problems for people all over the world. Billions of people depend upon the fresh water that comes from melting winter snows and glaciers for their drinking water. But when the snows don't come, and the glaciers are melted away, where will this water come from? This diminishing resource of fresh water is of major concern to the

World Food and Agriculture Organization. Gary Brassch explains their concern in this manner:

> According to the World Food and Agriculture Organization, half the human population drinks water that originates in mountains, and more than a billion people depend directly on flow from glaciers and seasonal snow. But now global warming jeopardizes every part of this hydrologic system. Snowfall elevations are rising, providing fewer raw materials to low elevation glaciers. Snow melts earlier and from higher elevations, pushing peak river flows earlier in the year. Run-off from storms and glaciers is already causing floods and pouring more water into the oceans, raising sea levels. Rivers are not as full in the summer and fall when demand for water intensifies. As glacier ice continues to dwindle, river flows, too will diminish. Mountain peoples will face drought, as will great low-land cities from China to the American West that depend, at least in part, on glacier water.[27]

This scenario is playing itself out all over the world. Even in the American West the result of glacial melt and dwindling snow pack in the Rocky Mountains is being felt. In 2004 writers from the National Geographic accompanied research scientists from the U.S. Geological Survey as they examined the rate of glacier melting in Montana's Glacier National Park. Writer Daniel Glick stated that "the results were positively chilling." He noted that when the park was established in 1910, there were an estimated 150 glaciers in the park. "Since then the number has decreased to fewer than 30," Glick reported, "and most of those remaining have shrunk in area by two-thirds."[28]

The article focuses on Sperry Glacier as an example. This spectacular glacier was measured at over 800 acres in 1901 and had melted down to "less than 250 acres" by 2004 at the time of the article. But Sperry Glacier is just an example of what is happening all over the world. The famed snows of Kilimanjaro have melted by 80 percent and are expected to be completely gone in the very near future. Glaciers and winter snows are disappearing from mountains all over the world. From the Alps, to the Himalayas, to the Andes of South America, the story is the same. Glaciers are disappearing at an alarming rate. As the National Geographic reports, "from the Arctic to Peru, from Switzerland to the equatorial glaciers of Irian Jaya in Indonesia, massive ice fields, monstrous glaciers, and sea ice are disappearing, fast."[29]

EXTEME WEATHER – WHEN THE ABNORMAL BECOMES NORMAL

Since 1970 the earth's average temperature has risen by nearly 1.4 degrees Fahrenheit. This does not sound like much of a rise. But not everywhere on the planet is the climate warming at the same rate. As we have seen, in the polar regions the average temperature has risen about 5 degrees over the past couple of decades. It has been this unprecedented rise that has caused the ice and glaciers to melt. We have also discovered that just a one degree rise in the global mean temperature has disrupted the planet's climatic balance and has precipitated unforeseen changes in climate patterns. Most climate scientists agree that Earth's global thermostat is very sensitive. As George Philander, a climate expert at Princeton University states, "continuing to fiddle with the global thermostat is just not a wise thing to do."[30] Just a small warming of the global average can set in motion numerous factors which can precipitate unknown and possibly drastic effects on the entire global climate.

It has been our climate's predictability and consistent weather patterns that have allowed humans to develop our current agricultural and societal systems. We have depended upon this reliability in order to determine where to build our cities, where to cultivate agricultural products, and even where to obtain our water. The face of our global map has been determined by the predictability of the climate that we have enjoyed for the past 6,000 years. Our cities, nations, and civilizations have been predicated upon either the hospitality or inhospitality of the climatic conditions in a particular region. Now this predictability is changing. Droughts are increasing in certain areas while flooding is occurring in others. The intensity and number of severe storms are increasing and the seasons are changing. Spring is coming earlier and fall later in many areas. Seasonal rains are disappearing in the place of either extreme drought or torrential rains. It seems as if unusual weather events are becoming so frequent that they are becoming the usual. As Gary Braasch explains in his book:

> ...greater changes and extremes in weather seem more and more common lately. Increasingly, news stories confirm many people's observations that spring is coming earlier, rainstorms are pelting down harder, snowfall is less predictable, heat waves more common, and droughts afflict larger areas. It is true that around the world many... long-term observations and scientific studies corroborate these impressions.[31]

According to Joseph Romm, the World Meteorological Organization has stated that "new record extreme events occur every year somewhere on the globe, but in recent years the numbers of such extremes have been increasing."[32] Climatic impacts and changes are occurring faster more frequently, and with more severity than most computer models have suggested. Extreme weather events are becoming the norm – and they are expected to increase as the global temperature rises.

Lester Brown of the Earth Policy Institute notes that meteorologists have recorded "that the 22 warmest years on record have come since 1980." He also observed that the six warmest years on record have "come in the last eight years."[33] This extreme heat pattern appears to be increasing in frequency and duration with each passing year. During the summer of 2003 Europe experienced its most deadly heat wave ever recorded. Over 35,000 people died as a result of this deadly heat wave. During the months of June and July "temperatures exceeded 104 degrees Fahrenheit over much of the continent."[34] All-time records were broken in London with temperatures soaring over 100 degrees. Roth, Germany, recorded 104.7 degrees, Grono, Switzerland, 106.7 degrees, and Amareleja, Portugal, a scorching 117.1 degrees.[35]

The consequences of this heat wave were unimaginable. Train tracks buckled, schools and businesses were closed, and thousands of elderly people without air conditioning perished in the heat. Temperatures in hospitals and emergency rooms remained unbearably high. As Robert Henson records, "no heat-wave in global history has produced so many documented deaths."[36]

In descending order, the five years with the highest global average annual temperatures were 2005, 1998, 2002, 2003, and 2004. During the summer of 2005 many cities in the United States broke all-time records for high temperatures and consecutive days with temperatures over 100 degrees. Reno, Nevada, set a new record of 10 consecutive days with temperatures at 100 degrees or hotter. In July, Las Vegas, Nevada, tied its all-time high of 117 degrees. Tucson, Arizona, tied its record of thirty-nine days with temperatures higher than 100 degrees. Grand Junction, Colorado, reached an all-time high of 106 degrees, with Denver following at 105 degrees. Newark, New Jersey, Raleigh, North Carolina, and Florence, South Carolina, all set records with temperatures over 100 degrees.[37]

A study conducted by Switzerland's Federal Office of Meteorology showed that since 1880 heat waves are lasting twice as long in certain parts of the globe, and the number of recorded setting hot days has tripled.[38] And along with this record breaking increase in heat waves comes record breaking drought. Research by the U.S. National Center for Atmospheric Research has confirmed that "the percentage of Earth's land area undergoing serious drought has more than doubled since the 1970's."[39] In an uncertain world where the climate is changing, one thing is certain; drought conditions and the number of heat waves are steadily increasing.

The increasing record heat in the western Atlantic is contributing to weather extremes in South America. For the first time in recorded history a hurricane formed in the South Atlantic and blasted southern Brazil in March of 2004. Its winds were recorded at 114 miles per hour and nearly flattened towns like Torres damaging almost 90 percent of the homes. In 2005 the worst drought in over 40 years lingered over the usually moist Amazon. Rivers which normally flow with water were turned to mud, killing the fish and cutting off access to over 900 towns. Economic disruption and hardship quickly followed and the area is still suffering from the effects of this record breaking drought.

In other parts of the globe, extreme weather events manifested themselves with frightening regularity during 2005. In February, widespread flooding and heavy snowfall in Pakistan and northern India killed at least 486 people throughout the country. Thousands were left homeless after several dams burst due to torrential rainfall. Flooding was also recorded in South America, Central America, China, Central Europe, Southeast Asia, Malaysia, and Northeastern United States. In January violent windstorms swept across Europe killing at least 13 people and leaving millions without electricity. The hurricane season brought hurricanes Dennis, Katrina, and Rita, ripping across the Gulf Coast area and into the United States. As Geoffrey Holland notes in his book:

> The hurricane season in the Atlantic in 2005 was the most active since record keeping began in 1851. There were twenty-seven named storms, fifteen of which became hurricanes. The worst, Hurricane Katrina, was the most destructive tropical storm of all time. Some estimates have suggested the economic losses of Katrina will ultimately exceed $125 billion.[40]

It was August 28, 2005, when Hurricane Katrina slammed into the Gulf Coast of the United States. The hurricane immobilized and devastated city after city along the Gulf Coast. Reports of miles upon miles of destruction came from Biloxi, Waveland, Bay St. Louis, and Slidell. Oil rigs were tossed about like toys, hotels and casinos were leveled and entire cities were flooded with a record surge of water from the gulf. Witnesses who viewed the devastation compared the effects to that of a nuclear explosion. And small wonder. *Newsweek Magazine* reported that "a hurricane like Katrina packs the energy of a 10-megaton nuclear bomb – exploding every 20 minutes. The winds were recorded at 140 miles per hour and the surge that hit the coast was some 29 feet high, the highest ever recorded."[41]

New Orleans, a city that lies below sea level and is protected from water by a system of levees was inundated as the levees gave way. In a matter of hours 80 percent of the city had been flooded and chaos had ensued. People were fleeing to high areas and onto the roofs of their houses. Many were trapped in their attics and died as the waters rose higher and higher. Looters began rampaging through the city breaking into businesses and homes. The city was without power, water, and communication. The police did what they could but found themselves unable to respond to the disaster that led to increasing lawlessness. Officers were fired upon and the police retreated into their stations as night fell.

New Orleans, a technological representation of modern civilization, was a city devastated. It had deteriorated into chaos in a matter of hours as the infrastructure disintegrated. Modern technology was shown once again to be no match for nature's fury. *Time Magazine* reported that "for the first time ever, a major U.S. city was simply taken off line, closed down. Food, water, power and phones were gone; authority was all but absent."[42] It was the first time since the Civil War that a major American city had to be evacuated.

But Hurricane Katrina was just one of numerous record breaking hurricanes that whirled their way through the Caribbean and the Gulf of Mexico in 2005. Billions of dollars in damage was done and thousands of lives lost due to hurricanes in 2005. Hurricanes Stan and Wilma missed the United States but had whirled through the gulf and struck Central America killing over 2,000 people and inflicting over 25 billion dollars in damage. Wilma was noted to be the most intense and costliest Atlantic Basin hurricane on record.

All in all, there were twenty-five named Atlantic storms in 2005. This number surpassed the old record of twenty-one set in 1933, and three of the 2005 hurricanes were among the six most powerful hurricanes ever recorded. The increase in the number and severity of the hurricanes is attributed directly to the warming of the ocean temperature by many experts. An extensive study conducted by Kerry Emanuel of the Massachusetts Institute of Technology found that since the middle of the twentieth century there have been approximately 4,500 storms that have brewed in the North Atlantic and the western part of the North Pacific. His study also demonstrated that the average power of these storms has increased by 50 percent in the last fifty years.[43] Hurricanes appear especially sensitive to climate change as warming ocean waters provide the energy which drives the storms.

Overall, 2005 was a year of weather records. Record snowfalls in Algeria and Japan, record hurricanes in the Gulf area, record flooding in many parts of the world, and record wind storms and heat waves. But this pattern is not unique to the year 2005. Weather related events are setting new records with unnerving frequency. Cold waves, heat waves, floods, droughts and other extremes are becoming the norm. These natural disasters and extreme weather events are occurring more and more frequently and leaving more and more societies in disarray.

In March of 2006 at least eighty-four tornadoes touched down in the United States over a two day period. This was the largest two day outbreak of tornadoes on record. In April another outbreak occurred with reports of sixty-three tornadoes sweeping across the states of Tennessee, Iowa, Kentucky, Arkansas, Missouri, Ohio, Illinois, and Indiana. In many places the thunderstorms which accompanied these tornadoes produced hail as large as softballs inflicting tremendous property damage. In 2003 a total of 562 tornadoes were reported during the month of May setting a new one month record. The old record had been set in 1992 with 399 tornadoes.[44]

The list could go on with heat waves in India, a record breaking thirteen feet of snow in Japan, cold weather and freezing conditions in Bangladesh and New Delhi, and a report of "bizarre weather" in the tiny kingdom of Lesotho, Africa. In January of 2003 the *Washington Post* reported that after this tiny country had endured devastating drought conditions, it had then experienced storms bringing flooding rain, hailstorms, tornadoes, and then an early frost during the summer months. The *Post* quoted Makhaabasha Ntaote, a seventy-year-old matriarch of the country as saying, "frost in the summertime! We never used to see weather like this. We don't know what to expect anymore from the skies. I think God is angry at us, but I don't know why." They simply "believe something has gone haywire with the cosmos. The weather patterns… no longer form patterns." The article continues by indicating that nearly one-third of Lesotho's population "will need emergency handouts this year" to sustain them, all this due to an extreme shift in weather conditions.[45]

Each story and each event could be examined in detail. Each one of them would reveal its own account of human suffering and the destructive power of nature. The research conducted for this book revealed so many bizarre and extreme events that it was impossible to list them all. From so many choices it was difficult to choose specific instances to illustrate the dramatic changes taking place in worldwide weather conditions. All of them had their own unique account of human beings overtaken by bizarre changes in the weather or enduring nature's fury. But one thing they all had in common was the marked recognition that these were unusual events that were far from the ordinary. The words "bizarre" and "extreme" were used consistently along with phrases such as "something has gone haywire" or "nature is out of control." To the people experiencing and researching these events there is no doubt that something very unusual is taking place with Earth's weather patterns. Both science and physical evidence point to one conclusion – climate change is a reality, and its effects are being felt with increasing severity and frequency worldwide.

AND EARTHQUAKES TOO

There is no doubt that the effects of global warming are consistently being manifest more frequently and more severely. It appears as if nature itself is rebelling against the brutal exploitation and increasing wickedness of mankind. Yet the effects appear to go beyond global warming. Earthquakes, which are not related in any way to global warming, have increased dramatically in the past few decades. So dramatic has been the increase in worldwide seismic activity that we would be remiss in not mentioning it when considering natural disasters. According to the USGS National Earthquake Information Center, there were a total of 16,590 earthquakes reported worldwide in 1990. By the year 2000 the number of earthquakes had risen to 22,256, and by 2006, the number of recorded earthquakes had risen to 28,854. The year 2004 was the most active as far as worldwide seismic activity with 31,194 earthquakes being recorded. This is almost double the total number reported in 1990.[46]

It was on December 26, 2004, that the most devastating earthquake in recent history occurred. It was a clear beautiful morning in the Southeast Asian countries that encompass the Indian Ocean. It appeared to be just another of many beautiful days, yet this one was to be dreadfully different. Nature was about to shake herself in a manner that would be felt around the world. A massive earthquake trembled along the earth's crust off the western coast of Indonesia. This Teutonic plate which usually moves only about 2.4 inches a year, suddenly slid almost fifty feet in one gigantic lurch. This massive seismic lurch sent shock waves through the ocean creating a tsunami that was felt more than 3,000 miles away. This massive wave resulted in the death of over 250,000 people and devastated countless villages, cities, and nations that surrounded the Indian Ocean. *Time Magazine* reported that this catastrophe was "like no other disaster in living memory..."[47]

Time reporter Michael Elliot quoted witnesses as saying that "it felt like doomsday" as the earth shook and "killer waves" drove upon the shorelines from Indonesia to Tanzania sweeping thousands upon thousands into eternity at one time. Whole resorts and villages were swallowed by the overpowering waves. The force of nature was relentless and man was helpless in its wake. The entire earth trembled. The power of this massive quake measured 9.1 to 9.3 on the Richter scale and scientists indicate that the entire earth wobbled on its axis. According to USGS seismological expert Ken Hudnut, Indonesian Islands in the vicinity were moved by as much as 20 meters, and the northwestern tip of Sumatra may have shifted as much as "36 meters."[48]

One cannot help but think of the words of the prophet Haggai, "For thus saith the Lord of hosts; yet once, it is a little while, and I will shake the heavens, and the earth, and the sea, and the dry land" (Haggai 2:6). But then Isaiah the prophet also prophesied that "the earth shall reel to and fro like a drunkard..." (Isaiah 24:20). If there was ever a day that the earth was literally shaken, it was December 26, 2004. Yet, as horrendous as this catastrophe was, we must consider that this earthquake was just one of an ever increasing number of seismic shocks. No longer can Jesus' warnings in Matthew chapter twenty-four be carelessly dismissed.

That something unusual and strange is happening in the natural realm on Planet Earth cannot be denied. Polar ice is melting, glaciers that have been in existence for thousands of years are disappearing, unprecedented heat waves and droughts are occurring, bizarre storms are happening, weather patterns are changing and now earthquakes are increasing dramatically. Not only is nature rebelling, but it appears that God is desperately trying to send mankind a message. Life on Planet Earth is about to change dramatically.

OTHER EFFECTS OF CLIMATE CHANGE

The effects of climate change go far beyond polar ice melting and severe weather related disasters. As the climate warms, the ecological system is affected. Animals and insects are being forced to the brink of extinction or are migrating to new habitats. A spider-eating wasp has been observed for the first time in Great Britain. Mosquitoes, which carry Dengue Fever and Malaria, have expanded their normal ranges apparently due to the warmer climate. As a result of this expansion the World Health Organization has noted a marked increase in the cases of both Dengue Fever and Malaria. In fact both diseases are being diagnosed in areas where they had been virtually unknown. According to WHO (World Health Organization), around two-fifths of the world's population are now living in areas affected by Dengue Fever, and almost half the world's population is now at risk of Malaria infection.[49]

Warmer and milder winters along with extended drought conditions have precipitated one of the world's largest die-offs of mountain and boreal forests in North America. Robert Henson of the National Center of Atmospheric Research describes this "die-off" in his book, *The Rough Guide to Climate Change:*

Across western North America, the intersection of pests and warming atmosphere has led to one of the world's largest forest die-offs. A series of major droughts and warm winters since the 1990's from Mexico to Alaska has transformed the

95

landscape across huge swathes, destroying millions of hectares of forest through beetle invasions and forest fires. The extent of both is unprecedented in modern records.[50]

Dr. Henson continues to explain the extent of this devastation to our forests by describing how "in 2002 alone, British Columbia lost 100,000 square kilometers (39,000 square miles) of lodge pole pines to fire and disease." Astounding as it may seem, Dr. Henson notes that the Canadian Government has predicted that by 2013 over 80 percent of the pine trees in British Columbia will be gone.[51]

All one has to do is drive through any western state or province in Canada and the United States and you can observe this catastrophe in the making first hand. In areas, entire mountain sides are brown with dead or dying pine trees. Throughout Arizona, where I live, you can find large stands of pine trees which have been devastated by bark beetle infestations. But it is not only in Arizona, it is throughout the west. This beetle which normally requires two years to reach maturity is now maturing in a single season due to the extremely warm summers and mild winters. Once again Dr. Henson explains, "It takes two bitterly cold winters in a row to keep the population (of bark beetles) in check. The combination of milder winters and warmer summers since the early 1990's has allowed the beetle to run rampant." This scourge has left entire forests littered with brown, dead, or dying trees.

The Bark Beetle is just one of many parasites attacking the western forests. The Mountain Pine Beetle, which was once only found in lower elevations and fed upon lodge poles and ponderosa pines, has moved to higher elevations and are now besieging the white bark pine in Utah at elevations as high as 10,000 feet. Dr. Henson also notes that across parts of "New Mexico, Arizona, Colorado and Utah, where record-setting drought took hold in 2002, pine beetles and other drought-related stresses have killed up to 90 percent of the native pinion pines trees..."[52] Simply put, the western American forests are under siege. The pines that once flourished in this arid mountain high country are dying off at a record pace. What is left are enormous amounts of dried and dead timber, the perfect fuel for forest fires.

This dead and dried timber is undoubtedly one of the reasons why wildfires in the United States have been so devastating in recent years. According to the National Climatic Data Center, dryer than average conditions over most of the country have contributed to burns in excess of 9.5 million acres in 2006 and over 8.5 million in 2005. These figures broke the old record of 7.4 million acres in 2000, and almost doubled that of the 4.5 million acres burned in 1960. The extended drought, forest die-offs from insect infestation and human encroachment have all contributed to the increase in wildfires.

But the primary cause can be attributed to climate change. It has been the shift in ocean currents and weather patterns that has brought about the extended drought conditions. Added to this are the warmer conditions and heat waves triggered by the increase in global temperature. This has led to a drying of the foliage and a prolific increase in insect infestation. As we have seen, these parasitic tree killing insects such as the Bark Beetle and Pine Beetle have moved to higher altitudes and more northerly climates due to warmer temperatures. All these conditions have placed great stress on the forests of North America, making them ripe for forests fires.

In October of 2007 wildfires broke out in Southern California. From Malibu to the Mexican border, over 16 separate fires raged while being whipped by the Santa Anna winds. Thousands of acres were scorched, over 2,000 homes destroyed and nearly one million people were evacuated. This was the largest evacuation in American history, exceeding even that caused by Hurricane Katrina. Over ninety aircraft and 6,000 firefighters were involved in suppressing the fires. The total cost of fighting the fires, including the damage inflicted, is estimated to exceed 1 billion dollars. This would be the most expensive fire season in California's history.[53]

The staggering 1 billion dollars attributed to the 2007 California wildfires is just the beginning. When all the fires and climate change related disasters are added to this figure, the amount assumes unimaginable proportions. The National Climatic Data Center records seventeen separate weather related events occurring in the United States from 1998 to 2002, which cost over 1 billion dollars each. These events include droughts, floods, fire seasons, tropical storms, hailstorms, tornadoes, heat waves, ice storms, and hurricanes. The most expensive of these events was the drought of 2002 which cost in excess of 10 billion dollars. These financial statistics do not even include the devastating hurricane season of 2005. Just the damage inflicted by Hurricane Katrina alone is estimated to be over 125 billion dollars.[54] The financial burden has become so staggering that some insurance companies are refusing to provide insurance against hurricanes in some areas along the Gulf Coast.

These statistics are from the United States. Worldwide, the figures are even more discouraging. Dr. Lester Brown, of the Earth Policy Institute, documents the findings of one of the world's leading reinsurance companies – Munich Re – in his book *Plan B 2.0*. He indicates that Munich Re published a list of forty-nine natural disasters which had incurred damages for more than 1 billion dollars between 1983 and 2004. Their list revealed a steady increase in the frequency and severity of these disasters. There were three during the 1980's, twenty-six during the 1990's, and from 2000 to 2004 there had been seventeen.[55] Dr. Brown presents the 30 billion dollar damage inflicted by Hurricane Andrew in 1992, along with the 30 billion dollar flooding devastation incurred along the Yangtze River basin in China in 1998, as examples of the "growing damage toll." He indicates that the insurers "are convinced" that because of the anticipated increase in storm severity and frequency, "future losses will be even greater."[56]

This astronomical rise in damage claims, along with the projected continued escalation in claims due to natural disasters, has produced profound concern in the insurance and reinsurance industry. Dr. Brown notes that "they are concerned about whether the industry can remain solvent under this onslaught of growing damages."[57] Dr. Tim Flannery concurs with Dr. Brown with his observation that "insurance industry leaders doubt that their businesses will be able to absorb the claims for much longer."[58] He explains the financial and insurance crisis in this manner:

> Over the last four decades the insurance industry has been reeling under the burden of losses as a result of natural disasters, of which the impact of the 1998 El Nino offers a fine example. Paul Epstein of the Harvard Medical School

calculated that, in the first eleven months of that year alone, weather-related losses totaled $89 billion, while 32,000 people died and 300 million were made homeless. This was more than the total losses experienced in the entire decade of the 1980's. Since the 1970's, insurance losses have risen at an annual rate of around 10 percent, reaching $100 billion by 1999. Losses at this scale threaten the very fabric of our economic system...[59]

Dr. Flannery continues by explaining that with a 10 percent increase in damages every year, the amount of the total damages incurred by natural disasters would soon reach the unbelievable amount of all "that humanity produced in the course of a year."[60] In other words, the damages inflicted from natural disasters would reach the point where they would be greater than the gross production of the world economy. But long before this point could ever be reached, the world's economic system would have collapsed under such a burden.

While this may seem beyond the realm of comprehension, this was exactly the concern of members of the United Nations Environment Program's (UNEP) financial services initiative when they met in Nairobi in February of 2001. Their primary agenda was to develop a plan on "how to cope with the rising toll of natural disasters." Their report indicated that projected future losses due to the increase in these natural disasters could reach an unimaginable 304.2 billion dollars annually. Klaus Toepfer, Executive Director of UNEP, stated that "the time to act is now... climate change should sound alarm bells in every national capital and in every community." He earnestly indicated that it was time to "move ahead" and nations should "start preparing... for the impacts of global warming."[61] These concerns were expressed in 2001, even before the Tsunami of 2004 and the devastating hurricane and cyclone seasons of 2004 and 2005. The cost estimations have risen considerably since that time.

There is little doubt that the increase in natural disasters and their severity is weighing heavily upon the minds of world leaders. That natural catastrophes have the potential of wrecking financial devastation to any nation, and even the global economy, is a distinct possibility. It is a possibility that cannot be ignored when confronted with the growing evidence and the increase in such natural calamities. Dr. Gerhard Berz, head of Munich Re's Geosciences Research Group, disclosed this concern by saying that "there is reason to fear that climatic change will lead to natural catastrophes of hitherto unknown force and frequency." He continued by explaining that "studies have indicated, disturbingly, that climatic changes could trigger worldwide losses totaling many hundreds of billions of dollars per year."[62]

Consider the United States of America. Even though this country is the most prosperous in the world – how many disasters on the scale of Katrina could this country withstand? Could there be numerous simultaneous or even consecutive disasters to the point where the infrastructure could no longer function? Could there be devastation so vast and with so many people dislocated or unemployed because of homes and jobs destroyed that the nation could no longer provide? Could the economic system be devastated to the point that it could not function nor cope with the financial extent of the damage?

These questions and others like them were the subject of an unclassified report released to *Fortune Magazine* by the Pentagon in 2004. The Pentagon report, dated October 2003, was entitled "An Abrupt Climate Change Scenario and Its Implications for United States National Security." The report had been commissioned by Pentagon defense advisor Andrew Marshall and was written by Peter Schwartz, a CIA consultant, and Doug Randall of the Global Business Network. According to the *San Francisco Chronicle*, these authors "are tough minded analysts, not your stereotypical tree-hugging environmentalists."[63]

The report opens by affirming that "there is substantial evidence to indicate that significant global warming will occur during the 21st century." The report continues by asserting that ignoring the evidence or assuming that the climatic changes will be gradual "may be a dangerous act of self-deception, as increasingly we are facing weather related disasters – more hurricanes, monsoons, floods, and dry-spells – in regions around the world." Swartz and Randall then emphasize that "weather related events have an enormous impact on society, as they influence food supply, conditions in cities and communities, as well as access to clean water and energy." Because of the potential impacts, they assert that "climate change and its follow-on effects pose a severe risk to political, economic and social stability."[64]

The report indicates that "catastrophic changes" due to climate change will precipitate "food and energy shortages" along with "dwindling supplies of water." The report anticipates that flooding will occur in some areas while others suffer drought. It predicts extreme weather events which will disrupt services and cripple national, state, and urban infrastructures. The report suggests that as these events unfold regional conflicts may develop as nations struggle to defend vital resources such as food, water, and energy, which are essential to maintaining their infrastructure. It also indicates that internally there could be widespread rioting and conflict as basic services and resources deteriorate. Schwartz and Randall dismally predict that as these events take hold, "priorities will shift," the goal will be "survival rather than religion, ideology, or national honor." They conclude their report by stating that global warming must "therefore be viewed as a serious threat to global stability and should be elevated beyond a scientific debate to a U. S. national security concern."[65]

As dire and unlikely as these predictions seem, a very similar scenario chillingly unfolded in the fall of 1998 in Honduras and Nicaragua. On October 29, Hurricane Mitch swept ashore with winds exceeding 200 miles per hour and a rain storm which dumped almost three feet of rain within a few days. The storm devastated the infrastructure and economy of both Honduras and Nicaragua in just a few days. Homes and factories along with entire communities were destroyed. Nearly all bridges and roads were washed away. Seventy to eighty percent of the transportation infrastructure was destroyed. Communications were shut down and entire portions of the country were isolated for weeks. The report of National Climatic Data Center (NCDC) stated that "the resulting floods and mud slides virtually destroyed the entire infrastructure of Honduras and devastated parts of Nicaragua... Whole villages along with their inhabitants were swept away in torrents of flood waters and deep mud that came rushing down the mountainsides. Hundreds of thousands of homes were destroyed." The mud-slides covered entire villages killing thousands of people and causing up to 1.5 million people to be displaced and left homeless.[66]

The onslaught of the storm was so vicious that 70 percent of the nations' agricultural crops were destroyed and over 11,000 people were killed and countless others never accounted for. Food, medicine, and water shortages were critical. The NCDC reported that "hunger and near starvation was widespread" and "epidemics, feared as malaria, dengue, and cholera" made their appearance."[67] Dr. Brown calculated that the destruction of the storm was so extensive that it exceeded "the annual gross national product of the two countries, (and) set their economic development back by 20 years."[68]

It was only with the assistance of other nations such as the United States and the United Nations that relief from this devastation was supplied. Should such a disaster (or multiple disasters) strike the United States with such crippling force, where would our relief come from? If the economic infrastructure of the United States was incapacitated, what country or institution would have the economic resources to keep our system operating until it could function again on its own? These are sobering questions that should be considered in light of some of the recent natural disasters which we have seen. More than once, nature has surprised us with a ferocious demonstration of her awesome power. Numerous times she has demonstrated her potential to incapacitate technology and wreck havoc on modern civilizations. One should consider just how fragile our modern infrastructure is when confronted with the devastating wrath of nature, and then consider that these demonstrations are being made more and more frequently.

Pondering the swift and immediate impact of a devastating natural calamity is one thing, but it is much more difficult to comprehend the slow but insidious impacts of climate change that are even now manifesting themselves. As difficult as it is to comprehend in the land of abundance, the grim specter of famine (or to use the more politically correct term – food shortage) is slowly manifesting itself.

In February of 2007 the Commodity Information Systems (CIS, Inc.), made an announcement via a press release, that a *"Global*

Grain Shortage of Historic Proportions (was) Ahead." Their announcement was based upon figures that indicated the "world had consumed more corn, wheat and rice than it produced in six of the last eight years."[69] This information had reaffirmed the Earth Policy Institutes announcement in 2006 that the world's grain harvest was projected to "fall short of consumption by 61 million tons." They then confirmed that this shortfall "marked the sixth time in the last seven years that production had failed to satisfy demand."[70] The announcement continued by citing that "world grain consumption has risen in each of the last forty-five years except for three." But now the world is experiencing a shortfall in which demand or consumption is greater than production. Dr. Brown continued by explaining that the "world's farmers must try to feed an additional 70 million people" that are added to the world's population every year. He stated that with unprecedented drought conditions, and with "water tables now falling and wells going dry in countries that contain half the world's people, including the big three grain producers – China, India, and the United States," meeting a hungry world's demand was becoming increasingly difficult. Dr. Brown then grimly noted that "while it is widely recognized that the world is facing a future of water shortages, not everyone has connected the dots to see that this likely also means a future of food shortages."[71]

Dr. Brown, who is a recognized expert in the field of agriculture, and has served as an international agricultural analyst with the U.S. Department of Agriculture's Foreign Agricultural Service, explained the dilemma facing the world. He advised that while the "widespread over-pumping of aquifers" and the loss of water resources to bourgeoning cities was critical, "the most dangerous threat to future food security is the rise in temperature." He stated that it was now recognized "that for each temperature rise of one degree Celsius, above the historical average during the growing season, we can expect a 10 percent decline in grain yields."[72] This rise in the global average is now affecting harvests over the entire planet. In short, he states that "spreading water shortages and rising temperatures are making it difficult for farmers to keep up with the record growth in demand." Marcia Baker of the *Executive Intelligence Review* provides the grim statistics:

Global wheat production for 2006 is projected to be 585.1 million metric tons (mmt), down dramatically from 618.85 mmt in 2005 and from 628.84 in 2004. The 2006 plunge in wheat production comes from the immediate impact of drought and other bad weather in Australia, in Kansas and other parts of the U.S. wheat belt, and lowered production in Brazil, China, India, and the EU-25 (European Union). In Australia, instead of a crop of 25 mmt, drought will cut the harvest to barely 11 mmt. These reductions combined, far outweigh the small increase of 0.4 mmt in Canada.[73]

The rise in global temperature that has precipitated the unprecedented heat waves and drought conditions in many parts of the planet are taking their toll on earth's usually abundant harvests. Australia is experiencing one of its worst droughts in 100 years. This drought has all but destroyed Australia's grain harvest and thousands of farmers are threatened with bankruptcy. Michael Byrnes, a Reuters News Service reporter writes that Australia, which is the world's second largest grain exporter, "will produce almost nothing this year (2007)." He writes that this "drought which has struck intermittently since 2002, and which farmers hoped had ended in April with rains that prompted them to sow their fields, returned three months ago and devastated the crops of entire farming communities." He quoted one farmer as saying that they are "in a state of disbelief, shock, and helplessness,"[74] as they watch their crops and futures wither away.

The British Broadcasting Company (BBC) released an article in September of 2007 indicating that the European Union was acting "on the world grain shortage." The article stated that the EU for the past fifteen years had enforced a requirement that "farmers set aside 10 percent of their land and let it lie fallow." The news article stated that European Union Officials were "temporarily" lifting this restriction so farmers could "boost grain production by up to 17 metric tonnes" to assist in reducing the world's grain short-fall. However, the European Union Officials also noted that "sharply increased demand and poor harvests" of their own "have recently shrunk... reserve stocks to almost nothing."[75]

The United States has also experienced the effects of drought and extreme heat over the past decade. In the year 2007 these conditions persisted and affected much of the "central, southeast, and eastern parts of the southern U.S." According to the National Climatic Data Center (NCDC), "average temperatures..." in the affected areas "were more than 10 degrees Fahrenheit warmer than the average in many parts of the country." Their report indicated that the "exceptional drought conditions" were exacerbated by a "devastating April freeze that killed off many budding plants and crops." The NCDC concluded by stating that "the combination of the exceptional drought and the prolonged heat wave has taken a heavy toll on the agriculture industry across the Southeast." They indicated that "many crops have been severely damaged" and that 81 percent of the Alabama corn crop is in poor or very poor condition." They advised that the "corn crops in many parts of Tennessee is forecast to be a total loss."[76]

The affects of the drought and heat wave extended far beyond the grain harvests. The NCDC report indicated that "between 40 and 52 percent of pasture and rangeland in Alabama, North Carolina and Tennessee was listed as being in 'very poor' condition." They stated that many "herd owners" had been forced to sell their livestock "due to a lack of water and vegetation."[77]

The impact of these world-wide drought conditions escapes the notice of most consumers in the industrial world. All that is usually noticed is a higher price for various food products in the grocery store. Usually a heat wave or drought is simply a minor inconvenience only affecting their electric bill as the thermostats are turned lower and the air conditioners work harder. Industrialized life revolves around consumer markets with neatly packaged and processed products. There is little or no thought given to the fact that most of these products (especially food) are originally harvested from the earth and are dependent upon a hospitable environment. That is – there is little or no thought given to this until there is none to be purchased.

Modern man's world is a secular business and market-oriented culture built entirely upon technology. There has been a total disconnect between modern man and nature. The idea that nature and not technology – may ultimately control the future of modern man is inconceivable. But a closer examination reveals that this disconnect between man and nature also reflects a disconnect between man and the God which created all things in nature. The idea that the God which created nature may have something to say about the future is utterly incomprehensible to modern man.

The prophecies of the scripture now appear to be coming into focus. The natural environment seems to be in turmoil and unusual events are becoming the norm. Our once hospitable planet seems to be rebelling against man and all that he has instituted in the name of progress. We have seen the evidence of a marked increase in earthquakes and natural disasters. The current and pending grain shortfalls indicate that the modern world is perched precariously upon the edge of a world-wide food shortage or famine. All it would take to push us over the edge would be some global catastrophic event. With what we have seen to this point, Jesus' words concerning "famines, and pestilence, and earthquakes" cannot be ignored (Matthew 24:7). His warning that there would be signs in the heavens "and upon the earth, distress of nations, with perplexity; the sea and the waves roaring" is taking on a whole new meaning (Luke 21:25).

Chapter 6

THE COMING ENERGY CRISIS – PEAK OIL

O ur world is about to change. A crisis is in the making that will affect every facet of our society and lives. It will be a permanent, dramatic, earth-shaking crisis which will threaten the very existence of modern civilization. The fact is that modern civilization as we know it has been built upon an abundant supply of cheap energy in the form of petroleum. This cheap supply of energy has fueled our modern industrialized society for the last 100 years, and it is about to come to an end.

What most people have not realized – or refused to accept – is that petroleum is a finite resource, and the end of this finite resource is now in sight. As Paul Ehrlich, in Richard Heinberg's book, *The Party's Over*, bluntly puts it, "…by early in the twenty-first century, the era of pumping 'black gold' out of the ground to fuel industrialized societies will be coming to an end."[1] Mike Bowlin, Chairman and CEO of Arco, confirmed this analysis by stating, "We've embarked on the beginning of the last days of the age of oil."[2]

To appreciate the enormity of the problem, one must understand that our nation – and all industrial nations – are almost entirely dependent upon the consumption of an inherently limited supply of petroleum. Industrial nations of the world have been consuming this finite resource in enormous amounts. It has energized our economies, built our cities, fueled our transportation, and provided the basis of our industry. It is not an exaggeration to say (if anything it is an understatement) that our modern civilization is almost exclusively built upon the use and consumption of fossil fuels.

The extent of our dependency staggers the imagination of those unfamiliar with petroleum and its manifold uses and versatility. There is hardly an activity in modern industrialized life that is not affected in some way by fossil fuels and petroleum products. Turning on a light switch, setting the thermometer in your house, driving your car, and using your cell phone, all of these daily activities are dependent upon fossil fuels. But the dependency goes far beyond the obvious. Plastics of all kinds are derived from petroleum products. This includes the plastic your food is wrapped in and the plastic casing of all our computers and technical gadgetry. Petroleum is used in chemicals which fertilize our fields, kill pests, and is even used in our pharmaceutical industry. Many of your children's toys are made from petroleum products. It's in your shampoo, toothpaste, and clothing softeners. It's in the asphalt you drive on, the tires on your vehicle and the paint on your house.

The list could go on almost indefinitely. Most of the food we eat has been raised on farms using enormous amounts of petroleum fueled machinery, petroleum based fertilizers, and pesticides. It has been refrigerated or frozen in petroleum energized refrigerators or freezers. It has been packaged and processed with petroleum products. And then it has been shipped in petroleum fueled transportation conveyances to our petroleum cooled and heated supermarkets. Our industry itself could not operate without petroleum energy, or the petroleum based products it either makes or uses in the production of products. Essentially – our economy – and thereby our society – is completely dependent upon petroleum products and would grind to a halt without them. It is a commodity that is no longer a luxury – it has become absolutely essential for the survival of our modern industrial civilization. Howard Kunstler, in his thought provoking book entitled *The Long Emergency*, emphatically states that "everything characteristic about the condition we call modern life has been a direct result of our abundant supplies of cheap fossil fuels."

Petroleum energy is so fundamental to industrialism and progress that our entire economic system depends upon it. It has energized our factories and industry thus creating our wealth. Over the last 100 years an economy has evolved which is entirely dependent upon tremendous amounts of cheap petroleum energy. Paul Roberts, an expert in the field of economics and technology describes "a new kind of economic order" that emerged during the twentieth century as a result of this new fossil fuel based energy:

> This new order engendered a powerful system of production practices and distribution networks, tailored to the reciprocal dynamic of supply and demand. It included a corporate business model designed for massive economies of scale, a financial structure to manage the large capital requirements, and political relationships to protect these investments. Just as significantly, around the new energy order arose a culture of energy consumption and a social and political awareness of the critical role that energy played in rising living standards and wealth, in national success and international power.[3]

Roberts continued by explaining the unique relationship established between energy, production, and the new economy in this manner:

> The pattern was clear: the more you produced, the more energy you needed. And conversely, the more energy you used, the more things you produced – and the wealthier you or... your employer or the state became. One might just as well re-label the expanding Industrial Revolution, the energy revolution, because the industrial economies of the nineteenth century simply could not have developed without the parallel emergence of energy economies to sustain them. And as industrialization spread, country by country, region by region, so did the demand for energy.[4]

Now, after a little more than 100 years, this essential energy source is about to become scarce. The global demand for petroleum based energy is going to exceed the available supply. Michael

Ruppert, in his book, *Crossing the Rubicon*, cites numerous experts as he describes the dilemma in this manner:

> Global demand for oil and natural gas is growing faster than new supplies are being found, and the world population is exploding. Currently the world uses between four and six barrels of oil for every new barrel that it finds, and the trend is getting worse... There are only about one trillion barrels of accessible conventional oil remaining on the planet. Presently the world uses approximately 82 million barrels a day. Even if demand remained unchanged, which it clearly will not, that would mean that the world will run out of conventional oil within thirty-five years... Since the world's population and the demand for oil and natural gas are increasing rapidly, by reasonable estimates, the world supply of conventional oil is limited to perhaps twenty years.[5]

But the problem is not that the world will deplete all of its oil resources within 20 or 30 years. The dilemma is that oil is a finite substance, and as the discoveries of oil around the world decline, the volume produced from these declining wells will no longer meet global demand. The point at which the world is producing its maximum amount of oil is the "peak" of production. After that point the production of oil will begin an inevitable and relentless decline. It is not that all the oil has been found and produced – it is that we have crossed the halfway point and all of the easily accessible and cheap oil has been found. The half that is left is harder to find, in more difficult places, and of poorer quality. As Paul Roberts notes, "oil companies and oil states will find it harder and harder to maintain current levels, much less keep up with rising consumption. Demand will outstrip supply...[6]

Roberts proceeds by describing the critical unfolding of the Peak Oil dilemma as a series of progressive and evolving events which ultimately culminate in a devastating crisis.

> ...the term "peak" suggests a neat curve with production rising slowly to the halfway point, then tapering off gradu-

ally to zero. In the real world, the landing will not be soft. As we approach the peak in production, soaring prices... will encourage oil companies and oil states to scour the planet for oil. For a time they will succeed, finding enough to keep production flat, stretching out the peak into kind of a plateau and perhaps temporarily easing fears. But in truth, this manic, post peak production will simply deplete remaining reserves all the more quickly, thereby ensuring that the eventual decline is far steeper and far more sudden. As one geologist put it, 'the edge of the plateau looks a lot like a cliff.' In short, oil depletion is arguably the most serious crisis ever to face industrial society.[7]

The problem is compounded by the fact that as the world's oil production begins its inevitable decline, the world's demand will continue to rise. Industrial nations must continue to consume more energy to sustain their current and growing economies. The developing nations such as China and India must consume even more as they enlarge their emerging economies. An article in the *New York Times Magazine*, published in August of 2005, cited the worldwide consumption of oil as growing from "79 million barrels a day in 2002, to 82.5 in 2003, to 84.5 in 2004."[8] This is an increase of almost 2 million barrels a day (bpd) every 2 years. At this time (2008) the world is consuming between 86 and 87 million barrels of oil per day. Peter Tertzakian, the Chief Energy Economist of ARC Financial Corporation, notes that these figures "translate into a staggering one thousand barrels a second."[9]

Tertzakian continues his world financial analysis by observing that "the world as a whole requires an increasing amount of oil every year to facilitate economic growth." He states that "pressure on the world's supply chains will keep building so long as the global economy keeps expanding. Any global economic growth at all necessitates more and more oil every year."[10] It is a cycle that cannot stop. Energy produces growth, and growth produces wealth. Without wealth the economy crumbles and industrial progress grinds to a halt.

In the final analysis, the industrial world needs energy. It cannot survive without enormous amounts of energy. This energy is supplied by fossil fuels and at this time there is no replacement in sight. The industrial world must have oil just as the human body must have oxygen. The significance of this basic fact is poorly understood by the general population of the world. Petroleum energy and the modern lifestyle "has lasted long enough for the people now living in advanced industrialized nations to consider it absolutely normal."[11] Even though our energy demands are obviously exceeding the world's ability to supply them, we continue pumping more and more oil from the ground to sustain our industrialized lifestyle. The demand continues to rise, but now there are signs that supplies are dwindling. It appears that the only thing that can stop the world's unquenchable thirst for oil is the limits of nature – and nature does not negotiate.

The question is not whether oil is a finite substance. That is an indisputable fact. Colin Campbell, a former Texaco and Amoco petroleum geologist and founder of the Association of the Study of Peak Oil, states that history cannot be changed, "nor resource limitations" associated with oil. He points out that oil is a resource "whose occurrence is controlled by Nature" and no engineer however skilled can overcome the natural limitations of this resource. He solemnly warns that "when geologists tell us that we are about to face a major change as the resources of available oil dwindle, we had better pay attention."[12]

When it comes to oil consumption the United States has no rival. In his book, *The End of Oil*, author Paul Roberts notes that "Americans are the most profligate users of energy in the history of the world." He explains that the United States is "a country with less than 5 percent of the world's population (and) burns through 25 percent of the world's energy."[13] Tertzakian observes that for the past fifty years "America has had no sizable competition for the world's energy resources." But he indicates that this situation is swiftly changing as other nations such as China begin to expand their industrial economy. He states that "as China awakens with its own rapidly growing energy needs, the tension over the global energy supply is mounting."[14] All nations now want their piece of the industrial pie.

The prosperous, but unsustainable industrial lifestyle enjoyed by the western nations has become intensely desirable to all other nations. This lifestyle is only possible through the consumption of energy – and lots of it. This energy comes from a swiftly diminishing supply of oil and all nations are now seeking their share.

THE U.S. PEAK AND A WAKE-UP CALL

The concept of what is now called "Peak Oil" originates with a distinguished petroleum geologist by the name of M. King Hubbert. Although Hubbert's reputation was already well established in the petroleum industry, he assured himself of a place in petroleum history when he predicted in 1956 that the U.S. oil production would peak between 1966 and 1972. This announcement was made at the meeting of the American Petroleum Institute in San Antonio. His prediction immediately ignited a storm of controversy. Almost everyone rejected his analysis. Economists, petroleum officials, and government agencies including the USGS dismissed his prediction as wild conjecture. The controversy raged inside the petroleum industry until 1970 when the United States production of crude oil "peaked," and then began a steady decline every year thereafter.

History has proven that Hubbert's prediction was correct. In 1970 the United States reached its maximum production level of just over nine million barrels per day. It has slowly but steadily declined ever since. Today (2008) the maximum production is a little over five million barrels per day. While the production levels have consistently declined since 1970, the consumption level has risen dramatically. Today the nation is using over twenty million barrels per day and importing approximately 60 percent of this twenty million to meet consumption demands.[15]

Aside from the fact that Hubbert's prediction was shown to be correct, it is the steadily increasing conflict between our rising demand and falling production that has made Hubbert's concept of Peak Oil vitally important. The concept – if not the mathematical formula – is relatively simple. Hubbert's principle of peak oil is based upon four fundamental laws.

1. Oil is a finite resource, and there are basic laws which describe the depletion of any finite resource.
2. Production has a beginning point, or value of zero.
3. Production will rise to a "peak," or maximum point which cannot be surpassed.
4. Once the "peak" has been passed – production will decline until the resource is depleted and returns to a point or value of zero.

Hubbert first described these simple principles in the 1950's but had actually begun his studies on resource depletion years earlier. Taking these basic principles and using statistical and physical methods, Hubbert found that he could calculate oil and natural gas supplies by documenting their production and consumption history. He noted that by plotting production history – using years and volume of production – on a graph would result in a bell-shaped configuration with a top, and tail on both ends. His analysis showed that the decline side of the curve would be a mirror image of the increase side. It was on the basis of this profile, and his estimate of petroleum reserves, that Hubbert was able to accurately predict the ultimate peak and decline of U.S. oil production fourteen years before it occurred.

What was noted from Hubbert's studies was that the production of oil tends to follow a bell-shaped curve. This bell-shaped production curve is described by Richard Heinberg in his book, *The Party's Over:*

> During the early phase, production increases rapidly as the easiest-accessed oil is drained first. However, beyond a certain point, whatever remains is harder to get at. Production begins to decline, even if more wells are still being drilled. Typically, the production peak will occur when about half of the total oil in the reservoir has been extracted. Even after production has tapered off, some oil will still be left in the ground: it is economically impractical – and physically impossible – to remove every last drop.[16]

What has been found – and history has shown – is that the production history of the United States conforms nearly perfectly to the production graph which Hubbert's figures produced. His calculations have proven to be distressingly accurate. But then as if to punctuate the point – the United States and the world received a wake-up call in 1973. Almost before the significance of Hubbert's calculations had set in, the Yom Kippur war broke out in the Middle East.

By the 1960's the United States was already consuming more oil than it was producing. This was of little concern at the time because more oil fields had been discovered all over the world – and more importantly – in the Middle East. As American oil field production declined, more and more oil was imported. This dependency on imported oil would steadily increase as U.S. production continued its relentless decline. But in 1973, with the economy booming and prosperity at an all time high, this was of little concern to the American people. That is, until the Arab nations imposed an oil embargo on the United States because of its support of Israel.

A coalition of Arab forces led by Syria and Egypt and backed by Soviet (Russian) technology conducted a surprise attack on Israel to regain land Israel had gained in the 1967 war. For the first two days the Arab coalition appeared to have the advantage, but Israel rapidly gained control in the war. During the course of the war, the United States and other western nations supported Israel politically and with weapons and supplies. In retaliation, Saudi Arabia's King Faisal convinced the oil producing Arab nations (OPEC) to place an embargo on crude oil supplies to the west – and in particular to the United States.

The effects of the oil embargo were immediate and dramatic. Prices of gasoline soared from twenty-five cents a gallon to over a dollar in just a few months. Americans had never experienced an escalation of fuel prices on this scale before. Gasoline was rationed and many gas stations ran out of fuel. Those that had gasoline limited the sale to ten gallons and experienced long waiting lines. Drivers were forced to wait as long as three hours to purchase the allotted amount. Thermostats were turned down in the winter and air conditioning was turned off in the summer. It was a time of turmoil as electric companies and customers endured brownouts and prices of commodities rose. Congress issued a 55 mph speed limit on highways and Daylight Savings Time was observed year round in an effort to conserve energy. President Nixon ordered the Department of Defense to create a reserve of oil to be used primarily for national defense in the time of emergency.

By the time the embargo had ended, the price of a barrel of oil had quadrupled. It had gone from three dollars a barrel to an unbelievable twelve dollars a barrel. The economic impact of this rapid price increase sent shock waves throughout the world. The entire world experienced an economic recession as inflation soared above ten percent and unemployment hit record highs. The era of economic growth which the world had enjoyed since World War II came to an abrupt end. The United States and the rest of the world had received their wake-up call. It would no longer be the western nations and the United States that would hold sole control of the global economy. The OPEC nations had succeeded in establishing that they would now play a key role in setting the price of oil and thereby maintain a strong influence on the world's economy.

Although the world had painfully learned the importance of petroleum, they had still not fully grasped that there could be an end to this precious commodity. The embargo was perceived by most people to be an "artificial shortage" created by "political policies." The connection between this shortage and the natural limitations of petroleum was somehow missed. Americans still generally believed that there was a limitless supply of this wonderful substance. It was oil companies, politicians, and suppliers that were to blame for the "artificial shortage." The idea that oil was finite, and at some point there might be an "authentic" and permanent scarcity was still beyond comprehension.

But there were still a few voices sounding the alarm. After he had delivered his prediction concerning the peak of U.S. production, Hubbert had committed himself to calculating the global production peak. Using the same principles he had used earlier, and figures he had available in reference to the world's petroleum reserves, he calculated that the world would reach its peak of production sometime between 1990 and 2000. Due to insufficient data and minor flaws in his calculations, Hubbert's forecast would prove to fall short of the actual peak by a few years. But what Hubbert had understood was the great social, political, and economic implications of a world peak in oil production. He grasped better than anyone else at the time how indispensable fossil fuels had been in the development of the modern industrial world. He understood the tremendous impact that a scarcity of petroleum resources would have on modern society. He attempted to convey this warning through articles and lectures until his death in 1989.

TAKING A LOOK AT THE WORLD'S PEAK

After Hubbert's death other petroleum geologists continued to work with his calculations and peak model. Making minor adjustments and using more available data they modified his predictions only slightly. Most of these experts calculated that the global peak of production could be reached sometime between 2005 and 2012. The United States Government also commissioned a study of the *Peaking of World Oil Production* by Robert L. Hirsch in 2005. This report provided a list of many notable experts along with their projected dates for the peaking of world oil production.

Projected Date	Source of Projection	Background
2006-2007	Bakhitari	Iranian Oil Executive
2007-2009	Simmons	Investment Banker
After 2007	Skrebowski	Petroleum Journal Editor
Before 2009	Deffeyes	Oil Company Geologist
Before 2010	Goodstein	Vice Provost, Cal. Tech.
2008-2010	Campbell	Oil Company Geologist
After 2010	World Energy Council	Non-Government Organization
2010-2020	Laherrere	Oil Company Geologist
2016	EIA (Nominal)	DOE analysis/information
After 2020	CERA	Energy Consultants
2025 or later	Shell	Major Oil Company
No visible Peak	Lynch	Energy Economist

From *Peaking of World Oil Production: Impacts, Mitigation, & Risk Management*
By Robert L. Hirsch, commissioned for the United States Department
of Energy, February 2005

It is interesting to note that while the general public in the United States manifests very little knowledge (and concern) about the anticipated peaking of world oil, the United States government has shown a remarkable amount of interest and knowledge concerning this event. Not only does the Hirsch report document this knowledge, but a 2004 report by the United States Department of Energy concerning the *Strategic Significance of America's Shale Oil Resource* also indicates a concern over this issue. The report indicates this concern by stating that "the disparity between increasing production and declining reserves can only have one outcome: a practical supply limit will be reached and future supply to meet conventional oil demand will not be available. This event," the report states, "is now inevitable." It continues by noting that the primary "question is when peak production will occur, and what will be its ramifications. Whether the peak occurs sooner or later is matter of relative urgency..."[17]

The report continues by acknowledging that many non-OPEC countries "have peaked and are currently declining." It then concludes by conceding that the peak of world oil may occur as soon as "2003," and notes with some apparent uneasiness that no prediction "extend(s) beyond the year 2020."[18]

The peak of world oil production is no longer a "fringe" theory. Overwhelming evidence has demonstrated that this is an event which is anticipated to occur shortly. As both Department of Energy reports indicate; the question is not "whether" peak will occur, but "when." It is this critical question of just exactly "when" this momentous event will occur that occupies the center stage today. Even such reputable periodicals as *The Wall street Journal* have addressed this subject. In November of 2007 the headlines on the front page read, "Oil Officials See Limit Looming on Production." Writers Russell Gold and Ann Davis confirmed that "a growing number of oil-industry chieftains" are conceding that "the world is approaching a practical limit to the number of barrels of crude oil that can be pumped every day." The article continued by stating that the date projected by these "oil-industry chieftains" could be "as soon as 2012."[19]

Gold and Davis quote such oil notables as Sadad Ibrahim Al Husseini, a former head of exploration and production at Saudi Arabia's national oil company. The article stated that he has expressed concern because "new discoveries (of oil) are tending to be smaller and more complex (difficult) to develop." Matthew Simmons, the chairman of energy investment banking firm Simmons & Company International, was quoted as conceding that "peak oil is likely already a crisis that we don't know about. At the furthest out, it will be a crisis in 2008 and 2012."[20]

As we have seen, the dates run anywhere from 2003 to 2020. When these times are considered in the light of the significance of the event – seventeen years is inconsequential. But the fact remains that most of the world's leading experts in geology and petroleum place the dates nearer the 2005 to 2012 bracket. It is interesting to note that economists, government agencies, and oil companies align themselves with the more liberal dates. But there is yet further evidence and data to consider on this most vital subject.

A significant piece of evidence is based upon the fact that the world's discovery of oil fields has already peaked. This pivotal milestone was passed in 1963 and duly noted by the United States Geological Survey (USGS).[21] It is a historical fact that has been well documented by the oil industry and the United States Department of Energy.[22] Since 1963 the rate of oil field discoveries has been falling worldwide. Except for a small increase right after the oil embargo of 1973, the oil industry has experienced a steady decline in the number and size of newly discovered oil fields. In his book, *The End of Oil*, Paul Roberts describes this peak in discovery and the consequent decline in the volume of oil produced:

> ...when one charts the average volume of oil that has been discovered each year since the beginning of the century, it becomes clear that new oil is indeed getting harder to find. Year by year, the volume of newly discovered oil – that is, the number of barrels found each year and recorded in the books as known or discovered reserves – climbs steadily upward from 1860 until around 1961, when it peaks. Since then, oil companies have found, on average, a little less oil

each year... In fact, since 1995, the world has used 24 billion barrels of oil a year but has found, on an average, just 9.6 billion barrels of new oil annually.[23]

The fact is – all the easy oil and larger fields are gone. Oil companies have scoured the planet but are failing to find the monster fields of the past. In spite of having more sophisticated equipment and newer technology, the oil companies still have not been able to locate oil fields matching those discovered before 1963. Dr. Leeb confirms this grim prognosis in this manner:

"World-wide oil exploration has suffered from declining returns for some time, despite the use of improved technology. It has been decades since the last giant oil reservoirs were discovered, and even large discoveries are becoming rarer... we can safely assume that virtually all significant oil deposits in the planet's crust have already been found. Further exploration will result in ever smaller discoveries, and in ever higher exploration costs per barrel of oil discovered."[24]

The last discoveries of significantly large fields were South America's Cantrell field, discovered in 1976, and Prudhoe Bay in Alaska, found in 1968. Since then the pickings have been slim and experts are not optimistic about things getting any better. Chris Skrebowski, the editor of *Petroleum Review*, published a report in 2004 which indicated that global oil supplies may have difficulty meeting demand as early as 2007. Skrebowski notes that "between a quarter and a third of the world's oil production is already in decline and it appears that giant new discoveries to replace lost capacity are becoming scarce."[25]

Richard Heinberg, in his book *Powerdown*, cites statistics from Skrebowski's report which indicate that "the rate of new discoveries of major new oil fields has fallen dramatically in recent years." He states that "there were thirteen discoveries of over 500 million barrels in 2000, six in 2001 and just two in 2002. For 2003, not a single new discovery over 500 million barrels was reported."[26] This serious decline in discovery of new fields and the lack of finding the large fields like those of the past are significant indicators that the world's oil reserves are diminishing fast.

What makes the decline in the world's discovery of oil fields even more significant is the fact that this was one of the factors which Hubbert used when calculating the peak of production in the United States. He had noticed that the discovery of oil fields in the United States had peaked in the early 1930's. He reasonably calculated that the industry could not long keep up significant production if the older fields were declining and the discovery of new fields was getting less and less. As we have seen – approximately forty years later his calculations and predications proved to be correct. The same logic holds true for the planet as a whole. The world cannot long maintain significant production if the fields which provide that production are aging and in decline. Production can only be maintained through new fields that match the demand. This is not happening – and has not happened in over forty years!

The oil fields of twenty-five of the forty-five significant oil-producing nations are past peak.[27] Every year they produce less and less oil as the world demands more. Outside of the Middle East, most oil producing countries are either at peak – or are past peak – and their production levels are declining just as the United States has since 1970. The world is consuming between five and six barrels of oil for every new barrel discovered. On the average the global demand for oil is increasing at a rate of about 2 percent a year.[28] Ultimately, the only way the world's growing thirst for oil is going to be satisfied will be through the vast reservoirs of oil found under the sands of the Middle East.

Michael Klare in his book, *Blood and Oil,* explains the importance of the oil reserves found in the Middle East and Persian Gulf region. He notes that "the overwhelming majority of the world's proven reserves are in just five nations: Iran, Iraq, Kuwait, Saudi Arabia, and the United Arab Emirates (UAE) – which together possess some 658 billion barrels of untapped petroleum, or 63 percent of known reserves. Add the supplies of neighboring Oman and Qatar, and the Gulf's total share rises to 65 percent, just shy of two-thirds of the world's total remaining petroleum supply."[29]

Ultimately, it will be the oil resources of the Middle East upon which the industrial nations of the world will rely for the fuel needed to maintain their energy intensive lifestyles. It will be Middle Eastern oil that will keep the economies and institutions of the industrialized world functioning. But of all the oil producing nations, it is Saudi Arabia that holds the largest reserve in the world. Under the sands of this desert nation lie 25 percent of all the oil reserves remaining on the planet. As an individual nation, Saudi Arabia alone holds reserves large enough to increase production that will keep pace with the 2 percent per annum increase in the world's growing economy.[30] If – and when – Saudi Arabia's production peaks, the world is in for a rude awakening. So far, the Saudis have been able to keep pace with world demand, but there are disturbing signs that even the vast oil fields of the Saudi Kingdom may be faltering.

Ghawar, one of the oldest Saudi oil fields – and the world's largest – was discovered in 1948 and began production in 1951. It has been one of the world's main supplies of oil since its discovery. This field has been pumping out oil at an enormous rate for over fifty-five years. According to Matthew Simmons, Chief Executive Officer of Simmons and Company and member of the National Petroleum Council, there are distressing signs that may indicate not only is Ghawar in decline, but also many other of the Saudi's older fields.[31]

Simmons conducted extensive research by examining "over 200 technical papers about Saudi Arabia's petroleum resources and production operations." He visited the kingdom in "2003 as a guest of Saudi Armaco (Saudi Arabia's national oil company)." The information gleaned from his research and visit was incorporated into his book, *Twilight in the Desert*. In this book he does a field-by-field assessment of key Saudi oil fields analyzing their production and capacities. Simmons notes that in many of these fields – including Ghawar – the Saudi's have been injecting sea water for some time. The injection of water into a well is a method used to increase pressure and assist bringing crude oil to the surface. According to petroleum experts, when water is injected into oil fields to increase pressure, this is a sure sign that pressure has decreased and that the field is reaching its peak. This practice – and including the fact that

no new significant discoveries have been made in over thirty years
– could spell serious trouble for the industrialized world. Simmons
explains the Saudi oil production plight in his book:

> Ninety percent of all the oil that Saudi Arabia has ever
> produced has come from seven giant fields. All have now
> matured and grown old, but they still continue to provide
> around 90 percent of current Saudi oil output. The king-
> dom's three most important fields have been producing at
> very high rates for over 50 years. High volume production at
> these key fields, including the world's largest (Ghawar), has
> been maintained for decades by injecting massive amounts
> of water that serves to keep pressures high in the huge under-
> ground reservoirs... When these water injection programs
> end in each field, steep production declines are almost
> inevitable.[32]

To complicate the dismal Saudi situation further, Simmons notes
that there does not appear to be much hope that the Saudi's will
discover any new fields to make up for the decline in their older
ones. He explains that their "exploration efforts over the past 35
years" have been disappointing. He notes that the "accounts of
Saudi exploration activities... confirm that there has, in fact, been
intensive exploration in Saudi Arabia for the past 30 years, and that
effort has brought only marginal success."[33] Simmons summarizes
the situation by stating that the evidence indicates that a Saudi peak
in oil production appears imminent. He warns that "the consequences of such an event... are of such monumental importance to
the world economies that to ignore the eventuality of this occurrence
is naïve."[34]

Credibility is supplied to Simmons' analysis by the oil market
report issued by OPEC every month. This report indicates that in
October of 2004 Saudi oil production was at 9.5 million barrels per
day. In October of 2005 Saudi oil production was still at 9.5 million
barrels per day. But in October of 2006 production had fallen to 9.0,
and October of 2007 it was down to 8.5 million barrels per day.[35]
This decrease in production seems strange when one considers that

the nation with the largest known reserves is reducing production at a time when world demand went from 81.7 million barrels per day to 85.7 million barrel per day. Interestingly, the report also revealed that the combined production of all the OPEC nations during this same period of time had remained virtually the same at around 30 million barrels per day.[36] This left the decline in Saudi production to be made up by other OPEC suppliers and the few remaining non-OPEC producing nations that have not yet peaked. Whatever the reason – the fact remains that Saudi oil production (and OPEC's) has not increased in the last four years.

It is also interesting to note that after the Hurricanes Katrina and Rita had stormed through the Gulf of Mexico inflicting damage on numerous oil rigs in 2005, Saudi Arabia had assured the United States that it would increase oil production to make up for the production which had stopped in the Gulf due to the storm. This increase never came. Once again in October and November of 2007, as prices broke all-time records and climbed toward the $100 dollar a barrel mark, Saudi Arabia had assured the world that they could increase production "by as much as 720,000 barrels a day"[37] according to the Wall Street Journal. This promised increase did not come. The December 6, 2007, issue of the Wall Street Journal reported that the cartel members had declined to increase production because they felt that "there was ample inventory of crude to keep consumers well supplied through the winter." While the OPEC ministers claimed the market was "well supplied," the International Energy Agency released a statement indicating that "the market remained 'clearly uncomfortable' over diminishing stockpiles of crude..."[38]

The evidence as a whole is not comforting. Discoveries of oil fields worldwide peaked in 1963. Most of the non-OPEC nations are either past peak or near their production peak. Fewer and fewer discoveries are being made and these are growing smaller in size. Saudi Arabia – the largest oil producer in the world – and the nation holding the largest reserves – appears to be faltering. Oil production from the OPEC nations as a whole has been flat for the last four years. All the while demand for oil in the industrialized world is still rising and developing nations such as China and India are increasing their energy intensive economies at record pace. All this together is a recipe for an economic disaster on a scale never seen before. Dr. Leeb assesses the situation by writing:

...there is more than enough evidence for us to believe a crisis of epic proportions is brewing... A world in which oil prices climb relentlessly higher will challenge civilization's leaders more severely than any other crisis in living memory – more than the Great Depression and World War II. The rapidly approaching oil shortage may be the greatest test of civilization and the world economy since the advent of the Industrial Revolution. In fact, unless our leaders act quickly and aggressively, our chances of surviving as a complex society are rather low.[39]

Few people today understand the implications of a global peak and the inevitable decline of oil production. We have lived so long in an energy extravagant manner that we have grown to think that endless energy is our "birthright." We cannot imagine a world without industrial and technological progress. We have grown accustomed to a modern energy intensive lifestyle and have come to believe that it is a normal condition of life in spite of its unsustainable nature. But the truth is – the petroleum energized age which we have enjoyed for the past 100 years is swiftly coming to an end. Richard Heinberg describes the end of our petroleum subsidized party in this manner:

Industrial societies have been flourishing for roughly 150 years now, using fossil energy resources to build far-flung trade empires, to fuel the invention of spectacular new technologies, and to fund a way of life that is opulent and fast-paced. It is as if part of the human race has been given a sudden windfall of wealth and decided to spend that wealth by throwing an extravagant party. The party has not been without its discontents or costs. From time to time, a lone voice issuing from here or there has called for the party to quiet down or cease altogether. The partiers have paid no attention. But soon the party itself will be a fading memory – not because anyone decided to heed the voice of moderation, but because the wine and food are gone and the harsh light of morning is come.[40]

LOOKING DOWN THE OTHER SIDE

It is after the world production of oil peaks that life as we know it in industrial societies will change. After peak, the supply of available energy resources will begin to diminish while the demand for energy will continue to rise. The current configuration of modern civilization demands energy. Without energy nothing works or nothing moves. As Paul Roberts states, our world is "completely dominated by energy. It is the bedrock of our wealth, our comfort, and our largely unquestioned faith in the inexorability of progress." He contends that energy, and more specifically petroleum energy, is "implicit in every act and artifact of modern existence."[41]

The demand for oil will continue to increase because it is our primary source of energy. Not only is it fundamentally vital for economic growth – but it is necessary simply to sustain the infrastructure of modern civilization. Our dependence upon oil goes far beyond an addiction. The modern industrial civilization needs oil just as the human body needs oxygen or blood. Our body is not addicted to oxygen – it cannot survive without it. So it is with modern civilization – it cannot exist without oil.

This assessment is not simply the dismal conjecture of a few apocalyptic doomsday prophets. Numerous authorities in various fields of expertise have described the same dilemma. Our world today has established its fundamental underpinnings of survival upon a resource that at one time was abundant and cheap. This resource now is becoming scarce and expensive. This crucial fact is recognized by scientists, economists, and government officials. The nature of the impending crisis cannot be overemphasized. In his book, *The long Emergency*, James Kunstler succinctly assesses the crisis by writing that "oil is the world's most critical resource. Without it, nothing works in industrial civilization..." He continues by reiterating that "everything about the condition we call modern life has been a direct result of our access to abundant supplies of cheap fossil fuels..." and "the age of fossil fuels is about to end."[42]

The fundamentals of these crucial facts are poorly understood by the world's population today. Other than knowing that the price of gas and electricity is going up for some complex political reason – generally there is no comprehension of what is occurring. Our modern society has existed for the last one hundred years using fossil fuel resources like there was no end. They were cheap and they were abundant. Our use of them in our daily lives became accepted as the norm. The generation since 1950 has known nothing other than a modern industrialized lifestyle and has come to accept it as their "birthright." All the accouterments and innovations of technology that are either directly or indirectly a result of petroleum energy are accepted as an entitlement. These things are here – this is our life – and that is simply how things are. No other thought is given much beyond this. Our lives are so consumed with everyday activities – all of which are grounded upon fossil fuel consumption – that we have no time for consideration of anything else.

Our world is in for a rude awakening. Never in the history of mankind has the world faced such critical times nor confronted such a momentous crisis as it does today. Mankind has confronted and survived numerous significant crises in past history. Many of these crises have affected entire nations, kingdoms, and even societies – but never in the history of mankind have we confronted a crisis that has the potential of affecting the entire planet. Globalism and our interdependent world economy have insured that every nation, society, and culture on the planet will be critically affected when the world's production of oil peaks. Kunstler describes the anticipated effects in this manner:

> The world production peak represents an unprecedented economic crisis that will wreck havoc on national economies, topple governments, alter national boundaries, provoke military strife, and challenge the continuation of civilized life. At peak, the human race will have generated a population that cannot survive on less than the amount of oil generated at peak – and after peak, the supply of oil will decline remorselessly. As that occurs, complex social and market systems

will be stressed to the breaking point, obviating the possibility of a smooth ride down the peak...[43]

Petroleum geologist Colin Campbell also sees the world peak of oil as a time of "great volatility." He stresses that the "growing physical shortages (of oil), must lead to a major economic and political discontinuity in the way the world lives." Essentially he states that "the world will become a very different place with a smaller population. The transition will be difficult, and for some, catastrophic."[44]

Geologist Jeremy Leggett, a former faculty member of the Royal School of Mines in London, also describes fundamental world reaction to peak oil:

Humans will no longer be able to run their lives and their industries on growing amounts of cheap oil. All we can expect thereafter is shrinking supplies of expensive oil... It will be a grim time. When it becomes clear that there is no escape from ever shrinking supplies of increasingly expensive oil, there will be a paroxysm of panic. Human society will face an energy crisis of unprecedented proportions, and that, plus the panic, will spark an economic collapse of unparalleled awfulness.[45]

Petroleum geologist Kenneth Deffeyes, Professor Emeritus at Princeton University, also confirms the dismal consequences resulting from shrinking oil supplies:

...it looks as if an unprecedented crisis is just over the horizon. There will be chaos in the oil industry, in governments, and in national economies. Even if governments and industries were to recognize the problem, it is too late to reverse the trend. Oil production is going to shrink... there will be enormous effects on the world economy... the industrialized nations will be bidding against one another for the dwindling oil supply.[46]

The Hirsch report on the *Peaking of World Oil Production: Impacts, Mitigation, and Risk Management*, which was commissioned for the United States Department of Energy in February of 2005, also warns of the menacing consequences of peak oil:

> Oil is the lifeblood of modern civilization. It fuels the vast majority of the worlds mechanized transportation equipment – automobiles, trucks, airplanes, trains, ships, farm equipment, the military, etc. Oil is also the primary feedstock for many of the chemicals that are essential to modern life... the upcoming physical shortage of world conventional oil (is) an event that has the potential to inflict disruptions and hardships on the economies of every country... the potential economic impact of peaking is immense and the uncertainties relating to all facets of the problem are large... the problem of the peaking of world conventional oil production is unlike any yet faced by modern industrial society.. (and) will almost certainly cause major economic upheaval.[47]

The warnings are almost endless. It would be impossible for me to list all those that have added their voice in sounding the alarm. These are not doomsday prophets. They are not fanatics lingering on the fringes of society with their placards announcing the "end is near." These are professionals and experts from a variety of disciplines. They are scientists, authors, economists, energy experts, and even government commissioned experts. All of them agree on two basic facts: the first is that the peaking of the world's production of oil is imminent, and the second is that "peak oil" is the most critical crisis that modern civilization has ever confronted. All of them are secular in their approach to this crisis. None of them approach this subject from a spiritual or biblical perspective – yet all of them are sounding an alarm that echoes the words of the prophets. We have truly entered into uncharted waters and are confronting a crisis the magnitude of which we have never faced before. By anyone's estimation we are living in "perilous times."

The world will not simply run out of oil as it enters this period of time referred to as "peak production." As we have seen – oil will continue to be produced but will exponentially decrease in volume. This decrease in production will begin slowly but will escalate the deeper the world goes into the downward curve of production. In fact, most experts predict that the top of the peak will resemble a plateau. The world oil producers will expend great efforts to maintain world production as demand increases. Desperate measures will be taken in exploration to find new reserves of oil. Oil resources will be exploited from every reserve and every place imaginable as the world desperately attempts to meet modern society's insatiable demand for energy. The intensified efforts exerted by oil companies struggling to meet the ever increasing demand will create this "plateau" at the top of the peak.

How long this "plateau" lasts will depend upon many variables such as weather, natural disasters, an economic slowdown (recession or depression), and military or terrorist conflicts, to name a few. There are any number of variables which can either escalate or diminish the demand for oil. As the supply of oil becomes restricted and prices rise, governments will institute conservation measures to reduce demand. Markets may become volatile and economies may contract, thus reducing demand. There are many variables which will come into play during this time of social and economic instability. For this reason the period of time at the top of the peak will be a "plateau" with many variations and minor ups and downs. But inevitably, the time will come in which the world will pass a critical point and the remorseless decline in production will begin as the world's reserves of oil begin to dwindle.

The time at the top of the peak will see rising prices, energy conservation, and economic instability as the market reacts to rising energy prices and numerous corresponding economic repercussions. Oil, the economy, energy conservation, and alternative energy sources will increasingly dominate the news and the media's attention. Undoubtedly there will be political finger-pointing as energy issues and the economy become volatile political issues.

During this time, governments will attempt to maintain their business as usual methods relative to industrial and market activity. The energy based industry and economy must not stop. Our economy is based upon exponential growth and it must grow in order to survive.

If the economy stops – everything collapses. It is this crucial need for industrial growth which creates a paradoxical dilemma for all industrial economies. To continue functioning they must consume enormous amounts of energy. Yet to consume energy is to deplete rapidly diminishing reserves of indispensable oil. Inevitably, economic collapse for energy intensive industrial economies will become unavoidable no matter what the choice.

Our modern industrial economy is much like a spinning top. For the top to continue standing upright it must continue spinning. The faster the top spins the stronger and better its perpendicular position is maintained. As the top's spinning momentum begins to slow it starts to sway and wobble – but it will continue to spin as long as there is sufficient velocity in its spin to keep it upright. As the top's velocity slows due to expended energy – it will reach a critical point at which the velocity can no longer maintain the top's perpendicular position. At this point the top will fall over. The economy is much the same. It must continue to grow in order for it to function. As growth slows, there is a critical point at which too many jobs and too much profit is lost. This results in a declining market which causes a loss of wealth. There is a certain "terminal point" at which these losses can no longer be sustained by the economy and the market collapses.

Although the illustration is simplistic – it accurately depicts the condition the world will face as the market begins to experience declining supplies of energy. It is fossil fuels – primarily petroleum – which supplies the market and provides the energy needed for economic growth. As the available supply of energy decreases so will the market. As the market decreases so will the wealth created by the market. This will result in a loss of jobs which will cause a further decline in the market and wealth. The market's deterioration will begin to accelerate – as available energy decreases – until the economy reaches a terminal point and collapses. Kunstler vividly describes this economic unraveling in his book:

> The global peak period itself will be a period of both confu-
> sion and denial. Then, as the inexorable facts of the world
> peak assert themselves, and the global production line turns

down while the demand line continues to rise, all major systems that depend on oil – including manufacturing, trade, transportation, agriculture, and the financial markets that serve them – will begin to destabilize... Once the world is headed firmly down the arc of depletion, fuel supplies will be interrupted by geopolitical contests and culture clashes. Eventually, economic growth as conventionally understood in industrial societies will cease, or continue in only a few places at the expense of other places... Global production will never again increase. After oscillating at peak a few years, production rates will inexorably drop, and then the question becomes: how steep the drop?[48]

The effects of this economic unraveling are almost too much for most people to comprehend. We have become so accustomed to an artificial reality which has been created by petroleum energized industrialism that we cannot imagine life outside of this paradigm. Industrial progress and technology have become so commonplace in our existence that we have accepted them as natural occurrences. But these are not natural. They do not emerge spontaneously out of nature. Industrialism and technology are products of man's ingenuity and not that of nature. It has been the combination of man's ingenuity and fossil fuels that has created the synthetic industrialized civilization in which we live.

It is only when we begin to comprehend just how dependent modern man is upon this industrialized system which he has created that we can understand the impact of the coming energy crisis. It is frightening to realize that one's very survival is contingent upon the industrial system in which we live. While there are a few self-sustaining agrarian people left today, most of the planet's population is dependent in one way or another upon the industrial system. It produces our food, our clothing, our homes, our jobs, our wealth, and every other convenience which we take for granted. It is only when we understand the extent of our dependency that the implications of the impending energy crisis hit home. As Dr. Stephen Leeb, an authority in economic issues and writer of numerous financial publications asks:

What will happen when oil supplies fall behind demand? We have built our modern civilization on the premise of unending growth – growth that needs energy. We have built a complex civilization that requires increasingly larger amounts of energy to maintain itself. What happens if growth is no longer possible?[49]

Dr. Leeb then provides his own solemn answer.

As energy supplies decline, the complexity of human enterprise will also decline in all fields, and the most technologically complex systems will be the ones most subject to dysfunction and collapse... Complex systems based on far-flung resource supply chains and long-range transportation will be especially vulnerable. Producing food will become a problem of supreme urgency... In a world of declining energy, the only government would be local. Highways and commercial buildings would fall into disrepair. The only industry possible would be cottage industry. People would be forced to repair things rather than buy new ones. Finding enough land for food production would be difficult. Most middle-class, professional jobs would be gone... Without cheap energy, our civilization would be unable to sustain itself much above the nineteenth-century level. In fact, it will be difficult to do even that, since we no longer have an infrastructure that works without cheap oil. Few people today have the knowledge or the skills to grow food, make clothes, manufacture items, repair tools, or build houses the way their great-great grandparents did. Self-sufficient family farms have become exceedingly rare.[50]

The threat of the looming energy crisis is one that will affect every community on earth. The very idea that modern civilization could collapse is so frightening and horrendous that it provokes an instinctive reaction to become shortsighted or disregard it completely. The implications are almost too horrific to comprehend. Our minds simply cannot grasp the enormity of a situation that has the potential to change our lives so drastically. It is easier to ignore or disregard the warning signals and go on with life as usual. The natural reaction is to pretend that all is well and the dark clouds that have darkened our life will quickly pass on by. As Dr. Leeb has said, the "reality is so frightening" that people would prefer "to pretend the problem does not exist."[51] Heinberg adds his thoughts by commenting that "the vast majority of people will continue to prefer happy illusions to the stark truth, no matter how compelling the arguments…"[52]

The undeniable fact remains that our world is about to change. Hiding our heads in the sand will not stop the inevitable occurrence of events that are taking shape around us. The evidence indicates that our modern technologically dependent world is on a collision course with a global crisis of catastrophic proportions. In fact, the evidence strongly suggests that our world is either very close to peak production or already there. The world peaked in oil field discoveries in 1963. Since then discoveries have been fewer and fewer every year. Most non-OPEC nations have already peaked. OPEC's production has been flat for the last three years and Saudi Arabia's production is falling. Most experts have calculated the peak of world production to be somewhere between 2005 and 2012, with a few projecting 2020 at the very latest. Whatever the date may be, the evidence strongly suggests that our magnificent energy intensive industrial civilization has arrived at its appointment with destiny. We may very well be approaching that point in time when every manmade institution is going to be shaken to its foundation just as the prophets have said (Hebrews 12:27).

Chapter 7

CONSEQUENCES AND CRISIS

As crucial as oil is to all industrialized societies it would be absolutely impossible to survive the post-peak era without severe consequences. The severity of these consequences of course is contingent upon many variables. It is also impossible to anticipate the full scope and impact that the decline of petroleum energy will have on industrialized societies. The impact will not be fully understood nor the extent of our dependency until we are fully committed and well into the declining curve of production. Nevertheless, there are some consequences that are obvious as we consider the results of a severe decline in the availability of cheap energy.

WAR AND INTERNATIONAL CONFLICT

As the supplies of petroleum products slowly begin to decrease, the pressure placed upon all societies and nations will be enormous. In an attempt to maintain their economies and basic infrastructures, nations will be desperate to obtain vital oil supplies. Kunstler supplies a dismal but discerning forecast by explaining that "the economic stress among virtually all nations, the rich and poor, the advanced and developing, will be considerable and is certain to lead to increasingly desperate competition for diminishing supplies of oil."[1]

For a country as dependent upon foreign oil as the United States, this situation is more than critical – it is a situation of national security at its ultimate. The United States with 5 percent of the world's population consumes 25 percent of the world's oil.[2] Oil is our major source of energy and is the key driver behind our economic growth. It powers our industry, heats our homes, provides the raw materials for many of our manufactured products, and is essential to our agricultural industry. "But it is in transportation that its role is most essential. At present, petroleum products account for 97 percent of all fuel used by America's mammoth fleet of cars, trucks, buses, planes, trains, and ships."[3] But as Michael Klare explains in his book, *Blood and Oil*, as vital as oil is to maintaining our domestic lifestyle, it is simply imperative to our national security:

> Just as petroleum fuels the economy, it also plays an essential role in U.S. national security. The American military relies more than that of any other nation on oil powered ships, planes, helicopters, and armored vehicles to transport troops into battle and rain down weapons on its foes... the fighting machines that form the backbone of the U.S. military are entirely dependent on petroleum. Without an abundant and reliable supply of oil, the Department of Defense could neither rush its forces to distant battlefields nor keep them supplied once deployed there.[4]

To express the dilemma more concisely if not bluntly, Secretary of Energy Spencer Abraham described it in this manner before the House Relations Committee in June of 2002:

> Energy security is a fundamental component of national security.[5]

It has been this principle that has been the cornerstone of the United States foreign policy since the 1973 oil embargo. It was during this embargo that the vulnerability of the United States was openly displayed for all to see. As the oil supplies were cut the economy of the United States went into severe withdrawal pains.

It became evident that even just a slight disruption of oil could cripple the nation. As the public experienced gas rationing, higher fuel costs, and energy shortages, apparently drastic measures were considered to remedy the situation. Michael Klare reveals that "according to recently declassified British documents, in December 1973, Secretary of Defense James R. Schlesinger told the British ambassador to Washington that the administration might consider using military force to seize Saudi oil fields if the embargo lasted much longer…"[6]

That the United States considers the flow of oil from the Middle East and the Persian Gulf to be a prime objective of its foreign policy was thoroughly established by President Carter in 1980. In what became known as the "Carter Doctrine," the president unequivocally established that the primary objective of the United States Military's Central Command was to insure the flow of Persian Gulf oil. He designated this flow of oil as a "vital interest" and told Congress that Washington would use "any means necessary, including military force," to keep the oil flowing.[7]

Today the United States consumes approximately 21 million barrels of oil per day. Of these 21 million barrels over 60 percent is imported. And as the United States' oil production continues its relentless decline, this dependency will become even more severe. The Department of Energy anticipates that by the year 2025 the United States will be consuming approximately 28.3 million barrels of oil per day.[8] Our reliance on imported oil could exceed as much as 80 percent by this time. The farther we go into the future, the deeper our dependency on foreign oil will be and the greater perils we will face.

The United States is not the only industrial country confronting this frightening dilemma. The world's growing thirst for oil is approaching a staggering 87 million barrels per day, which translates into an astounding 1,000 barrels per second. Our thirst for oil is insatiable and is growing every day. Any growth at all in the world's economy demands oil. The dependency is such that our world cannot survive in its current economic configuration without oil. As the world's population and economy grows so does the unquenchable demand for all resources – and especially oil.

As the world's demand for oil increases, so does the competition for this precious but diminishing commodity. This competition has apparently already begun as nations like India and China enter into the technological and industrial scene. Pulitzer Prize winner Thomas L. Friedman reports that China is "obsessed with acquiring secure oil supplies" and has stretched its political ties into the Middle East in an attempt to insure future oil needs. He writes, in his book, *The World is Flat,* that "in 2004 China (also) began competing with the United States for oil exploration opportunities in Canada and Venezuela."[9] Of course this is necessary because China has no domestic oil supplies of its own to speak of. Kunstler explains China's unpleasant predicament in this manner:

China has even less oil than the United States has left, with four times the population. China has ramped up its industrial economy that is now the world's second largest consumer of oil, surpassing Japan in 2004. In fact, it could be said that China has launched the last industrial economy of the oil age, and gotten it under way too late in the game. China's oil imports doubled over the past 5 years and surged nearly 40 percent in the first half of 2004 alone. At the current rate of growth in demand, China alone, of all the world's nations, will consume 100 percent of currently available world exports in 10 years – assuming no growth in demand elsewhere in the world and assuming no falloff in global production.[10]

It does not take a rocket scientist – or a biblical prophet – to sense the already escalating tensions in this global competition for oil. At a petroleum supply meeting in Europe in 2003 it was openly proposed that the United States' invasion of Iraq was "simply for the control of oil."[11] When one considers the evidence and observes where the U.S. military forces have primarily been deployed in the last twenty-five years, this seems entirely feasible. But whatever the reason, this is exactly what other nations such as the European Union, Russia, China, and even many of the Islamic nations believe. Oil is the lifeline of industrial economics and production, and as Kenneth Deffeyes observes, "if the world oil shortage becomes sufficiently painful, there could be a temptation for a military seizure of the oilfields...."[12] With the Middle East holding 60 percent of the world's remaining oil reserves, and every other industrial nation consuming far more oil than they produce, the potential for conflict is enormous. Kunstler once again provides the grim diagnosis:

> A military contest over oil could eventually inflame a theater of war stretching from the Middle East to Southeast Asia, and it could leave the oil production infrastructure of many countries shattered in the process. Such a conflict might be the Last World War.[13]

Michael Klare, the professor of Program Peace and World Security Studies at Hampshire College, confirms this grim analysis in his thought provoking book entitled *Resource Wars*. He summarizes the situation in this manner.

> Of all the resources... none is more likely to provoke conflict between states in the twenty-first century than oil. Petroleum stands out from other materials... because of its pivotal role in the global economy and its capacity to ignite large-scale combat. No highly industrialized society can survive at present without substantial supplies of oil, and so any significant threat to the continued availability of this resource will prove a cause of crisis, and in extreme cases, provoke the use of military force.[14]

He continues by stating, "that conflict over oil will erupt in the years ahead is almost a foregone conclusion." He then points out that "of all the world's major oil producing areas, the Persian Gulf region is the one most likely to experience conflict..." Klare explains that this area is of the utmost importance because it "possesses nearly two-thirds of the global petroleum supplies" and is therefore "certain to remain the focus of intense world-wide competition as energy demand rises in the decades ahead."[15]

This focus has already manifested itself as both China and Russia have made extensive efforts to extend their spheres of influence into the area. Klare notes with some alarm that "Russia continues to arm the former Soviet republics in the Caucasus and Central Asia" and has "deployed combat forces in these areas." He observes that both China and Russia have provided "arms and military technology to Iran" and China has conducted "joint military exercises with Kyrgyzstan." He states that all of this is evidence of "the intense competition among major powers for control over the possession and distribution of energy" which flows from this area. Klare predicts that this intense competition "will lead to a larger conflict."

In his book, *Blood and Oil,* Klare outlines the geopolitical maneuvering which is even now occurring as the major industrial powers attempt to secure vital energy supplies. His primary focus is on China, Russia, and the United States as they attempt to exert an enormous amount of influence in this area. He describes the alignment of powers as they are emerging in Central Asia and the Middle East. He notes that both China and Russia are "bolstering" ties with their suppliers "by providing them with arms, weapons, technology, and other forms of military assistance." He then describes the military and "security" agreement that Russia and China recently made with nations in the Gulf/Caspian area:

China has established formal security ties with states in the greater Gulf/Caspian area and helped form a new regional security institution to legitimize and facilitate its expanding military involvement in Central Asia. This treaty organization was created at a 1996 meeting in Shanghai, of China, Russia, Kazakhstan, Kyrgyzstan, and Tajikistan – the Shanghai Five, as they came to be called. The resulting accord, the 'Agreement on Confidence-Building in the Military Field Along the Border Areas' is aimed at averting border clashes and promoting military-to-military cooperation.[16]

Russia has furthered its Middle Eastern alliances even further than China. *Global Challenges Research* reveals in numerous articles exactly how Russia has moved to strengthen its influence in this area beginning with Turkey. An article in May of 2005 noted that until recently Turkey had been "one of the most faithful allies of the United States," but since this time it "has progressively become a supporter of Moscow's interest in the Middle East." The article continued by explaining that "today's Turkey is part of the Islamic world" and has much more in common with the Russian Eurasian policy than it does with the United States. This commonality in purpose and policy has grown to the point that Turkey along with Russia has extended their alliance to Iran and Syria. According to the article, this alliance was a direct result of Russia's "desperate efforts to return to Middle Eastern politics as a superpower." This desire is the fundamental purpose behind this "quadrilateral alliance" between Russia, Turkey, Iran, and Syria. [17]

The Russian alliance with Turkey now includes a "military cooperation agreement and agreement on military personnel training" which was signed in 2002. This agreement has included the Turkish purchase of "Russian weapons" including "helicopters, armored vehicles, and automatic rifles." Further strengthening this alliance is the fact that "Russia and Turkey have become leading trade partners. The volume of the trade has grown from $200 million dollars in 1990, to $10 billion in 2004 with an estimated growth rate of 15 to 20 percent a year." *Global Challenges Research* notes that Turkey is quickly leaving "the American sphere of influence" and joining itself more and more strongly to the Russian policy in the Middle East.[18]

This alignment should make any student of biblical prophecy sit up and take notice. That nations today are beginning to align themselves just as the prophets Daniel and Ezekiel prophesied should send chill bumps up and down ones spine (Ezekiel 38: 1-8 and Daniel chapter 11). It should also be noted that an alignment of nations which holds the potential for fulfilling the prophecy concerning "the kings of the east" spoken about by John in the Book of Revelation has occurred (Revelation 9:14-16 and Revelation 16:12). These events should cause even the most skeptical to reconsider the prophetic implication of current events.

FOOD SHORTAGES AND FAMINE

We have entered a phase of history early in the twenty-first century that will leave no person or group untouched by this great watershed. We have entered into an energy transition period where life will go from great complexity and sophistication to simplicity and basic essentials. Energy will be at a premium and human survival skills will be the new capital. Life will become increasingly local and materially modest as this transition takes place. As Heinberg points out, "we have arrived at a point where global societal collapse – meaning a reversion to a lower level of complexity – is likely and perhaps certain over the next few decades."[19]

As the world reaches peak production and the supply of oil begins to dwindle – so will the amount of available energy which has powered modern industrial progress. Technological and industrial progress requires an enormous amount of energy. As the available supply of energy diminishes, the technology and industry that is dependent upon this energy will also be reduced. A society can never progress any further than the energy available to power that progress. At peak oil, all industrial civilizations will have reached their technological and progressive peak. Without an enormous amount of available cheap energy modern societies will endure a forced energy transition from complexity to simplicity.

This transition from industrial complexity to simplicity will be incremental. Though we will describe numerous severe and exacting circumstances, it would be a mistake to assume that these events will occur immediately or even soon. The entire transition may take years. There is no way to calculate exactly how long the world may perch atop the production "plateau." However, it would also be a mistake to assume that these events will be so gradual in their appearance that life will go on unchanged. In fact, because of the numerous unknown and unpredictable variables which may occur during this time, the disorders and instabilities of post-peak may assert themselves rather quickly. The truth is, humanity is entering into uncharted waters and we are confronting circumstances with which we have had little or no experience to guide us. All we can say for sure is that there are violently stormy waters ahead of us and our civilization will be tested as never before.

It is apparent that the early effects of the energy peak are either very near or already upon us. Our industrial system is an integrated entity, and it will respond to the decline in energy as a system. Different areas of the world, and even different areas within the United States, may feel the effects of energy depletion differently, but they will all be affected. Although these effects will occur simultaneously, they may be felt more severely or even sooner in one location rather than another. As we have already indicated, the more complex and technologically dependent areas will be affected sooner than others. Cities and urban areas will feel the debilitating effects sooner and more severely than rural areas. Locations that are dependent upon transportation and imports for basic essentials will be more deeply affected than those that are locally self-sufficient. But for all the variables one thing is sure, everyone will face a period of dire and unprecedented difficulty.

Kunstler provides a pointed comparison of "post-peak" existence to our current life. This comparison vividly illustrates the drastic transition which will occur:

> The circumstances of the Long Emergency (post-peak existence) will be the opposite of what we currently experience. There will be hunger instead of plenty, cold where there was once warmth, effort where there was once leisure, sickness where there was health, and violence where there was peace. We will have to adjust our attitudes, values, and ideas to accommodate these new circumstances and we may not recognize the people we once were. In a world where sheer survival dominates all other concerns... life will get much more real.[20]

The incremental descent of society to a more simplistic life will be difficult for the millions of people who have been raised in a modern industrialized environment. As society makes this difficult transition from complexity to simplicity, the knowledge of the natural environment will slowly take preeminence. Basic skills and crafts will replace technical and business knowledge. Those who understand the principles of husbandry and have the skills to live off the land will be those who have the best chance of survival. Craftsmen and artisans will be in great demand – the ability to work with one's hands and fashion needed items will be essential. Those skills which society has lost over the last one hundred years will have to be replaced. Knowledge of nature, the land, and the artistry of craftsmen will have to be relearned. Knowledge and skills that our great grandparents took for granted will have to be regained in order to survive.

One of the most critical circumstances of the post-peak era will be in the area of agriculture and food production. The current population of 6.5 billion people is already pressing the limits of agricultural sustainability. Studies from various experts, including Dr. Tim Flannery of the University of Adelaide in Australia, and results from a study published by the National Academy of Sciences in 2002, indicate that the demands of human population exceeded the planet's natural sustainable limits sometime between 1980 and 1986.[21] The United Nations Food and Agriculture Organization has predicted that 64 of 117 third world countries will be unable to meet their agricultural needs sometime before 2010.[22] It has only been through advanced technology which initiated the "Green Revolution" that the world has been able to marginally sustain the current population to this point.

The effects of industrialization and technology on agriculture are not given much consideration by most people. Even though they enjoy the benefits in their supermarkets, little thought is given to how these products were grown, harvested, transported, and marketed. But without the benefits of petroleum energized machinery, petroleum based fertilizers and pesticides, and a petroleum fueled transportation system, none of these benefits would be available. Almost every facet of our industrialized food production system is distressingly dependent upon petroleum energy. From the planting and harvesting, to the transportation, refrigeration, packaging, and marketing – every step is vitally dependent upon petroleum products in some manner.

As we have previously seen in chapter three, without petroleum based agricultural technologies world grain production would drastically fall. The research conducted by Kunstler for his book, *The Long Emergency,* revealed that "the so-called Green Revolution of the late twentieth century increased world grain production by 250 percent."[23] It was the introduction of petroleum technology which increased the natural carrying capacity of the planet. If petroleum fuels and other petroleum based technologies were withdrawn – or even diminished – there would be a dreadful decrease in agricultural productivity in all areas. Using corn production as an example, Dr. Pimentel, a recognized authority in agriculture from Cornel University, contends that "if fertilizers, partial irrigation, and pesticides were withdrawn, corn yields would drop from 130 bushels per acre to about 30 bushels."[24] Though the decrease would vary according to crops – a drastic decrease in harvests and productivity of all grain crops would inevitably occur as the availability of petroleum products decline.

But the already serious problem is exacerbated by the fact that the world grain production is already in decline. An article written by Gwynne Dyer in the *Energy Bulletin* addresses our current food production situation:

> The miracle that has fed us for a whole generation now was the Green Revolution: higher-yielding crops that enabled us to almost triple world food production between 1950 and 1990 while increasing the area of farmland by no more than ten percent. The global population more than doubled in that time, so now we are living on less than half the land per person than our grandparents needed. But that was a one-time miracle, and now it's over. Since the beginning of the 1990's, crop yields have essentially stopped rising.[25]

Dyer continues by noting that "for the sixth time in the past seven years the human race will grow less food than it eats" and "the world's food stocks have shrunk by half since 1999." These statistics and analyses are confirmed by numerous authorities including Dr. David Pimentel and Dr. Lester Brown. The problem with grain production is already critical even without a reduction in petroleum products. Dyer asserts that "there is no doubt that the situation is getting serious." She then bluntly states the obvious by pointing out that "at some point not too far down the road we (are going) to reach the point of absolute food shortages."[26]

The critical question now becomes: If the world is already facing the potential of grain and food shortages – what are the implications of a drastic reduction of available petroleum supplies? The implications are almost too horrific to consider. If the world's population of 6.5 billion people has been sustained by artificial methods via petroleum technologies – what will happen when these technologies are no longer operational? If a population of 2 to 3 billion people is actually the limit of earth's natural carrying capacity – what happens to the other 3 to 4 billion people when technology fails? These questions will become of the utmost importance as the world reaches its peak production of oil and begins its decline into the post-peak era. Heinberg attempts to answer these difficult questions in his book, *The Party's Over:*

> Expanding agricultural production, based on cheap energy resources, enabled the feeding of a global population that grew from 1.7 billion to over 6 billion in a single century. Cheap energy will soon be a thing of the past. How many people will post-industrial agriculture be able to support? This is an extremely important question, but one that is difficult to answer. A safe estimate would be this: *as many people as were supported before agriculture was industrialized* – that is, the population at the beginning of the twentieth-century, or somewhat fewer than 2 billion people.[27]

The primary focus in the coming years as petroleum products slowly begin to disappear will be on agriculture. People have to eat to survive, and the production of food products will have preeminence above all else. All jobs associated with technology, finance, entertainment, and tourism will become obsolete. As the transportation infrastructure deteriorates, the food products that have filled our supermarkets will begin to disappear. The transportation supply chains necessary to supply American supermarkets will be fragmented. Shipments will become fewer and farther in between. Americans will stream to the supermarkets to find the shelves empty. When the occasional shipment does arrive with vital commodities – they will be few and very expensive. Most will not be able to afford these precious items and there will definitely not be enough to go around. All manufactured items will become scarce and expensive. Those that cannot afford these items – or find them already gone – will endure extreme privation unless they possess agricultural skills and land. Those who are dependent upon marketed food products and live in areas unsuitable for farming are going to suffer.

While the scenarios presented here may seem extreme to many people, consider that these are the social conditions that must exist as the events predicted by John in Revelation chapter six occur. After the third and fourth horsemen of the Apocalypse (famine and death) make their appearance on Planet Earth, humankind will be confronted with circumstances in which one quarter of the population of the earth will die. Although John does not describe the social and living conditions which will exist during this time in detail, it should be apparent that life during this time cannot be the same as it is today. It will be a time of extreme hardship, privation, and suffering. Drastic changes will have occurred in a very short period of time. I am simply, but very emphatically, attempting to point out that according to numerous secular experts, the depletion of crucial energy supplies to an energy dependent society will produce strikingly similar results as those foretold by the prophet John almost two thousand years ago (Revelation 6:5-8).

DISEASE AND PLAGUES

As we have seen, our modern infrastructure is almost totally dependent upon energy provided by fossil fuels. This dependency is manifest nowhere more critically than in our public healthcare system. Taken as a whole, our public health system is a highly energy intensive enterprise. The hospitals, clinics, pharmacies, and emergency response units which provide the backbone of our healthcare system all rely on enormous amount of energy. The technical and medical equipment which is used thousands of times a day and in almost every medical evaluation are for the most part dependent upon energy derived from fossil fuels. But once again, this sickening dependency goes far beyond the apparent.

The northeast blackout of 2003 which occurred throughout parts of northeastern and Midwestern United States and Ontario, Canada, provided ample evidence of this dependency. On the hot humid summer afternoon of August 14, a massive power fluctuation affecting the electrical transmission grid began a cascading effect which precipitated massive power outages covering some 9,300 square miles. The blackout affected portions of Michigan, Ohio, Pennsylvania, New Jersey, New York, Connecticut, Vermont and Canada. Over 50 million people were affected.

In New York City, workers streamed out of high-rise apartments and businesses to find the streets in a gridlock because traffic signals at all of the city's 11,600 signalized intersections had stopped operating. The subway system ground to a halt stranding more than 400,000 passengers in tunnels under the city. The city's extensive commuter rail network closed down leaving hundreds of thousands stranded at the start of the evening rush-hour. Many of the tunnels and bridges into Manhattan were closed or access to them was restricted.[28] Although the effects on transportation and traffic were felt more severely in New York City, all major metropolitan areas were affected as the power grids in their areas failed.

Emergency services personnel responded to the high-rise buildings answering thousands of frantic calls from people trapped in elevators. At the same time, emergency personnel were also attempting to extricate the hundreds of thousands of people trapped in the subways beneath the city. All other calls were put on hold. Emergency responders were hampered by the traffic gridlock and thousands of people streaming into the streets. The *Journal of the Society of Critical Care Medicine* reported that during this time over 5,299 calls for EMS service came in. (This figure does not include the 175,000 hotline calls.) But in addition to these calls, the EMS responders received thousands of calls related to "respiratory" distress, "cardiac" problems, and other medical emergencies. Statistics in all categories rose significantly as electrically dependent respirators, ventilators, assist devices, nebulizers, oxygen compressors, and cardiac equipment failed.[29]

Although the power outage lasted only for two to three days, critical deficiencies were noted in the public health system. In a 2006 report released by the Association of Schools of Public Health, it was reported that "despite having emergency generators, four of the seventy-five hospitals in the city (New York City) were temporarily without electricity when the blackout occurred." It was also noted that "several hospitals" depended upon "steam produced by electrically powered systems to sterilize hospital equipment," which failed when the blackout occurred. As the power failed and interruptions in service were experienced, fears that "vaccine spoilage" may have occurred as a "result from a loss of refrigeration."[30] While for the most part backup generator systems took over during the blackout, the consequences of an extended – or permanent – blackout were grimly revealed. The public health system cannot operate in anything but its most basic form without modern energy dependent technology. Without fossil fueled energy, the system and its supporting technology would collapse and many people dependent upon this system would perish or suffer horribly.

Energy dependency manifests itself in many other crucial ways. The report noted that high-rise apartment buildings in large cities which were dependent upon electric pumps to raise water from the street level to residents failed. These buildings were left without water, which created not only drinking water problems, but also deterioration in sanitary conditions as toilets no longer worked. This water problem was also manifest in all areas which were dependent upon electrical power to pump water from wells. In many areas public sanitation facilities were interrupted and water could no longer be treated. The blackout caused "the accidental release" of millions of gallons of untreated sewage into waterways in and around some urban areas. Residents in numerous urban areas were given instruction to boil water before using it. Problems appeared with "discarded perishables" from food products that had spoiled as refrigeration failed. Trash pickup was interrupted and trash containing spoiled food remained on the streets as "the contractors had difficulty hauling away the increased volume of refuse." The deteriorating sanitary conditions and the increased volume of refuse raised concerns that the "rodent population" would "grow as a result of the increased food supply."[31]

Overall, the blackout disrupted communication systems including cellular telephones and cable television networks. It induced fuel shortages as many gas stations were unable to pump fuel due to the lack of electricity. Transportation and supply was disrupted as trucks were held up for lack of fuel, and traffic problems were compounded as many motorists simply drove until their vehicles ran out of gas and left them on highways and streets. Wall Street, the United Nations, and numerous airports were shut down. Over seventy auto and parts plants were shut down, along with eight oil refineries, eight steel production mills and plants, thirty chemical and petrochemical refining facilities, and countless other corporate and private businesses. The United States Department of Energy placed the estimated total economic loss at approximately 6 billion dollars.[32]

The 2003 blackout starkly reveals our complete reliance upon a modern technologically energy based system. Nowhere is this energy more vital than in our public health system. Whether the dependency is directly related to our hospitals, clinics, or our emergency response units, it is also indirectly related to our communications network, transportation system, sanitation facilities, and industry. Our industrialized infrastructure is so integrated that no system stands independent of the other. All of our systems, networks, and industries are ultimately dependent upon an abundant supply of cheap energy supplied by some form of finite fossil fuels. Although most of our electricity is produced by natural gas rather than petroleum, the appalling dependency is the same. Natural gas (one of the triads of finite fossil fuels which include, petroleum, natural gas, and coal) is confronting the same peak and depletion scenario as petroleum. As any one of these sources falter, our entire integrated system begins to flounder.

As our energy supply is diminished or disrupted, our entire public health and sanitation network is threatened. It has been these systems which have protected the developed nations from communicable diseases and parasites which have plagued lesser developed nations. Water and sewage treatment, medical research, the production and distribution of antibiotics and vaccines, our hospitals and medical equipment all require energy. Should the amount of available energy begin to decrease, the United States and other developed nations will confront an ever increasing threat of severe epidemics and increased disease related deaths.

Not only will sanitary conditions deteriorate, but the availability of medicines and technology based treatment will also decline. It was noted in the report by the Association of Schools of Public Health that "the heavy dependence of modern infrastructure on electricity can lead to public health effects when power is lost." The report documented not only equipment failure and possible blood and vaccine spoilage, but also among other things, "a robust increase in diarrheal illness."[33] This increase revealed just how quickly microbes and parasites seized advantage when sanitary conditions deteriorated even only marginally in three days.

Unsanitary conditions are the breeding ground for all manner of infectious diseases along with plagues of every sort. Heinberg documents how vital sanitary conditions are to health in general by citing statistics relating to the consequences of unsanitary conditions and waterborne infections:

Today, infectious diseases already cause approximately 37 percent of all deaths world-wide. Waterborne infections account for 80 percent of all infectious diseases globally, and 90 percent of infectious diseases occur in the less-consuming countries. Each year, a lack of sanitary conditions contributes to approximately 2 billion human infections causing diarrhea, from which 4 million infants and children die. Even in industrialized nations, waterborne diseases pose a significant health hazard: In the U.S. they account for 940,000 infections and approximately 900 deaths each year.[34]

Even as the world is coping with new strains of diseases, bacteria, and viruses that have become immune to our antibiotics, the threat of energy depletion immeasurably increases the dilemma. Infectious diseases such as the Black Plague (*Yesinia pestis*), which wiped out 50 to 60 percent of the world's inhabitants in 541 A.D., and another 40 to 50 million people in the fourteenth century, has made a recent resurgence in spite of medical technology. As recent as 2002, public health officials in California detected the plague in rodents in twenty-two counties. Malaria, Diphtheria, Dengue Fever, and other infectious diseases are being reported as increasing world-wide. Many long-familiar diseases that were formerly thought to have been eradicated, or in control, are making a come-back.[35]

Meanwhile new diseases are emerging: Hantavirus, Lyme disease, Creutzfeldt-Jakob disease, Legionnaires' disease, West Nile Virus, Hemorrhagic Fever viruses such as Ebola, and AIDS are all presenting immense challenges for an already strained public health system. As Heinberg notes, the "public health systems are already taxed beyond their limits. But what will be the impact of reduced energy availability on those under-funded and over-extended systems?"[36]

The implications of the post-peak energy depletion in the area of public health alone are almost too horrible to imagine. As sanitary conditions erode and the availability of medicines, medical tech-nology, and resources diminish, the recurring plagues which have tormented mankind for centuries will undoubtedly make horrific recurrences. Transportation systems which have rushed medicinal relief to developing countries will be disrupted. The supplies of anti-biotics and vaccines will decline as industry slows. Refrigeration and preservation methods will be disrupted; equipment and supplies will be limited as the infrastructure and systems contract. The diseases which are even now threatening mankind will literally overrun all defenses as the infrastructure deteriorates. As Dr. Richard Krause warned as long ago as 1982, "Plagues are as certain as death..."[37]

SOCIAL DISTRESS

It is difficult to even imagine the horrors of a society in collapse. Yet as horrific as the implications are, one must attempt to visu-alize what will happen in an industrialized society which has been constructed around the use of cheap fossil fuel energy as this energy source begins to disappear. Denial and disbelief will be pervasive.

The implications are so horrendous that they defy comprehension. A culture raised with the belief that perpetual progress and innovation are naturally occurring conditions will have a hard time dealing with decline and regression. To a generation raised to believe that cheap energy is a birthright – it will be hard to imagine a world without it. Yet this is the very prospect our world is facing. The days of cheap energy which powered our industry are coming to an end.

The law of energy and energy conservation is one of the most basic laws of science. Work or progress, and the amount of work or progress accomplished are directly contingent upon energy and the amount of energy expended. It is impossible to have progress or industry without energy, and the level of progress or industry is directly contingent upon the amount of available energy. As energy declines – industry will decline. As industry declines – technology will decline. As technology declines – progress will decline. Whether we want to face the fact or not, we are in for a period where technology and progress are going to decline. Life is going to become much more labor intensive and local.

The loss of skills and knowledge needed to survive in a world without cheap energy is going to be immeasurable. Retrieving this knowledge is going to be difficult. Community and common cooperation in labor and the sharing of knowledge and skills will be vital for survival. People thrust into very difficult circumstances will quickly realize that they have to work together in order to make it through those times. Values and community bonding that have been lost in the last one hundred years will have to be replaced in a hurry. Even children will quickly become introduced to carrying their part in family and community labor. Adolescence will quickly disappear and childhood will be cut short as children will be expected to carry their weight and assist in "grownup" responsibilities. Norms of accepted conduct will change drastically. There will be little tolerance for excuses or justifications. The only thing that will matter will be getting the job done and doing what is necessary to survive. Laziness will be intolerable as everyone will be expected to carry their own weight.

Life will become focused on practicality and reality. The luxury of idealism will die along with affluence and leisure from which it came. Irony, hipness, coolness, along with designer fashions will seem utterly inexplicable to people struggling with reality and trying to produce enough food to get through the winter. People will make, repair, or scavenge for what they need. The consumer culture will die and fade away as national chain stores and malls whither.

As the infrastructure and transportation systems begin to deteriorate, many cities will become uninhabitable. Power failures will become more and more frequent. Over time the electrical grids will deteriorate as the resources to maintain such an extensive system shrink. Sewage systems will not work. Large buildings dependent upon elevators, modern sanitary facilities, engineered heating and air-conditioning will be abandoned and useless. As the infrastructure deteriorates, so will every other facet of modern civilized society. What occurred in New Orleans during Hurricane Katrina will be repeated in city after city. Without electricity, basic utilities, sanitary systems, and food, the cities will deteriorate quickly into chaos and violence. Millions will flee into the surrounding countryside searching for the basic necessities of life – food, clothing and shelter.

As available energy diminishes it will be difficult for the vast metropolitan and suburban areas which were established all over the United States during the era of cheap energy to continue. The infrastructures needed to sustain these areas will begin to falter. As these energy dependent infrastructures weaken, the government will undoubtedly focus its efforts on keeping certain strategic locations and cities inhabitable and functioning. This will require enormous amounts of energy – not to speak of the resources for maintenance – therefore these cities will be strategically selected. But most cities and even middle-sized towns will be devastated by failing power supplies, deteriorating infrastructures, the loss of jobs, failed markets, and a collapsing economy. People without money, jobs, food, and nowhere to find these things will become desperate. The symptoms of a civilization in collapse will manifest themselves very quickly at some point.

Dr. Leeb has noted that "the more complex the society, the more energy flow it needs," and as such is subject to the greatest dysfunction as energy supplies begin to decline. He grimly points out that the United States is the highest energy consuming nation on the planet, consuming 25 percent of the world's energy resources, and by virtue of this energy consumption has become the most complex and energy dependent society in existence. He then describes the logical outcome as complexity begins to deteriorate:

> A real decline in complexity would mean shortages of food and other items, a breakdown of law and order, and a corresponding reign of terror. Malnutrition and starvation… could become widespread, resulting in a much lower population. Diseases would be harder to prevent and control. Cities and towns across the continent might come to look like New Orleans after Katrina. Civilization could truly collapse.[38]

Dr. Leeb stresses the seriousness of the situation by stating emphatically that "the next crisis," which he attributes to "a shortfall of energy production – could be our doom." This analytical economic authority then seems to assume a prophet's robe as he states:

> The collapse of modern civilization would be a catastrophic event, far worse than the popping of the technology bubble. Never mind the financial hardship that would befall almost everyone – the end of our civilization, and its complex division of labor, would result in mass starvation and a level of violence and chaos not seen since the end of the Roman Empire.[39]

I realize the scenario presented in this chapter is very disturbing. But while the portrayal of events is disturbing and shocking – it is also the logical conclusion to which one should arrive based upon the facts as we know them. When presented with the facts concerning peak oil, and the likely consequences of the decline in energy, most people initially react with shock, disbelief, and denial. It is only after absorbing the facts and re-examining the evidence that they finally proceed through the emotions of despair, anger, and finally an acceptance of the crisis that our world is facing. It is difficult to grasp the drastic and imminent changes that lie just ahead for mankind. It is very hard indeed for most people to comprehend just how fragile the foundation is upon which our modern civilization rests.

But once again, it is important to note that what has been presented has been from secular authorities and based upon the physical evidence of circumstances that are unfolding at this time. They have presented a disturbing scenario based upon evidence which indicates that our world is confronting a time of impending economic collapse, famine, anarchy, disease, and resource induced wars. One would have to be spiritually blind not to see the theological implications. The circumstances described by authority after authority bear a remarkable resemblance to the words of Jesus and other prophets. They describe in great detail not only the circumstances leading up to these events, but also the events themselves. These experts describe the particulars of what Jesus simply referred to as "wars and rumors of wars," along with "famines, and pestilences," or plagues. Jesus stated that the last days would be marked by the "distress of nations" and men being filled with "fear" because of "those things which are coming on the earth." While these things will be addressed in greater detail in later chapters – one would have to be blind not to see that our world is entering into an era such as we have never seen before. The undeniable fact is that we are a generation of crisis!

Chapter 8

AN ECONOMY IN CRISIS

The consequences of Peak Oil will be enormous and will affect all facets of modern civilization. The central factor of course is the affect that a shortfall of energy will have on the economic stability of industrialized nations. As we have seen, most of the difficulties will arise as economies begin to unravel as the available supply of energy decreases and industrialization as we have known it for the last one hundred years begins to deteriorate. The repercussions of this crisis alone are enough to devastate the infrastructure of any industrialized nation in the world. But even as we reach the point where the world production of oil is peaking – the United States' economy is already far weaker than the general public realizes, and is even now reeling from other issues that are cause for serious concern. Any one – or a combination of any of these problems – presents serious economic difficulties for the United States. Add the complication of an increasingly acute energy crisis to the mix and the implications are absolutely unnerving.

For the past half century the United States has been the most powerful economic force in the world. We have become so comfortable in this position that we seem to accept it as an inevitable fact of life just as the rising of the sun or the air we breathe. As Americans we seem to accept that we may have economic difficulties from time to time – but to even consider that the economic system which has provided us with such abundant prosperity may falter is beyond comprehension. Our confidence in the power of technology and the might of industrialization has endowed us with an unwarranted perception of invulnerability.

The past glories of our great country have obscured our vision of present realities. We are entirely too optimistic about our civilization's chances of surviving the current economic malaise. As with countless fallen civilizations before us, we have become far too overconfident and proud. We have been blinded by overconfidence and therefore find ourselves repeating the mistakes of every fallen civilization before us. We assume that our particular civilization is somehow immune to the forces which have brought devastation and ruin to societies throughout history. It is undoubtedly because of this inherent blindness that no society in the history of mankind has ever had a real awareness that their society or economy could actually collapse. They all seemed oblivious to the indicators of impending disaster and chose to ignore those occasional radical voices that would sound an alarm. Therefore, we as other civilizations before us, have paid little attention to problems and warning signs. And just as others before us, we may well ignore these problems until they become severe enough to threaten our present lifestyle. Of course – by then it will be too late.

At the close of World War II the United States emerged as the most dominant economic power in the world. Europe was virtually in ruin and Japan was devastated. The United States' economic and manufacturing infrastructure provided the basis for the reconstruction of Europe and Japan while supplying a major portion of the world's agricultural needs at the same time. At the close of the war, the United States was the richest nation in the world and therefore the leading lender in the world. We were the greatest manufacturing nation in the world, and our exports supported our economy and provided a standard of living unparalleled in the history of civilization. Our manufactured products fueled and built our economy.

Today we are a service oriented economy and our exports have evaporated. We now import far more products than we produce and have become the largest consumer nation in the world. Items that are "Made in America" have almost become a relic of the past. In just a few decades the country that was once the richest lender nation in the world has become the most indebted nation in the world. This rapid transition in the American economy has virtually gone unnoticed. Or at least unappreciated as far as the repercussions this transition will bring in the not too far distant future.

An economy that was once vibrant and self-sustaining has now become crippled and dependent. While America's economy still grows and expands – the foundation upon which this economy rests has greatly eroded and is swiftly washing away. While we are impressed with the extravagant and affluent lifestyle which we have fashioned, we do not realize the manufacturing and economic basis upon which this lifestyle depends is quickly evaporating. Our national debt exceeds 10 trillion dollars and is growing every day. Our manufacturing sector is hemorrhaging and moving to foreign countries at a dizzying pace. Consumer debt has reached record proportions of over 9 trillion dollars inclusive of both credit card and mortgage debt. Most Americans now spend more than they earn. Our trade deficit is the greatest in the world and the dollar is falling in value. Social Security and Medicare are in crisis – and the price of energy is rising. The United States is in dire economic trouble and yet this country continues its extravagant partying lifestyle just as if everything will continue as it always has.

Wall Street prognosticator Peter Schiff indicates that the United States economy has reached the point where inevitably our "dollar-denominated assets are going to collapse" and our "standard of living will be painfully lowered." Based upon his vast experience in economics he summarizes the problems confronting the United States economy in this manner:

> The economy of the United States, long the world's dominant creditor, now the world's largest debtor, is fighting a losing battle against trade and financial imbalances that are growing daily and are caused by dislocations too fundamental to reverse… In the short space of a couple of decades, and causing surprisingly little anxiety among economists, the nation has undergone a radical transformation in terms of its economic infrastructure and its economic behavior. A society that saved, produced, created wealth, and was a

major exporter has become a society that stopped saving, shifted from manufacturing to non-exportable services, has run up record national and personal indebtedness, and uses borrowed money to finance excessive consumption of unproductive imported goods.[1]

Schiff then grimly observes that, "there is going to be a day of reckoning and its already overdue."

NATIONAL DEBT, CORPORATE GREED, AND PUBLIC COMPLICITY

These are truly perilous times for America. Politicians, economists, legislators, and other government officials all agree on this one fact. They may argue and disagree as to what should be done and what the appropriate course of action should be to get us out of the mess we are in – but all will agree that these are critical times. Senator Byron Dorgan, in his book, *Take This Job and Ship It*, confirms that these are "dangerous times" for America. He contends, along with Schiff and many other economists that it has been our fiscal and trade policies that have "made us the world's biggest debtor nation," which in turns "threatens America's future."[2]

Currently our nation's budget deficits range in the 400-to-500-billion-dollar-a-year range. (These figures are from 2007, prior to the 2008-2009 government bailouts and the proposed 2010 budget of President Obama which exceeds 3 trillion dollars.) These red ink operating expenses coupled with trade deficits of over $700 billion a year are adding to our current national debt. The budget deficit is financed entirely by borrowing, and the trade deficit is financed by foreign capital purchases of our bonds, stocks, real estate, and other assets. This adds up to an enormous 1.2 trillion dollar deficit per year. I know this is a lot of money – but think about it. Talk about living beyond ones means. This is 1.2 trillion dollars beyond the total yearly revenues of this country. And just like your family or personal budget – the only way to make up for this deficit is to borrow or sell assets, and that is exactly what our country is doing.

Foreign countries and investors are buying American assets at an alarming rate, and we in turn are borrowing against existing assets to finance the remaining deficit. As a result of this unsustainable economic policy our national debt has exceeded 10 trillion dollars and is growing every day. I don't know about you, but I cannot even imagine what 1 trillion dollars is – much less 10 trillion. All I know is that one million seconds comes out to about eleven and a half days. One billion seconds calculates to thirty-two years, and one trillion seconds calculates to an unimaginable 31,720 years. That's in time increments of seconds! I still can't grasp just how much money that is. But the scary thing about it is – I don't think anybody in Washington can even imagine what it is either. At least judging from the way they spend our money and glibly toss these figures around, they either don't know how much money this is or they don't care.

But just how did this great nation which was once the richest lender nation in the world become so indebted and dependent upon foreign creditors? While the intricacies of national debt, budget and trade deficits are complex and beyond the scope of this book, suffice it to say that America has gone from a nation which produced and sold more than it purchased, to a nation which consumes and purchases more than it produces and sells. In short – our outgo or expenses now far exceed our revenues or income. No matter what economists or politicians say, the result is the same for a nation as for an individual or household. To be solvent, there must be a source of income which exceeds the debt. Our national budget deficit is unsustainable and can only continue in this manner for a short time. As Senator Dorgan succinctly states, "wealth is measured by what you produce, not what you consume."[3] A nation cannot remain economically sound being a nation of consumers. It must have a solid foundation of manufacturing and production. Without manufacturing and production which creates real wealth (products as opposed to money), a consumer nation is doomed to become mired ever deeper in debts and deficits which it cannot pay.

How did America get itself into this mess? How did we go from being a self-sufficient nation of innovative craftsmen and artisans to indebted consumers? At what point did we go from a nation which produced its own food on family owned farms, manufactured its own products made by the hands of skilled self-employed craftsmen and artisans, to wage paid consumers of a service oriented society?

The story is an old one that has been repeated time and again. The truth is that America sold its soul to the devil. Being lured by mass production and an enormous amount of new products, Americans allowed a corporate system to arise which first enticed them with promises of a better more prosperous life, then provided them with prosperity they had never dreamed of, and is now deserting them for more profitable markets and cheaper labor. As the multi-national corporations which have evolved in the last fifty years leave this country they are taking the wealth, jobs, and prosperity with them. But as they exit this country in search of a cheaper labor force, they leave America productively destitute, in debt, and still addicted to a consumer lifestyle which they created.

There was a day when the prevailing culture in America was the corporate mass marketer's worst nightmare. Frugality and thrift were central to the famed "Protestant work ethic." These were values formed by a combination of Christianity and the harsh realities of frontier life when America was young. Early Americans believed in hard work, participation in community, temperate living, and devotion to spiritual life. Their basic rule of life was that one should not desire more material things than could be used effectively. They taught their children to "use it up, wear it out, and make do, or do without."[4] These values held preeminence throughout the eighteenth and nineteenth centuries until they were slowly eroded by a new economic system and perspective of life which arose with the Industrial Revolution.

As the Industrial Revolution, technology, and innovation picked up steam in the nineteenth century, large corporations and business enterprises emerged which were created for one purpose – to make money – large quantities of money. Industrial mass production created products on a scale never seen before. These products were marketed to the public by retailing giants. Technology created more modern, diverse, and innovative products. These were produced by mechanized manufacturing giants and sold by large retailing firms. Americans were enthralled by science, innovation, technology and industrialized manufacturing. The new manufactured products were

quickly assimilated into American life and a new culture was born
– the consumer culture.

Historians Gary Nash and Julie Jeffrey note the drastic change
which occurred in the American culture near the end of the nineteenth and the beginning of the twentieth centuries. They indicated
that "fully 83 percent of the labor force was engaged in agriculture"
and lived in the rural areas of the country on self sustaining family
farms.[5] This demographic was to make a dynamic shift resulting in
a massive transition which would affect all facets of American life.
John Gordon would describe this massive transition in the American
society in his book, *An Empire of Wealth,* in this manner:

> In the half century between the end of the Civil War and the
> beginning of World War I in Europe, the American economy
> (and society) changed more profoundly, grew more quickly,
> and became more diversified than at any earlier period in the
> nation's history. In 1865 the country... was still basically an
> agricultural one. Not a single industrial concern was listed on
> the New York Stock Exchange. By the turn of the twentieth
> century, a mere generation later, the United States had the
> largest and most modern industrial economy on earth, one
> characterized by giant corporations undreamed of in 1865.[6]

Industrialization along with massive corporations would reshape
the economic and political structure of the United States. A rural
self-sufficient agrarian society would slowly be replaced by a wage-
earning dollar oriented society completely dependent upon corporate America and modern technology for survival. The geographical
and social landscape of America would change within a generation.
Large cities which were the hubs of industrial manufacturing and
marketing would emerge and the exodus from the farms and rural
areas would begin in earnest.

The transition would be enormous. At the beginning of the
twentieth century 83 percent of Americans lived in rural areas and
derived their living from farming. By the end of the century most
Americans would live in the cities and urban areas while those
that derived their living by farming would decrease to less than 1

percent. Skilled craftsmen and artisans, which had been a vital part of American society, would have almost disappeared being replaced by the mass production of modern factories. Dr. David Korten, from Stanford University Graduate School of Business and a recognized specialist in economics and organization theory, notes that it was during this time that a "shift from a social economy of household and community production to a primarily monetized economy took place in America." He indicates that the basic institutions of home, family, and community, were slowly displaced as "large corporations came into ascendance."[7] He continues by explaining that "large corporations became increasingly skillful in creating desire for their products through marketing." As more and more people become employed by these corporations, and the nation's economy became dependent upon their productivity, even the government began to encourage corporate growth and consumer based commerce as a way of maintaining employment and economic growth.

William Leach, author of *Land of Desire*, describes this new economic system which materialized in the United States during the twentieth century:

> The United States was the first country in the world to have an economy devoted to mass production, and it was the first to create the mass consumer institutions and the mass consumer enticements that rose up in tandem to market and sell the mass produced goods. More effectively and pervasively than any other nation, America... forged a unique bond among different institutions that served to realize business aims.[8]

In short, it was the discovery of petroleum in 1859 which powered the Industrial Revolution and industrialized manufacturing. In turn it was industrialized manufacturing that became the fundamental underpinning of the American economy by employing American citizens and producing manufactured products which were sold not only to Americans, but also exported to other countries. The wages and products provided by these large corporate manufacturing firms endowed Americans with a prosperous lifestyle never before seen in the history of civilization. Industrialization and large corporations became associated with "the American way of life." The citizens depended upon them for the constantly new and innovative products and wages, and the government depended upon them to supply the bulk of its Gross National Product (GNP). The wealth, prosperity, and economic security of the United States became almost entirely dependent upon these large industrialized corporations.

All one has to do to understand the extent of our dependency upon these large industrialized manufacturing corporations is look around our home or workplace. Drive down the street or go to the store. Look at everything around you. Almost everything in your home has been manufactured by an industrial corporation. Your clothing, your furniture, materials which built your house, cleaning materials, food products, toys, and appliances, all are manufactured by an industrialized corporation. The computer I am writing with even now. The telephone you talk on, the shoes you wear, the shampoo you wash your hair with. The towel you dry off with after taking a shower. Everything we have in an industrialized society is manufactured, produced, or shipped by some corporate business. Think of your job. Either you work directly for one of these corporations or you are indirectly dependent upon them for your business, supplies, products you sell, or earnings from those who work for them and do business with you.

Our personal and national financial well-being is entirely dependent upon an economic system sustained by industrialized corporate manufacturing. Self-sustaining Americans who derived their living from the land or by the work of their hands as craftsmen, artisans, or farmers are almost nonexistent today. Even the small family owned and operated businesses are swiftly disappearing because they find it impossible to compete with the large corporate system. Almost everything and everybody has been assimilated into this vast industrialized system.

This brings us full circle and to the point where we can answer the question of how we got into this financial and economic mess. Once again look at the products which fill our homes. Only this time we need to examine the manufacturer's tag. You will undoubtedly be hard pressed to find something that is made in the U.S.A. The fact is that most of the products we buy at the market and use in our homes and businesses are made in countries outside the United States. Most of those items you find that are made in the United States will either have parts from other countries, or are manufactured with machinery that is made in other countries. Since the advent of globalization after the middle of the twentieth century, corporations have increasingly become multi-national corporations and have time and again moved their manufacturing locations to foreign countries where labor and raw materials are cheaper.

Manufacturing corporations have left the United States consistently since the middle of the 1970's. They have gone to foreign countries where there is an abundant supply of cheap labor and little or no government regulation or taxes. Business profits have increased exorbitantly due to these enormous savings and corporations have become major political and economic forces in the global system. But just as manufacturing corporations have left the United States to increase their profits, other retail marketing corporations such as Wal-Mart have emerged making billions of dollars by selling these cheaply produced foreign manufactured items in the United States. Good paying manufacturing jobs have left the country, and products once produced here by American workers are now made in other countries. But to add insult to injury – these products that were once made in this country by American workers are now imported from other countries and sold to Americans by giant retailing corporations.

Lou Dobbs, the author of *Exporting America* and an economic and political analyst for CNN, states that "the power of big business over our national life has never been greater." He observes that all across America industries "from steel to appliances to automobiles, paying manufacturing jobs are being exported out of the country, leaving behind workers and communities struggling with how to recover." He explains that these "corporate pullouts run the gamut from manufacturing to high-tech."[9] All over the country good-paying manufacturing and high-tech jobs are lost as corporations leave the United States and set up business in foreign countries. Communities are left with high unemployment rates and people are searching to find jobs that usually pay less and have little or no health benefits.

The United States is left with an ever increasing burden of health and social care from people who now have none, and now must import products no longer made in the U.S.A. As a result – our national and state fiscal budgets expand because of the increased burden of social services and our trade deficit increases as exports of domestically made products decrease and our imports of foreign made products increase.

It does not take a brain surgeon to figure out that when American industries close up shop and move to a foreign country, the loss of good paying jobs tends to cause economic problems. The problems begin locally where people are put out of work and the supply of good jobs begins to disappear. When you consider that the poverty level in this county has risen consistently since 2001,[10] and the disparity between the rich and poor continues to grow ever larger – you know something is wrong. Middle class America is disappearing before our eyes. The wealthy are getting richer and more and more of the middle class are finding themselves in lower paying jobs with fewer benefits.[11]

The shift from a well paid manufacturing based society to one established upon low paid service and consumption oriented corporations is nowhere illustrated better than the comparison between General Motors and Wal-Mart. In 1970, the largest and most profitable corporation in the United States was General Motors. Thousands of Americans worked in General Motors plants and those of their subsidiaries. The employees were paid well and received good retirement and health-care benefits. Most people who worked there stayed for all their working lives. The largest corporation in America today is Wal-Mart. The average salary is only $18,000 a year and the turnover rate is nearly 70 percent. Most of their employees have neither retirement nor health-care benefits.

General Motors, like other manufacturing companies, has been closing its plants and cutting jobs. Between 2000 and 2005 General Motors cut 29,000 jobs. In November of 2005 GM announced that it planned on cutting 30,000 more jobs by 2008 and shutting down nine of their factories.[12] Where have these jobs gone? It's hard to tell where all of them have gone – but one thing is for sure – they are no longer here in the United States.

In his book, *Take This Job and Ship It,* Senator Dorgan provides example after example of American corporations that have closed down plants and factories in the United States in order to move production to other countries where labor is cheaper. He describes the "GE April Fool's Day layoffs of 2005." At the General Electric refrigerator plant in Bloomington, Indiana, nearly five hundred people learned they were going to lose their jobs on that day as General Electric planned to "discontinue production of mid-line, side-by-side refrigerator models" because they were not competitive on cost or product features. Senator Dorgan explains that what the employees were not told is that General Electric had already planned on setting up operations in Mexico where they would manufacture the same type of refrigerators.

He continues by citing such examples as how IBM in 2005 planned on laying off 13,000 workers in the United States and Europe and hire more than 14,000 in India. Kraft Foods stopped making their Fig Newton cookies in America and moved their production to Monterrey, Mexico. La-Z-Boy purchased the long time American company of Pennsylvania House Furniture in 2000, and closed the Lewisburg plant and moved to China thus "eliminating 425 jobs." Throughout the book he provides example after example of American companies which have closed their manufacturing plants and factories in the United States to move to other countries. He explicitly describes how this manufacturing evacuation has affected the economy of the United States by significantly adding to the growing trade deficit and national debt.

His heartrending account also provides personal glimpses into lives that have been changed by this evacuation of American companies. Countless individuals and families that have worked at well paying jobs which supported their families and communities have been forced to find lesser paying jobs with no benefits in order to survive. Many have been forced to uproot their families where they have lived for years and move to new locations looking for any kind of job which usually pays even less.

Senator Dorgan notes that as these corporations leave the country and "move their jobs overseas," they "don't give a second thought to basing their decisions on factors that completely ignore the impact on our country or its workers." He states that "they deal in cold, hard cash" and have "abandoned any pretense to patriotism" or care for local communities in the United States. He continues by asserting that they are "international enterprises owing no allegiance to the country in which they were chartered." He explains that their "strategy is to define globalization pragmatically in their (own) corporate self-interest."[13] In their pursuit of profit these multi-national corporations are dismantling America's manufacturing base. This manufacturing base has been the foundation of the country's economic strength for years. But it is not only American jobs that are lost. As manufacturing and jobs move overseas so do billions of dollars in United States currency as trade deficits climb ever higher.

In his book, Lou Dobbs listed over 750 American based corporations that are "either sending American jobs overseas or choosing to employ cheap overseas labor instead of American workers.[14] The list included such well known American companies as Albertson's, Amazon.com, American Uniform Company, Anheuser-Busch, Bank of America, Black and Decker, Boeing, Bristol Myers, Caterpillar, Circuit City, Cooper Tire and Rubber, Dow Chemical, Dupont, Eastman Kodak, Emerson Electric, Franklin Mint, General Electric, Goodrich, Goodyear Tire and Rubber, Hamilton Beach/Procter Silex, Hewlett-Packard, Honeywell, Ingersol Rand, John Deere, Johnson and Johnson, Kellogg, Kraft Foods, Kwikset, Lockheed Martin, Levi Strauss, Maidenform, NCR Corporation, Osh Kosh B'Gosh, Procter and Gamble, Toys R Us, Tyco International, Underwriters Laboratories, United Technologies, and Xerox to name a few. This list was compiled in early 2004 and we can be sure the list is much larger now.

Our country has signed numerous trade agreements with other countries starting with GATT (General Agreement on Trade and Tariffs) after World War II. Since then we have signed other trade agreements such as NAFTA, CAFTA, and WTO. With each of these agreements our trade surplus has decreased while our deficits have risen. For example – in 1994 when NAFTA (North American Free Trade Agreement) passed, the United States had a 1.3 billion dollar trade surplus with Mexico. According to Senator Dorgan, by 2004 this trade surplus had turned into a 45 billion dollar trade deficit and we have lost over 750,000 American jobs. Many of these jobs were high skilled manufacturing jobs including automobiles, automobile parts and electronics. Our bilateral trade agreement with China has resulted in a record setting trade deficit which has increased by over 200 billion dollars a year since we negotiated the agreement.

The *Los Angeles Times* reported that in 1950 the United States garment industry employed over 1.2 million people in our country. By 2001, that figure had fallen to 566,000. That same year, 83 percent of all apparel sold in the United States was imported from other countries. Even Levi Strauss closed its last two American plants in San Antonio, Texas, in 2004. These "American" classic jeans are now made in other countries such as Mexico, Bangladesh, and China. Fruit of the Loom, an American company which once employed as many as 10,000 employees in various plants in Kentucky, outsourced their production to other countries in 1998. A former employee reportedly stated that "nobody in the area buys Fruit of the Loom underwear anymore." Can you blame them?

The list could go on almost endlessly. But the truth is that American manufacturing jobs and wealth has been siphoned away by other countries. The richest lender and manufacturing country in the world has become the greatest debtor and consumer (importing) country in the world in just a few short decades. Our debt is growing beyond our means to repay. At some point the United States economy will not be able to bear this enormous amount of debt any longer. Peter Schiff explains our economic debacle in this manner:

> Our current account deficit, which is somewhere around $800 billion and growing and is mainly a trade deficit, is being financed by borrowings from foreign countries like China and Japan that export to us. This is debt we cannot repay because we have become a nation of borrowers and consumers instead of savers and producers... Yet we continue to spend like drunken sailors on imports from foreign countries... in the process building massive trade deficits that we finance with money borrowed from our trading partners, money we can't repay because of budget deficits and mounting national debt.[15]

Schiff continues by explaining that the enormous economic pressures currently being applied to the dollar are the result of its loss of value on the international market. He states that "the declining dollar is the result of an American economy characterized by declining production, inadequate savings, reckless consumption, soaring household debt, (and) ballooning federal deficits..." He grimly predicts that sooner or later "foreigners are not going to want our dollars anymore." He states that they will unload their dollar reserves by buying American assets while refusing to finance our debt by not exporting any of their manufactured goods to the United States any longer. He explains that the domestic supply of American dollars will "shoot up" as these nations unload their devalued dollars and prices will soar.

There is an enormous amount of evidence that indicates this scenario is playing out as this time. One would have to be blind not to have noticed that the value of the American dollar is continuing its fall on international markets. On November 8, 2007, headlines in an article released by the *Associated Press* read, "Stocks fall sharply as dollar sinks." The article spoke "about a dollar that just keeps getting weaker" and other currencies such as the "euro" reaching an all time "record against the dollar."[16] On November 27, 2007, *The Wall Street Journal* featured an article that confirmed that the "Dollar Retreats Against Rivals." The article noted that "concerns about the health of the financial system have led to strains in money markets... prompting banks in nations such as Canada and 'the euro zone' to step in with liquidity (monetary) injections."[17] Headlines related to the declining dollar were consistently found in almost every issue of *The Wall Street Journal* throughout 2007 and well into 2008.

As noted in the previous articles, foreign investors are even now stepping in with monetary assets buying stocks in a devalued American market. As American companies struggle financially due to rising energy prices and overextended credit issues due to the "mortgage meltdown," foreign investors are snapping up American assets and purchasing huge blocks of stock in American companies. On January 10, 2008, *The Wall Street Journal* announced that "Citigroup, Merrill Seek More Foreign Capitol." The article stated that "two of the biggest names on Wall Street are going hat in hand, again, to foreign investors" begging for help. The article continued by revealing that Merrill could get as much as "$3 billion to $4 billion" from Middle Eastern governments and "Citi could get as much as $10 billion" from other foreign governments.[18]

All of this is done of course to prop up a disintegrating American economy by financing our consumer borrowing and runaway deficits. Extraordinary efforts are being made to keep the markets active by inducing consumer spending. This is what keeps the sinking economy afloat – but at the same time produces more and more debt. This is why Schiff notes that the economy and dollar cannot possibly continue this cycle forever, and we have found ourselves in the middle of "a crisis which cannot be prevented."[19] Continuing to borrow to keep an economy afloat that is sinking precisely because of excessive borrowing is insane. Yet to stop borrowing is to allow the economy to come apart immediately and catastrophically. We are simply prolonging the inevitable. At some point the chickens are going to come home to roost and every American is going to pay a price that none of us can afford for purchasing cheap imported goods at Wal-Mart on our maxed-out credit cards.

The battle against inflation, recession, a falling dollar, and rising prices is already well underway. Energy prices are rising as the price of oil went over $100 a barrel for the first time in January 2008. Wheat and grain prices "soar" as concerns over supplies and dwindling stockpiles grow according to *The Wall Street Journal*.[20] Unemployment is rising and what's left of U.S. manufacturing is slowing down and setting off alarms.[21] The mortgage meltdown continues, and many major lending firms are nearing collapse. In fact many of them (as we have already seen) are being propped up by outside and overseas investors along with government bailouts.

The January 11, 2008, issue of *The Wall Street Journal* states that Countrywide Financial Group, America's largest mortgage lender, is "tottering" near collapse and seeking a "rescue deal." The article states that "Countrywide's fall and expected rescue mark a milestone in the unfolding international financial crisis." The article continues by acknowledging that the crisis is "spreading – and authorities are struggling to contain it." The writer notes that "a weakening economy and rising mortgage delinquencies have begun to feed off each other in a dangerous spiral."[22] Since that time the list of casualties to the economic meltdown include Bear Sterns, IndyMac, Bancorp, Freddie Mac, Fannie Mae, Merrill Lynch, Lehman Brothers, A.I.G., Washington Mutual, and Wachovia to name a few. Giant financial institutions are being shaken and falling. The experts are using terms such as; crisis, turmoil, collapse, and alarms when writing about our economy today. They concede it is "deteriorating quickly" and growing feebler every day. The concern is real and the symptoms of an economy in severe distress are genuine.

Yet for the most part Americans continue their sleep-walk toward disaster. As Associated Press business writer John Wilen notes in an article published in January of 2008, "consumers have done an amazing job of ignoring high oil prices, not to mention falling home prices." He noted that one consumer appeared to be completely "unfazed as oil approached its milestone, although rising oil prices are making it more expensive for him to gas up his just purchased 2008 Infinity FX SUV."[23] Generally Americans are oblivious to the severity of the crisis emerging around them.

Anymore I shudder when I hear Americans arrogantly state that the United States is the richest, most powerful nation in the world. Those that make this statement apparently have no concept that our wealth is artificially based upon an abundance of subsidized consumer merchandise and not productive capacity. It is virtually impossible for the most indebted nation in the world to be the richest. Our real wealth of manufacturing and self-sustaining productivity has long since been siphoned away. (Keep in mind that real wealth consists of manufactured products or yield which one produces – and not an accumulation of products made by someone else or even money which is only a medium of exchange.) Americans have definitely confused conspicuous consumption with legitimate wealth creation by production.

As far as the strength of our once mighty financial system goes, it is being shaken to its very foundation. According to *The Wall Street Journal*, this is the "worst crisis since the 1930's with no end in sight."[24] We have lived to see the American financial institution shaken to its foundation and teeter dangerously close to a total collapse. Citigroup (the nation's largest banking institution), Merrill Lynch, Lehman Brothers, and Countrywide (the nation's largest mortgage lender) have all suffered devastating financial losses. A.I.G. along with Freddie Mac and Fannie Mae have been rescued only by loans and bailouts. General Motors and Chrysler, two of America's largest remaining manufacturing industries have suffered serious losses and have extended their hands begging for a lifesaving "bailout."

The January 16, 2008, article in *The Wall Street Journal* concisely sums up the situation with headlines which read, "World Rides to Wall Street's Rescue." The article opens by conceding that "the latest signs of America's sinking financial fortunes" are evidenced by the fact that "investors from as far afield as Japan, Korea, Singapore, Saudi Arabia and Kuwait" have had to "come to the rescue of Wall Street." The writer of the article indicates that this "infusion" of capitol into U.S. financial institutions signifies "a dramatic shift in power." The article lists numerous other companies, including Morgan Stanley, Bear Sterns Co. and UBS AG, that have sought foreign capital to shore up collapsing financial fortunes.[25]

Professor Anthony Sabino, a professor of law and business at St. John's University in New York, notes this drastic shift in fortunes. He indicates that in the past it has been "the U.S. economy and wealth of the U. S. that has come to the rescue of nations and businesses across the world," but now fortunes have changed.[26] This change of financial fortunes definitely signifies "a shift in financial clout" according to *Wall Street Journal* analyst Nick Timiraos.[27] On January 18, 2008, *The Wall Street Journal* indicated that this "turmoil… is beginning to rock a foundation of the financial system" and the economic outlook is "worsening."[28] The United States has lost its productive capacity and is having to support its consumer addiction and financial institutions by borrowing exorbitant amounts of money and selling financial assets. For the first time in history foreign investors are rescuing American institutions, and our own Federal Government has been forced to invest over a trillion dollars of borrowed money into the private sector in a desperate attempt to rescue the floundering economy. The bill for our excessive consumption, borrowing, and reckless spending by both the government and public appears to be coming due.

But nevertheless, as Peter Schiff observes, "to consume, you have to either be productive or borrow, and you can only borrow so much for so long... it is a situation that cannot go on indefinitely."[29] There must be a day of reckoning. It is impossible even for the United States to defy the relentless forces which have humbled every great empire before us. We are not immune to disaster or collapse. The laws of economics are as immutable as any other and the United States is on a collision course with an economic disaster of epic proportions. Once again, Schiff provides us with a concise analysis of the situation which we are confronting:

> Because Americans are not saving and producing but are borrowing and consuming, we have become precariously dependent on foreign suppliers and lenders. As a result, we are facing an imminent monetary crisis that will dramatically lower the standard of living of Americans... Our days as the dominant economic power are numbered. The dollar is going to collapse, and Americans are going to experience stagflation on an unprecedented scale in the form of recession and hyperinflation.[30]

There will be run-a-way inflation, severe recession and or depression, and a scarcity of manufactured items from our former trading partners. Businesses will collapse and the American economy will suffer great hardship and dislocation. Schiff frankly summarizes the situation that will evolve when the value of the dollar drops to the point that creditor nations can no longer afford to finance our debt. "We don't have the factories to make new things. And goods are going to stop being shipped into this country. All those container ships are going to stay in China." He grimly but emphatically predicts that the problem has already reached the point that collapse cannot be avoided. He states that "the looming dollar crisis cannot be prevented, only delayed, and only at the cost of exacerbating the collapse."[31]

THE CONSUMER CULTURE – MORE IS NOT ENOUGH

William Leach opens his classic book in which he chronicles the transition of the American society from an essentially self-sustaining agrarian culture to a dependent consumer culture with this statement:

> From the 1890's on, American corporate business, in league with key institutions, began the transformation of American society into a society preoccupied with consumption, with comfort and bodily well-being, with luxury, spending and acquisition, with more goods this year than last, more next year than this. American consumer capitalism produced a culture almost violently hostile to the past and tradition, a future-oriented culture of desire that confused the good life with goods. It was a culture that first appeared as an alternative culture – or as one moving largely against the grain of earlier traditions of republicanism and Christian virtue – and then unfolded to become the reigning culture of the United States.[32]

As we have seen in the previous section, great corporations predicated upon profit margins and production rose out of and in tandem with the Industrial Revolution. These great engines of industry transformed the American landscape economically and politically. But the transformation of the American society was not only material but spiritual. The pre-industrial culture had instilled principles predicated upon responsibility, trusting God, hard work, self-discipline, sacrifice, and duty and respect toward family and community. At the heart of the new culture was the quest for pleasure, security, comfort, and material well being. It was a culture of seductive prosperity that whispered "amuse thyself and take care of yourself."[33]

Christopher Lasch, in his national bestseller, *Culture of Narcissism*, notes this dramatic change by observing that prior to the Industrial Revolution "the Protestant work ethic stood as one of the most important underpinnings of the American culture." He describes this fundamental "underpinning" in this manner:

176

The self-made man, archetypical embodiment of the American
dream, owed his advancement to habits of industry, sobriety,
moderation, self-discipline, and avoidance of debt. He lived
for the future, shunning self-indulgence in favor of patient,
painstaking accumulation...[34]

The rise of industrialization, along with the giant profit motivated
corporate businesses, dramatically transformed the pre-industrial
American culture and world-view. It produced a distinctively new
American culture which would become disconnected from the traditional family, community values, and religion in any conventional
sense. It would be a secular business and market oriented culture,
with the exchange and accumulation of money at the foundation
of its moral sensibility. The cardinal features of this culture would
be acquisition, consumption, and pleasure as a means of achieving
happiness and measuring success. The necessity of this change was
driven by the fact that an economy based upon mass production
would require not only an economic organization of production, but
an organization of consumption and leisure as well.

The transition to a culture based upon consumption and leisure
would stand in stark contrast to the former culture rooted in the
principles of the Protestant work ethic which embraced moderation,
personal industry, and self-discipline as its foundation. The new
system would be forced by necessity to re-educate the populous.
"Mass production," according to a Boston department store owner
in 1919, "demands the education of the masses; the masses must
learn to behave like human beings in a mass production world."[35] Of
course this new behavior would consist of consuming the commodities which would be produced by the new manufacturing system
which was turning out enormous amounts of new products every
year. Lasch explains that the "modern manufacturer has to (or is
forced to) 'educate' the masses in the culture of consumption." He
continues to explain how fundamental this is to an economy based
upon industrialized manufacturing:

The mass production of commodities in ever-increasing
abundance demands a mass market to absorb them. The

American economy, having reached the point where its technology was capable of satisfying basic material needs, now relied on the creation of new consumer demands – on convincing people to buy goods for which they are unaware of any need until the 'need' is forcibly brought to their attention by the mass media.[36]

Out of this need to perpetuate a consumer society arose an enormous and interrelated financial and economic system which now distinguishes not only the United States, but all other industrialized nations today. It would consist not only of the fundamental manufacturing sector, but also mighty banking and retailing institutions which would greatly enhance and enlarge the credit system so consumers could finance what they did not have the means to purchase at the time. In concert with the manufacturers and retailers, corporate businesses would implement marketing techniques through the creation of mass media distributors on a scale never seen before. This combination of corporate manufacturing, corporate retailers, credit institutions, banks, corporate marketing, and a commercialized entertainment establishment, would completely transform American society. It would create a self-perpetuating economic system completely different than anything the world had ever seen.

As this system grew and expanded, so also did the effects on the fundamental nature of the American culture. In his book, *The Age of Abundance*, writer Brink Lindsey notes that it was "Protestant morality" which "first started to crumble under the weight of machine-made bounty." He emphasized that the "old suspicion of luxury and sensual pleasure relaxed and gave way..." And slowly "the ascetic restraints of thrift and deferred gratification loosened and unwound."[37] The result was that the "American character began to change." Lindsey further examines this dramatic change and chronicles the transition in this manner:

The alteration was gradual, but over the course of decades the cumulative effect was fundamental. By the 1950's when the postwar boom ushered in the age of abundance,

America's dominant culture was far removed from the pre-industrial Protestant consensus of the century before... The substance of the change was this: from a scarcity-based mentality of self-restraint to an abundance-based mentality of self-expression. The aversion to material luxury was the first thing to go, as Americans reveled in wave after wave of new, factory-made comforts and conveniences... "enough" proved an everlasting receding horizon.[38]

Lindsey continues by asserting that "the continuing expansion and growing complexity of the division of labor, impelled forward by the consumerist consensus, worked to undermine traditional resistance to the new mass hedonism." He observes that eventually "affluence became a playground chase for self-assertion and personal fulfillment." The old Protestant work ethic and all the values it had once embraced was cast aside as an archaic relic of the past. America totally immersed itself into an industrialized and corporate sponsored consumer culture. The older culture was superseded by a new culture. It was a new culture of corporations and investment banks which moved almost overnight into control of the everyday lives of Americans.

Leach dryly describes this as "a transformation which put money into a position of eminence in the lives of Americans." He states that because of this new manufacturing market "pecuniary values (or market values) would constitute for many people the base measure of all other values."[39] Money and market values would be the measuring stick and fundamental base upon which everything in the new culture would be based. Everything from labor to talents, even to marriages and entertainment would be rooted upon a monetary foundation. Home, family, community, and even religion would succumb to this all consuming monetary based value system. Nothing that had any meaning could now exist outside of this new culture.

The old world in which Americans owned and worked their own land, built their homes with their own hands and sweat, worked with tools and possessed skills which made them self-sufficient artisans and craftsmen was quickly fading into the past. They were no longer a self-sufficient community oriented people. As Leach notes, they were now compelled to "rely on money incomes – wages and salaries – for their security and their well-being." They were a people who had become "dependent on goods made by unknown hands" in an industrialized factory.[40] The corporations now produced not only the commodities which filled their lives, but also the salaries by which these commodities were purchased.

The pursuit and manufacture of material commodities far beyond the basics of food, clothing, and shelter slowly created a society completely dependent upon those commodities. Things that at one time would have been considered a luxury became necessary for existence in the new world. Automobiles, washing machines, electric lights, vacuum cleaners, indoor plumbing, central heating, and countless other commodities became essentials of existence. Progress manifested an amazing ability to transform luxuries into necessities in a very short time. There was a complete disconnection from this new world created by industrial manufacturing and the former one man had known since creation. Brink Lindsey attempts to describe this disconnection in this manner:

> There is no making sense of the world we now inhabit until we confront the yawning chasm that separates our age from the vast bulk of human experience. The mundane, everyday, taken-for-granted circumstances of life of contemporary America's affluent society are, from the perspective of the other side of the chasm, the stuff of flightiest fantasy. We live on the far side of a great fault line, in what prior ages would have considered a dreamscape of miraculous extravagance.[41]

Ours is no longer a society based upon the necessities of existence – it is one based upon the pursuit of ever more innovation, pleasure, and luxury. These things, and the lifestyle created from them, have proven to be powerfully seductive. Miraculous innovations which would have once been considered luxuries and excessive extravagances, have become accepted as the very basics of life. Life can hardly be imagined without these innovations or the environment of entertainment created by them. These things have become the essence of the "American way of life," and at the center of this new economy and culture is the profit-driven corporation.

Of course this pursuit for "more" has a price tag. Many of the commodities produced by the manufacturing sector of the industrialized system were far more expensive than the average consumer could afford. It was from this culture of need and desire that our current system of credit and finance arose. Things that consumers could not afford to pay for at one time could now be "charged" or financed over a period of time. Large corporations would now not only produce the commodities, but they would also finance the purchases, and consumers could work for them in order to pay their charges. This system of dependence would continue to expand exponentially. An entire society and culture would become completely dependent upon this system by the middle of the twentieth century.

One facet of the dependence of the American society upon this system is the enormous amount of consumer debt with which we are now confronted. The total U.S. consumer debt which includes all installment debt (except montage) reached 2.46 trillion dollars in June of 2007. In 2004 – before the end of the real estate boom – U.S. consumers had accumulated more than 6.8 trillion dollars in mortgage debt. This is a staggering total of over 9 trillion dollars in debt. According to *USA Today*, Americans are buying "bigger houses, fancier cars, and charging more on their credit cards than ever before."[42] American's insatiable appetite for more and better has been the primary factor in this accumulation of enormous debt.

American's appetite and demand for gadgets, toys, and novelties has steadily increased since the 1950's. People's expectations and demands are greater than ever before and continue to rise. The kinds of things that were considered to be luxuries as recently as 1970 are now found in most of the homes in the United States and deemed to be necessities. Things such as dishwashers, clothes dryers, central heating and air-conditioning, color and cable TV, are essentially standard fare in American life. In 1970 there were no microwave ovens, VCR's, CD players, cell phones, fax machines, compact discs, personal computers, or video games. These commodities are now taken for granted and most people would feel deprived without them. Today's Americans have more stuff and a much higher material expectation than any previous generation in history.

This material demand for bigger, better, and more is illustrated nowhere more clearly than in the American housing market. Since around 1950 the average home in the United States has grown larger while the average family has become smaller. Around 1950 the average size of an American home was 750 square feet. By the end of the 1950's the size had increased to 950 square feet, and by the end of the 1960's it had reached 1,100 square feet. Today the average size is anywhere from 1,850 square feet to 2,300 square feet with a three car garage and room for a motor home and jet-skies. The garage space alone in many homes today have as much square footage as an entire family had in the 1950's.[43] The American home has truly become a symbol of conspicuous consumption and material growth.

We have more clothes, more shoes, more personal hygiene items, more domestic gadgets, more appliances, more tools, and more transportation conveyances than any generation in history. We have more of everything and still it is not enough. We have become a culture infected with greed and a desire for material possession. It is an addiction worse than that of any drug. America has sacrificed its moral values, family bonds and sense of community to accommodate this addiction. But more than this – most of these commodities supplied by our industrialized corporate system have been financed through our credit cards and mortgages. We have borrowed in excess of 9 trillion dollars to support our desire for larger homes, new gadgets, and more commodities and conveniences.

The manufacture of these items consistently raised the American standard of living throughout the twentieth century. As industrial manufacturing grew so did the prosperity and lifestyle of the American public. At first, wages essentially grew in proportion to the growth of manufacturing, but slowly the addiction to commodities caused the public consumer debt to outgrow income. This imbalance grew slowly after the 1950's but accelerated at a frightening pace after 1970.

Of course it was during this time that technology and progress created the global market, and free market economics began to replace the old economic order. Manufacturing companies began to leave the United States in search of cheaper labor and greater profit margins. The high paying manufacturing jobs began to disappear but the debt still grew. After 1970 more and more Americans have found themselves in lower paying service oriented jobs. To accommodate their consumer addiction they began to make up the difference through credit purchases and by mortgaging the equity in their financed homes. For the first time ever, U.S. households have assumed more mortgage debt than the GDP (Gross Domestic Product) of our country.[44] Never in the history of the United States has a generation been so deeply in debt.

Americans today are not only deeper in debt than any other generation, but they are steadily increasing this debt. For the first time since the Great Depression the average American is spending more than he earns. A report from *MSN Money* revealed that "43 percent of American families spend more than they earn each year," and the "average household carries some $8,000 in credit card debt." The report also indicated that "personal bankruptcies have doubled in the past decade"[45] as more and more Americans find that their income does not keep pace with their desires.

The concern over the disparity between income and expenditures is echoed by Herb Greenburg of *MarketWatch*. In an article published in September of 2007 he stated that "Americans are living well beyond their means." He indicates that the data is "overwhelming that households are spending more than their income" and "households are going into debt like never before."[46] What started out as a deficit of 50 billion dollars in the 1990's has swelled to an enormous 2.46 trillion dollars as of June, 2007. What Americans seem to have forgotten, is that there is no free lunch. Someone is going to be forced into picking up the tab sooner or later – and it appears that the check is now on the table.

This unfolding of economic circumstances has created an atmosphere ripe for the perfect economic storm. In an attempt to make a complicated set of circumstances simple, suffice it to say that the public and national financial practices of the past few decades have finally merged into the appalling conditions we now confront. Free trade policies have eroded our manufacturing and job market. Trade deficits have reached record highs. Our national debt has spiraled out of control mounting to over 10 trillion dollars including both installment loans and mortgages. Added to this is the fact that American jobs have gone overseas and Americans are making less now than they are spending. The housing market bubble has crashed and the values of their mortgaged homes are falling. Many now owe more than the value of their homes and this trend will continue into the foreseeable future.

The house of cards built by the United States economy over the past few years is shaking, and according to Stephen Leeb it is getting ready to fall. He explains that even as near as the 1980's the United States "had the luxury of a relatively un-leveraged economy." But he emphasizes that things are much different now:

> Today's economy is far more burdened by debt than it ever has been. Not only is government debt at record highs, but every measure of consumer debt is far greater than in the 1980's. For example, today mortgage debt represents about 50 percent of home equity, while in the late 1970's and early 1980's the figure was about 40 percent... Today over 70 percent of a record amount of consumer lending is secured by homes.[47]

Leeb continues by explaining the importance of home values to the economy. He indicates that "home values" are of the utmost importance to the economy because "more people own homes than own stocks." He further stresses that "the average person has more wealth tied up in his or her home than in the stock market."[48] It is for this reason that if "home prices suddenly started to fall," and if mortgage payments began rising rapidly because the adjustable rates of sub-prime loans matured, this could create havoc within the economy. When people begin to default and foreclosure rates begin to rise, this could very well create a domino effect in our house of cards. Once again Leeb explains:

> With mortgages such a large portion of home values, many home owners would doubtless be forced to sell their homes

(and many will suffer foreclosures). Home prices will tumble further, and the resulting downward spiral could easily be curtains for the economy.[49]

He states that at this time the Federal Government will begin a desperate battle to keep the economy going. He explains that the battle will primarily be between fighting inflation on one hand and a recession or depression on the other. To fight inflation the Federal Government would be forced to raise interest rates which would slow the economy. But in an economy that is already slowing and consumers are already spending less money, this would be catastrophic. As we have already seen – in an economy structured as ours – the only alternative is to promote consumer spending and growth. If the economy stalls or stops growing, if consumers stop spending, the whole house of cards comes tumbling down. Therefore, as Leeb acknowledges, "unable to fight inflation without risking an economic meltdown, from which our society might never recover, policymakers will put all their efforts into keeping the economy growing."[50]

Keeping the economy going, however, will turn out to be an almost insurmountable task. As we have already seen – this is simply a vicious cycle. The fundamental problem with the economy is overspending and the dwindling job market in the first place. Now to keep the economy going the Federal Government must attempt to promote more consumer spending which will only increase the debt load and escalate the falling value of the dollar, not to mention raising the already record breaking Federal deficit. Ultimately, as the economy contracts, the job market will dwindle further. As Leeb grimly notes, it is a vicious cycle where the "battle royal" will clearly be between "the destructive forces of inflation and depression." The only question is which of these forces will be the one which brings the house of cards down.

Leeb is not the only economist who has foreseen the events that are unfolding at this time (January, 2008). Peter Schiff, in his timely book, *Crash Proof*, confirms Leeb's observations.

Anybody who thinks the real estate bubble can have a soft landing simply can't be aware of the overbuilding, the number of properties bought by people unable to afford them who were planning on flipping them, and the second and third vacation homes bought with money borrowed against inflated home equity... There's going to be a recession combined with inflation and it's going to be an extremely bad situation.[51]

He also explains that as the Federal Government strives to stave off the inevitable slowing of the economy a vicious cycle will begin. His summary mirrors that of Leeb and others.

It's a spiral that will feed on itself and ultimately cause the American economy to implode.[52]

In an attempt to convey an accurate picture of a very compli-cated economic situation I have relied heavily upon the summaries of experts in the field of economics. But as I gathered material for this chapter I was amazed at how the projections of these experts began to materialize even as I wrote. Part of my research has consisted of compiling scrap books of newspaper and magazine articles related to this research. Altogether this has been quite an accumulation. As I sit in my office I am confronted with numerous articles which confirm the analysis of these experts. *The Wall Street Journal* contains articles almost every day relative to the Federal Government's fight against inflation, recession, the slowing market, the credit crisis, and the weakening job market, to name a few points. In fact as I look at the January 10-11, 2009 issue, there is an article entitled, "Yearly Job Loss Worst Since 1945." The article opens its bleak discourse in this manner.

The worsening U.S economy hit the nation's work force hard in December, as the unemployment rate climbed to 7.2 percent and brought the total number of jobs lost last year to just over 2.5 million – the worst since 1945.[53]

The article continues by indicating that "of those, 1.9 million (jobs) vanished in just the final four months of the year." The writers quoted President Elect Obama as saying that "clearly, the situation is dire." They continued by noting that "manufacturing, often a bell-wether for the U.S. economy shed 149,000 jobs in December" alone. Government leaders are worried that the self-reinforcing spiral of tightening credit and weaker growth, along with the shrinking job market could push the economy over the brink. As I read these articles I could not help but notice how closely it reflected the prognosis of both Leeb and Schiff.

Article after article reinforced the prognosis that the once strong and vibrant economy of the United States is reeling. Yet another issue of *The Wall Street Journal* featured an article which indicated that "the consumer leg of the economy, which had been remarkably stable throughout the housing downturn, may now be tottering." The article continued by affirming what our prognosticators have already told us. It cites J.P. Morgan's chief economist saying, "We're in the teeth of the storm"; it then states, "consumer spending fuels around 70 percent of domestic output (GDP) so a pull-back could severely crimp the economy." The article concedes that American households are "in terrible shape," and "they don't have any reserves to really fall back on."[54] It continues by indicating that rising energy and fuel prices are further exacerbating an already grim situation.

The grim news continues as I thumb through page after page. The auto market is slowing,[55] Honeywell has closed one of its Phoenix, Arizona, plants and is laying off 240 employees as it moves "most of the jobs overseas."[56] Another related article on January 13 states that "since 2001, Arizona has lost more than 10,000 high paying jobs in the semiconductor industry, through consolidation and plant closures." The article stated that the job losses were the result of a "move to shift production from U.S. plants to new facilities in Asia."[57] The bad news continues as the Wall Street Journal affirms that Hewlett-Packard announced plans to lay off 24,600 workers. The accompanying article noted that "they're basically replacing more expensive U.S. employees with overseas employees who will work for less."[58]

These are only a few of the dozens of articles collected. But the common thread of all of them is that the United States economy is in dire trouble. We are in debt, our economy is crumbling, our assets are being purchased by foreign investors, the value of the dollar is eroding, and the job market is shrinking. Yet in spite of all this, the American consumer sleeps on in an optimistic coma induced by an affluent lifestyle based upon glories and strengths long gone. Even if Peak Oil were not a consideration, our economy is in dire straits. Our foundations have been destroyed and our house of cards is about to fall. Once again Schiff provides with the prognosis of our economic condition:

> The U. S. economy is a house of cards. It has an impressive facade, but its interior structure has deteriorated beyond the point of no return. One strong wind will topple it... The impending economic collapse has been so long in the making, so complex as to be comprehended by only a small handful of economic analysts, and so skillfully concealed by parties who benefit from various elements of it that when it happens, it will happen suddenly and catch its victims unaware and unprepared. The consequences for the unprepared are potentially horrific...[59]

We are coasting downhill to destruction and nobody seems to notice. "For when they shall say, Peace and safety; then sudden destruction cometh upon them... But ye brethren, are not in darkness, that that day should overtake you as a thief" (I Thessalonians 5: 3 and 4).

Chapter 9

THE COMING ECONOMIC POWER SHIFT

There is no dispute concerning the fact that the United States emerged from World War II as the most dominant military and economic power in the world. This industrial success, and the period of great affluence that followed World War II undoubtedly set the stage for developments which would ultimately lead to the precarious economic situation in which we now find ourselves. Though these developments would unfold one small and seemingly insignificant step at a time, they would cascade ever more quickly in later years and culminate into the treacherous economic situation as it exists today.

However, in the aftermath of World War II the United States emerged as an industrial and military superpower. The war itself had reignited the American industry that had stalled during the Great Depression and was now creating new jobs and prosperity on a level never seen before. The exigencies of a wartime economy had brought about a quadrupling of manufactured output. By the end of the war the country was expanding industrially, economically, and technologically at an unprecedented rate.

The great industrial strength of the United States insured its status as the leading exporter of manufactured goods. The country also held the world's largest reserves of gold and its currency was fully backed by this gold. No country in the world could rival the position of the United States in industrial strength and economic stability. A world which lay in devastation after the war would now look to the United States for industrially manufactured products and monetary loans for reconstruction. It was this worldwide confidence in the strength of the economy of the United States that would set the stage for developments which would soon follow.

THE RESERVE CURRENCY STATUS

At the close of World War II the devastated economies of Europe and Asia were in desperate need of reconstruction. Manufacturing had been devastated, international trade markets destroyed, and many nations' currencies were almost worthless. The pressing need for worldwide economic and diplomatic stabilization led to the Bretton Woods Monetary Conferences of 1944 – 1945. In Carroll, New Hampshire, forty-four nations sent representatives which convened at the Mount Washington Hotel and created what was to become known as the Bretton Woods Agreement. A plaque was erected at this site commemorating this event. The plaque describes this momentous event with the following words:

> In 1944 the United States government chose the Mount Washington Hotel as the site for a gathering of representatives of 44 countries. This was to be the famed Bretton Woods Monetary Conference. The Conference established the World Bank, set the gold standard at $35 an ounce, and chose the American dollar as the backbone of international exchange. The meeting provided the world with badly needed post war currency stability.

The Bretton Woods agreement established the World Bank and the International Monetary Fund (IMF) and provided that the U.S. dollar would be the currency by which other nations and financial institutions were to settle foreign exchange accounts. This agreement essentially determined that the dollar would hold the coveted position of being the primary currency in which transactions for vital commodities such as gold and oil were to be made on the global market. Therefore, any nation that was involved in international trade was behooved to accumulate foreign exchange reserves of dollars.

The fundamental reason the dollar was originally accepted by the world as the reserve currency in the Bretton Woods agreement was due to America's unequaled industrial and economic strength. This unrivaled strength provided three essential components which the world economy needed in a reserve currency and the nation which secured it.

1. The United States was the leading industrial manufacturing power and thus the leading exporter of much needed manufactured products.
2. The United States was the richest nation in the world, thus having the ability to fund loans to assist in the reconstruction and development of other nations thereby becoming the world's leading creditor nation.
3. The United States possessed the largest gold reserves of any nation and secured the value of its currency with a fixed gold standard. The U.S. dollar was fully redeemable in a fixed quantity of gold.

The importance of the status as the world's reserve currency cannot be overemphasized. This agreement essentially established that nations and international financial institutions were to conduct international transactions in American dollars. These international commodity transactions that were conducted in dollars would have the effect of directly and indirectly subsidizing the economy of the United States. It has been this status that has allowed the United States to run up record trade deficits by the selling U.S. treasury bonds or securities (IOU'S) to other countries. Other countries hold these bonds (IOU's) as credit based upon the strength of the United States economy and faith that the United States will be able to redeem these bonds – with interest of course.

It is important to note that none of the components which made the United States economy and its currency so attractive as a reserve currency now exist. Were a similar accord attempted today the dollar would not come close to qualifying for a comparable status. The United States is no longer the leading exporter of manufactured goods – but the leading importer. The United States is no longer the leading creditor nation – it is the leading debtor nation. The United States dollar is no longer backed by gold or any other commodity of intrinsic value – it is a floating currency whose value has been in steady decline for the past decade. There has been a vast transition in the American economy between 1944 when the Bretton Woods Agreement was made and today. The economy that was once the anchor and bulwark for the world is now indebted, dependent, and in serious trouble.

This great transition from strength to dependency has occurred over the space of some sixty odd years and can be attributed to several essential factors. The first factor that began to affect the strength of the United States currency was the enormous governmental spending that began during the 1960's. There were the escalating expenses of the Vietnam War along with the space program and the funding of societal entitlement efforts such as President Johnson's Great Society programs. In order to finance these projects the Federal Reserve was forced to increase the supply of money. In other words, the Federal deficit was monetized – financed by – printing more money. This increase in the supply of printed money into the public sector resulted in the dollar falling in value as the supply of gold which backed it essentially remained the same.

This devaluation of the dollar was greatly exacerbated by the unexpected arrival of peak oil production in the United States in 1970. The United States had began purchasing foreign oil by the middle of the 1960's, but now the dependency was magnified as domestic production began its inevitable decline while demand continued to rise. The United States was forced to purchase ever increasing quantities of oil from foreign sources thereby increasing the deficit and devaluing the dollar even further. As European nations became concerned about the falling value of the dollar, they began redeeming their dollars for gold which led to the second essential factor leading to our economic problems of today.

The second major factor was when President Nixon abandoned the gold standard in August of 1971. As William Clark notes in his book, *Petrodollar Warfare*, "by the summer of 1971 the drain on the Federal Reserve's gold stocks had become critical." He continues by detailing how the British Ambassador had attempted to redeem "$3 billion for its fixed exchange value in gold of $35 per ounce (approximately 5.3 million ounces, or 2,600 tons of gold)." He indicated that at this time President Nixon "opted to abandon the dollar-gold link entirely, thereby going to a system of floating currencies on August 11, 1971."[1] This decision was momentous. As Peter Schiff notes, "the significance of that repudiation (of the gold standard) cannot be minimized. It was the national equivalent of declaring bankruptcy."[2]

With the break in the gold standard, the Bretton Woods Agreement had virtually ended. Market forces would now determine the value of the dollar, and the falling value of the dollar resulted in a substantial rise in inflation during the early 1970's. In spite of Nixon's efforts to alleviate the inflationary pressures on the dollar with a wage-price freeze early in the 70's, the rate of inflation continued to rise significantly throughout that decade.

Clark points out that it was "the combined forces of a free-floating dollar, the emerging U.S. trade deficit, and massive debt associated with the ongoing Vietnam War (that) contributed to both the volatility and devaluation of the dollar in the 1970's."[3] He reveals that it was during this time that the newly formed Organization of Petroleum Exporting Countries (OPEC) "began discussing the viability of pricing oil trade in several currencies." This marketing agreement was to include "a basket of currencies" from many industrialized nations including Europe, Japan, and Canada – and of course the United States.

President Nixon recognizing the drastic effect that this would have on the United States economy quickly initiated "high-level talks with Saudi Arabia to unilaterally price international oil sales in dollars only."[4] With the abandonment of the gold standard, the old Bretton Woods Agreement had essentially been nullified. The status of the United States dollar as the reserve currency was in serious jeopardy as OPEC considered abandoning the dollar as the primary trading currency for oil. As Clark records, "in 1974 an agreement was reached with New York and London banking interests that established what became known as petrodollar recycling" and "a few years later Treasury Secretary Blumenthal cut a secret deal with the Saudis to ensure that OPEC would continue to price oil in dollars only."[5]

The significance of this agreement cannot be overemphasized. It was enormous. This agreement secured the dollar's status as the world's reserve currency even without the backing of gold or any other commodity of intrinsic value. What this agreement did was to insure that every nation that purchased oil on the international market would have to do so with American dollars. As we have already seen – oil is virtually the life-blood of every industrialized nation. Without oil industrialized nations and their economies do not function. With this agreement all nations would now be forced through their need of oil to continue their trade in dollars. The dollar's status as the world's reserve currency was effectively secured by this agreement. Its value was now determined solely by its trade status for oil. Its value has nothing to do with any commodity of value held by the United States. In his book, *Petrodollar Warfare*, Clark further elaborates upon the significance of this agreement:

> One component was the requirement that OPEC agree to price and conduct all of its oil transactions in the dollar only, and the second was to use these surplus petrodollars as the instruments to dramatically reverse the dollars falling value via high oil prices. The net effect solidified industrialized and developing nations under the sphere of the dollar. No longer backed by gold, the dollar became backed by *black gold...* It is easy to grasp that if oil can be purchased on the international markets *only with U.S. dollars*, the *demand* and *liquidity value* will be solidified, given that oil is the essential natural resource for *every industrialized nation.*[6]

As we have seen in the previous chapter, the next essential factor in the decline of the United States economy was the rise of multinational corporations (globalism) and the subsequent Free Trade Agreements which led to the outsourcing of American manufacturing jobs. As manufacturing jobs and companies abandoned the

United States for other nations offering cheaper labor and more lenient environmental standards, the manufacturing sector of the United States began to shrink. This of course precipitated a decline in manufacturing and export trade with other nations. Slowly over the course of some thirty years the United States shifted from a major exporting nation to a major importing nation. With this shift in marketing the United States began to run up enormous trade deficits with other nations. This trade deficit is financed by the sale of securities to other nations in exchange for their manufactured products. These American securities can be saved to their maturity date (usually twenty years) and then returned to the United States to be redeemed with interest, or they can be exchanged on the international market for commodities such as oil.

I trust that it has become clear at this point just how fragile the economy of the United States is. Should the dollar be abandoned as the reserve currency – or as the currency used to purchase market commodities – especially oil – the value of the American dollar would plummet as other nations would no longer need it. The billions of dollars which they hold in securities would be abandoned for other currencies and the United States would be flooded with inflated dollars as all those abandoned dollars return home. The price in goods imported from other nations would rise drastically as the value of the dollar falls.

This scenario is not only possible, but according to many economists is becoming more probable every day. William Fleckenstein, the president of money management firm of Fleckenstein Capitol and writer for MSN Money, writes that "the United States, individually and collectively, is swimming in an ocean of debt that has been rapidly ratcheting higher." He explains that this enormous debt has caused the U.S. dollar to be "less attractive to hold than other currencies"[7] on the international market. Fleckenstein then emphatically explains what the outcome of a loss of confidence in the dollar by foreign nations is likely to have.

> "The United States has been spoiled: the U.S. dollar has been the world's reserve currency for almost a hundred years. Today that status is threatened... If the United States

continues on its current path, the U.S. dollar will be chronically weak, and it is a virtual certainty that it will no longer be the world's sole reserve currency."[8]

Fleckenstein concludes by summarizing the United States' public and national debt debacle by saying that "you couldn't have created a more precarious environment if you had tried."[9]

Peter Schiff confirms this analysis with the same bluntness. He states that the value of the dollar has steadily fallen because of "declining production, inadequate saving, reckless consumption, soaring household debt," and "ballooning federal budget deficits." He adds that these irresponsible economic activities will soon result in the fact that "foreigners are not going to want our dollars anymore" and at that time the reserve status of the dollar will be history. He indicates that "once the dollar loses its reserve currency status and collapse ensues, the process of returning to economic viability will be a painful one."[10]

The pathetic truth is that Americas is broke. We are living on credit and the debt is growing. Each day as the debt load increases the value of our dollar falls. The average American is living in a house they can't pay for, driving a car they can't afford, and shopping at Wal-Mart for imported Chinese gadgets they feel they can't live without. They are saving nothing, consuming without limitations, and confident in their belief that this unsustainable lifestyle will continue forever. And this points us directly to the last essential factor leading to horrible economic mess in which we find ourselves. It is the overwhelming and unsustainable national and public debt which the United States has accrued over the past few decades.

The American public is broke, the government is broke, and we are living in a fantastic dream world if we think it will continue. William Bonner and Addison Wiggen, in their thought provoking book, *Empire of* Debt, point out the extent of America's debt burden:

The total value of all assets in America is only about $50 trillion. Current (accumulative) U.S. debt is about 37 trillion. Add to it the present value of Federal Government liabilities and America is broke. Busted. Bankrupt. No bread. Like nothing. It couldn't pay its debts even if it wanted to.[11]

The full scale of the "implicit" financial liabilities of the United States was fully revealed in 2003 in a paper released by Jagadeesh Gokhale, a senior economist at the Federal Reserve Bank of Cleveland, and Kent Smetters, the former deputy assistant secretary of economic policy at the U.S. Treasury. The paper proposed the question as to whether the United States could pay all of its future expenditure commitments, even if it had the ability to acquire all the revenues it expected to receive in the future having to use it all today. "The answer is a decided no. According to their calculations, the shortfall would amount to $45 trillion."[12]

Keeping in mind that the calculations presented by Gokhale and Smetters were submitted in 2003, prior to the "sub-prime mortgage meltdown" and the huge purchase of American assets by foreign companies late in 2007 and early in 2008. The liabilities of the U.S. debt load have increased substantially since that time and are growing ever larger. In fact the February 1, 2008, issue of *The Wall Street Journal* carried an article indicating that the newly released budget for the Federal Government had broken the $3 trillion dollar mark for the first time ever. The article continued by stating that this massive budget would increase "federal deficits, to about $400 billion for both fiscal 2008 and 2009…"[13]

The implications of this vast debt are enormous. According to the article, the debt has now become so great that the U.S. Government could be in jeopardy of "losing its Triple-A credit rating, something that has never happened since Moody's Investors Service began grading U.S. securities in 1917."[14] It is this Triple-A rating that allows the Federal Government to borrow cheaply from other nations through bonds and securities. The American debt load has reached such enormous proportions that serious questions concerning the ability of the United States to make good on its outstanding debts are being raised. This is of great concern to foreign investors who hold enormous amounts of U.S. securities.

As the debt load increases the value of the dollar falls. As more securities to finance this debt are sold, the value of the dollar falls.

As the Federal Reserve prints more money to cover these securities, the value of the dollar falls. As the value of the dollar falls, so does the value of the securities held by foreign investors. Inevitably, as the securities lose their value there comes a time when the only financially prudent thing to do is let go of "dollar" securities and invest in something more stable. Every time the Federal Reserve prints more dollars and sells more securities to carry this debt, foreign investors cringe.

THE RISE OF THE EUROPEAN UNION AND THE EURO

There is no doubt that the status of the dollar as the reserve currency is in serious jeopardy. As we have seen, one of the major factors which secure this status is that for the past few decades OPEC has chosen to use the dollar as the trade currency for oil. But now the falling dollar, the enormous debt load, and the mortgage meltdown of 2007 which has threatened the stability of the economy of the United States, has put enormous pressure on this status. Venezuela, Indonesia, Iran, Kuwait, and the United Arab Emirates have all began to push for OPEC to go to a "basket of currencies," or a more secure "monetary peg." Even now it is a serious point of debate among the oil-rich Persian Gulf States. Something that was inconceivable a few short years ago is now seriously being considered. *The Wall Street Journal* addressed this issue in a November issue in 2007:

> For decades, oil-rich Persian Gulf states have pegged their currencies to the dollar. Now that link is stoking a bad bout of inflation in their red-hot economies and putting policy makers in a dilemma: Break the dollar peg and risk undermining the U.S. currency, or keep it and face growing local discontent.[15]

The article continues by quoting Sultan Nasser al-Suweidi, the governor of the United Arab Emirate's central bank. He stated that the Gulf States have "reached a crossroads." Essentially the decision is whether the OPEC nations should continue to suffer the effects of inflation as the dollar's value deteriorates, or abandon the currency allowing the economy of the United States to be "undermined." Simon Derrick, chief currency strategist at the Bank of New York Mellon Corporation, described the "pressures" as being broad. He summarized his concern in *The Wall Street Journal* article by simply conveying that the Gulf Nations have "pegged themselves to a falling currency."

The concern has grown to the extent that "decoupling" from the United States economy was "a major topic" in the January 2008 meeting "of the world business and political elite at Davos, Switzerland." The fear is how much of an impact a faltering U.S. economy will have on the rest of the world.[16] The concern is great enough that the international financial elite are now discussing the possibility of "decoupling" from the U.S. economy. The stage appears to be set for an economic transition of monumental proportions. The dollar which has been the foundation of a strong American economy for years is now faltering along with the American economy. The strong manufacturing base along with the gold backed dollar is long gone. The mighty creditor nation is now pitifully the greatest debtor nation. Its assets have been devoured and the bill is coming due for an exorbitant and unsustainable lifestyle.

Peter Schiff confirms that "the replacement of the dollar with the euro as the reserve currency is already being mentioned in international financial circles as a distinct possibility."[17] An *Associated Press* article also revealed that as early as 2005 the Economic Forum in Davos, Switzerland, had discussed transferring the reserve status to other currencies including the Euro. Fan Gang, director of the National Economic Research Institute of the China Research Foundation, had delivered the following opinion at this meeting:

> The U.S. dollar is no longer... in our opinion (seen) as a stable currency, and is devaluating all the time, and that's putting (bringing) troubles all the time. So the real issue is how to change the regime from a U.S. dollar pegging... to a more manageable reference, say Euros, Yen, dollars – those kind of more diversified systems.[18]

The sad fact is that not only is the transfer from the dollar to other currencies (and more specifically the euro) being discussed, in some cases this transfer has already begun. Russia has diversified her deposits from the dollar to the euro along with Kuwait. Iran has switched its oil payments from the European Union to the euro and has proposed an Iranian controlled oil Bourse (market) which would market oil using the euro. China has significantly increased its central bank holding of the euro "to facilitate the anticipated ascendance of the euro as a second World Reserve Currency."[19]

The transfer is already underway and the dollar is simply holding on by a thread. This thread is continually stretching as the value of the dollar continues its decline and the euro increasingly gains strength. This transfer to the euro as the World Reserve Currency makes sound economic sense for the rest of the world. While this transfer would be devastating for the United States, it is the most reasonable course for the international market as a whole. William Clark explains this reasoning in his book *Petrodollar Warfare:*

> From an international trade perspective, the EU economy is much more balanced than that of the U.S. The EU nations have done a more effective job constraining their debt formation/dependence on foreign capital, while retaining much of their crucial domestic manufacturing base. Because of this past management of its respective economic zones, the EU is poised to become a major pole of global power.[20]

This transfer of economic power is happening right before our eyes, yet most Americans seem oblivious to this momentous fact. The European Union has grown increasingly stronger as the United States has grown increasingly weaker and more dependent. When this transfer of economic supremacy occurs, it will have a drastic affect on the economy and standard of living in the United States. T.R Reid outlines this emerging economic shift in his enlightening book *The United States of Europe*:

> The threat facing the United States is that the euro, a strong currency backed up by some of the world's strongest econo-

mies, is beginning to look like a reliable alternative to the dollar... The members of OPEC, the cartel of oil-exporting countries, are already moving toward selling their product in euros... The explosive increase in euro-based international transactions suggests the worrisome possibility that foreign investors may have found a place other than the United States where they can safely store their money... There are indications that central banks, like the People's Bank in China, began putting significant portions of their reserves into euro bonds rather than dollar bonds beginning around 2003. If this trend continues – and most economists say that it will – it will be much harder for America to continue its import-and-borrow pattern of consumption... To put it simply, the success of Europe's common currency could bring America's financial house of cards tumbling down... If all that happened, Americans would wake up to the revolution in Europe in the most painful way.[21]

Most Americans are not even aware that their lifestyle is going to change drastically in the very near future. The transfer of economic supremacy to the European Union is already well underway. All that needs to occur is for OPEC or the international banking institutions to transfer their reserve holdings to the euro. This would bring immediate economic chaos to the United States whose economy and debt have been supported by the dollar's reserve status. The influx and tidal wave of returning dollars would cause inflation to skyrocket out of control. The value of the dollar would fall to levels never even imagined. There would be no imports of gadgets, commodities, or products which we have become accustomed to and no manufacturing of our own to make them. Stores shelves would be bare and fuel and energy prices would soar. The American dream would turn into a nightmare overnight. Clark documents the assessment of a former U.S. government analyst who confirms the drastic consequences of a transfer to the euro by the OPEC nations:

The effect of an OPEC switch to the euro would be that oil consuming nations would have to flush dollars out of their (central bank) reserve funds and replace these with euros. The dollar would crash anywhere from 20 – 40 percent in value and the consequences would be those one could expect from any currency collapse and massive inflation (think Argentina currency crisis, for example). You'd have foreign funds stream out of the U.S. stock markets and dollar denominated assets, there'd surely be a run on the banks much like the 1930's, the current account deficit would become unserviceable, the budget deficit would go into default, and so on. This could result in your basic 3rd world economic crisis.[22]

Schiff also foresees the dollar conceding its supremacy to the euro. He indicates that the ensuing "collapse" will be "a painful one" and could be "cataclysmic." Once again he provides us with a solemn warning:

The impending economic collapse has been so long in the making, so complex as to be comprehended by only a small handful of economic analysts, and so skillfully concealed by parties who benefit from various elements of it that when it happens, it will happen suddenly and catch its victims unaware and unprepared. The consequences for the unprepared are potentially horrific...[23]

The only disagreement I have with Schiff is that this impending crisis is not comprehended by most people not because it is so complex, but because they don't want to comprehend it. It is a classic case of denial. Our nation has become so accustomed to – no, demanding of – the positive and therapeutic that we generally refuse to accept anything that is considered negative, pessimistic or even realistic. But more specifically – the impending crisis confronting us is so momentous in its consequences that it is hard to imagine – much less accept. The only rational way to explain this apparent denial of facts is in the context of a psychological refusal to accept the obvious when one is confronted with a disaster or crisis that is so enormous that the mind cannot grasp its implications. Such is our case. The United States has become so accustomed to an abnormal lifestyle that it has become normal. But beyond that – we cannot imagine any lifestyle other than this abnormal, extravagant, consumer based, pleasure oriented one that we have contrived – and to even consider that it is going to end is simply preposterous and beyond comprehension.

But yet one cannot help but see the resemblance in Schiff's warning that this crisis will "happen suddenly and catch its victims unprepared" and the words of the prophets. Jesus himself said, "And take heed to yourselves, lest at any time your hearts be overcharged with surfeiting (excesses and overindulgence), and drunkenness, and the cares of this life, and *so that day come upon you unawares*" (Luke 21:34). Our nation is in the midst of a wild extravagant party. We have overindulged and given ourselves to excess but time is running out. Our extravagant party is unsustainable. Our nation with only 4.5 percent of the population consumes 25 percent of the world's energy resources and almost 30 percent of the world's natural resources.[24] Yet somehow we will not accept that this manner of living is unacceptable and unsustainable by any standard – including the biblical one.

Chapter 10

THE DECLINE AND FALL
OF AMERICA

Any of the numerous crises that are converging upon us early in the twenty-first century have the potential of drastically altering life as we know it. Any of these crises could bring about circumstances which could critically affect the quality of life in any industrial society. But consider the possibilities should any number of these crises occur simultaneously, or even happen in quick succession. The consequences could be beyond comprehension. It is absolutely impossible to imagine the results of a world inundated by global disasters, radically changing climate patterns, economic collapse, epidemics, and international conflicts. But this very scenario seems to be taking shape as we enter the twenty-first century. All of the evidence indicates that the perfect storm is heading our way.

As we consider these grim possibilities, we need only examine the current position of the United States. Consider for instance the very real possibility of our current economic crisis merging with a drastic decline in oil production as the world's oil supply becomes restricted due to a terrorist attack, some drastic change in the political dynamics of the Middle East, or even as the world's production of oil peaks. The economic repercussions on an already reeling economy would be unimaginable. Rising energy prices would drive the price of every manufactured item and imported commodity higher. As the price of oil and energy escalated, the prices of all commodities would continue to rise. Our already unsustainable national debt and trade deficit would soar even higher. As the worldwide competition for petroleum resources increased, and other nations such as China observed the value of the billions of dollars in U.S. securities which they hold securing U.S. debt begin to fall, the possibility of nations transferring their assets to other more secure currencies would increase. A transfer or change in the coveted position of the world's reserve currency would not only become likely – but unless the current meltdown of the U.S. economy miraculously changes – this change becomes inevitable at some point.

Rising oil and commodity prices alone could drive inflation to the point where the U.S. economy could not sustain itself. Especially, as we have already seen, how a decrease in oil equals a corresponding decrease in energy, which means that the productive output of this nation would enter into a relentless decline. Inflation, declining production, unemployment, along with rising trade and budget deficits alone contain the recipe for disaster. Whether other nations such as Japan, Russia, China, and numerous others which hold U.S. backed securities would release them before or after the collapse is inconsequential.

The bailout from the U.S. dollar could very well occur as a slow process before there is a transfer of the reserve currency status to another currency. This action would simply prolong the inevitable collapse. The U.S. economy would agonizingly suffer through the effects of a dying and declining economy as inflation, unemployment, and rising debt slowly unraveled the economy and eroded the "American way of life." The economic collapse would resemble the slow death of some unfortunate creature trapped within the constricting grasp of a boa constrictor. Every phase would simply add to the constricting pressure as the economy slowly withered until it collapsed under the pressures.

On the other hand, the change in the reserve currency status could occur suddenly and precipitate a rapid bailout from the U.S. dollar. This change would bring about a drastic and sudden collapse of the U.S. economy as billions of dollars would flood the world market as nations released them in a panic. The value of the dollar would collapse overnight. With the dollar no longer the trade currency for petroleum (or any other commodity for that matter) the price of oil in the United States would skyrocket overnight to unbelievable levels. It would continue this rapid ascension as the dollar deteriorated in value. Almost every aspect of the industrial lifestyle which has characterized the "American way of life" would grind to a halt. The government would struggle to simply maintain enough energy to keep vital aspects of the infrastructure functioning. The rest of society would be left to their own resources. At a certain point societal collapse would become unavoidable.

Either way – the economic collapse of the United States and the dollar is inevitable. The numerous and continuing pressures that are being placed upon the dollar and the U.S. economy will inevitably take their toll. The dollar cannot continue its decline in the world market, and the U.S. cannot continue to run up trillions of dollars in enormous and unprecedented debt without the bill coming due at some point.

As we can see, there are simply too many possible scenarios which could bring about the collapse of the U.S. economy to enumerate. It is useless to even speculate which of these scenarios will happen first. The current credit crisis and the domino effect of the mortgage meltdown itself could have catastrophic consequences for an already over burdened economy. When you add the energy crisis, the financial obligations of our geopolitical involvements, and the ever increasing cost of our bailout programs, the financial burden becomes almost unbearable. Mix in a natural disaster on the scale of Hurricane Katrina or another terrorist attack and the results are cataclysmic. The possible catastrophic scenarios are unending. There are any number of circumstances which could materialize at any time. The stage is set for an economic catastrophe of epic proportions. With an economy already in dire trouble, any of these catastrophes, or any combination of them could be the straw that broke the camel's back.

OUR REALITY CHECK IS IN THE MAIL

While we do not know the specific details of how the coming events will unfold – we can get an overall characterization as to how world events will transpire in the very near future. Not only have numerous secular experts in various fields afforded us the richness of their knowledge and expertise – but the Bible also provides us with a prophetic guideline as to how world events will develop as these crises assert themselves. What has been amazing during the years spent doing research for this book is exactly how more and more of the physical evidence which is being presented by secular experts is conforming exactly to what the prophetic writings of the Bible has portrayed for centuries.

In chapter two we saw how the prophetic timetable of events, which were to precede the second coming of Jesus Christ, was prophesied to begin essentially with the resurrection (or rebirth) of the nation of Israel in 1948. We also determined that Jesus himself had prophesied that the generation of people which saw this momentous event (or was alive during this time), would live to see the fulfillment of "all these things," including what is referred to as the "tribulation" period, the second coming of Christ, and end of the age – or world as we know it (Matthew 24:21 and 29-35).

One point should have become exceptionally clear as we examined the numerous crises which have emerged during the latter part of the twentieth and the first part of the twenty-first centuries. This point is that all of these crises are projected by the experts to climax or assert themselves significantly prior to the middle of the twenty-first century, or 2050. The world population is expected to reach an unsustainable level of somewhere between 9 to 12 billion people. Essential resources such as water and arable land are going to become increasingly scarce, causing shortages, drought, and famine, thus exponentially increasing the unsustainable level of population growth. Food production that began to decline in the late 1990's will continue to decline due to numerous factors including water shortages, climate change, and a continuing deterioration of arable land due to erosion and mineral depletion. Given the fact that most experts estimate that the planet exceeded its natural carrying capacity somewhere around 1986, this makes the declining food production a major concern to an ever increasing population.

Emerging new deadly and evolving diseases are predicted to bring pandemics on a scale never seen before due to the size of the world's population and the nature of the new diseases. This situation is exacerbated not only by our ever increasing population, but the fact that deadly diseases are evolving faster than our medical technology. They are growing ever more immune to any known antibiotics and no known cures are even on the horizon. Wars, food shortages, and water pollution and depletion will only intensify this already critical situation. Medical experts are already predicting that these new deadly diseases could assert themselves at any time. In fact according to most health experts we are overdue for an epidemic of historic proportions. As Dr. Richard Krause of the United States National Institute of Health warned the United States Congress in 1982, "Plagues are as certain as death."[1]

Petroleum geologists, energy experts, and current data all indicate that the world's reserves of petroleum are being depleted at an alarming rate. Most experts have predicted that the world will reach the peak production of oil reserves somewhere between 2005 and 2015, with most petroleum geologists leaning nearer to 2012 or before. We have already examined the devastating results which this critical event will bring. All industrial economies will be affected and growth will essentially stop. Economies will destabilize and resource wars will erupt as nations struggle to maintain their economies by competing for the ever declining life source of industrial societies. The peaking of the world's production of oil will precipitate a time of global turmoil such as this world has never seen. As James Kunstler has observed, "once the world is headed firmly down the arc of depletion, fuel supplies will be interrupted by geopolitical contests and culture clashes. Eventually, economic growth as conventionally understood in industrial societies will cease..."[2] He continues by explaining that oil is so vital that all nations will literally be forced out of necessity to fight for this vital commodity in order to maintain their industrial integrity. He states:

A military contest over oil could eventually inflame a theater of war stretching from the Middle East to Southeast Asia, and it could leave the oil production infrastructure of many countries shattered in the process. Such a conflict might be the last World War.[3]

He summarizes the grim scenario with the prognosis that, "even the nonreligious observers must regard with awe the potential that the Middle East now holds for setting off a civilization-ending war, a virtual Armageddon."[4]

All of these events are predicted to occur sometime prior to 2050, and all of these crises are asserting themselves at this time. But even as these momentous civilization changing crises are emerging – the United States is confronting an economic crisis of epic proportions. This is a crisis that has the potential of effecting economic devastation that surpasses the Great Depression. Record breaking national debt, record breaking government budget deficits, record breaking consumer debt, a declining dollar, and a withering manufacturing sector all indicate that we are headed for an economic disaster such as the United States has never experienced. As I have previously stressed – these conditions alone should be enough to alarm even the most stoic. But even as I write, the credit crisis is asserting itself and the dollar which once reigned supreme in strength is fading away and nations are "decoupling" from the dollar and investing in other currencies. The United States is in serious jeopardy of losing its reserve currency status which is the only factor that has sustained our record breaking indebtedness thus far.

In 2008 when the Senate Select Committee on Intelligence was briefed on "potential threats to the nation," one subject took preeminence over global terrorism, nuclear proliferation and regional conflicts. "This year," according to an article in *The Wall Street Journal*, Michael McConnell, the Director of National Intelligence, "went beyond the conventional world of sypcraft" and specifically addressed "the impact a weak dollar could have on national security." The summary of his address was that nations are already "de-linking their currency pegs to the dollar" and transferring their assets to other currencies. The article stated that "a perfect storm for dollar desertion may already be brewing," and "when our intelligence chief starts talking like a central banker, you know there's a problem."[5] The potential for economic collapse is real, and when an economy collapses every other facet that a nation deems necessary for national security goes with it.

With all of these crises seemingly asserting themselves as this time – the potential for a cataclysmic economic crisis and a complete collapse of our social system and infrastructure cannot be ignored. The pressures placed upon the economy of the United States by the growing burden of welfare, Medicare, Social Security, and lingering international conflicts cannot be sustained indefinitely. Something must give somewhere and at some time very soon. No expert in the world expects this status quo to continue very far into the future – much less beyond 2050. Our world – and more specifically the United States – is facing a crisis of momentous proportions. Our reality check is in the mail and is expected by many experts to be arriving very shortly.

Could it be that the Bible offers some insight or guide as to the unfolding of these momentous events? Could it be that prophets over 2,000 years ago provided an outline of geopolitical events that would transpire as the world approached the end of the age? And, could these events reflect what we see happening all around us today? I believe they do – and I believe it does. I believe the Bible not only offers us insights, but also provides us with a very accurate guide as to the sequence of events that are unfolding along with their possible consequences. When one considers the details of the prophecies and measures them against the events that are now unfolding around us – the similarities are remarkable. In fact, so remarkable are they that one can no longer consider them to be a coincidence. There are simply too many events and too many specific circumstances that are coming together to logically believe that the similarities between what is happening today and what the prophets foretold are coincidental.

But it is not only biblical prophets that are warning of coming plagues, famines, resource wars, and global conflict – it is secular authorities in all fields of expertise. It is not just some white robed doomsday prophet standing on the street corner warning of an impending economic disaster and the collapse of industrial society – it is financial experts and economists who are heralding this imminent crisis. It is not only preachers and religious students who are warning of impending food shortages, increasingly severe natural disasters, and potential global epidemics – it is scientists and respected secular experts who are sounding the alarm. It is not radical extremists who are warning of the possibility of global conflict – it is respected intelligence experts and authorities in world security who are admonishing us of this grim possibility. It is apparent that secular authorities in all fields of expertise are expecting and warning us of the very same catastrophic scenarios which the Bible describes as being characteristic of the last days.

The fact is that these events that were at one time so far in the future that they could only be seen through the spiritual eye of a biblical prophet are now so close that anyone should be able to see them. In other words, **we are so close to what the prophets prophesied about as future events – that they are now occurring as current events!** If we simply look around us, we should be able to see them with our natural eyes. We have climbed over the last prophetic mountaintop and are now looking down into the valley of the present and personally witnessing what was once hidden from past generations. **We have arrived at the appointed time of destiny and are now seeing the fulfillment of all things!** The "signs of the times" all indicate that this is truly the generation "upon whom the ends of the world are come" (I Corinthians 10:11).

It cannot be a coincidence that Jesus spoke of a time when there would be "wars" and nations rising against other nations, while indicating that at the same time there would be "famines and pestilences (plagues)" and natural disasters. This is exactly what secular experts are predicting for our generation today. While some skeptics may point out that the world has always experienced wars, famines, and plagues, we must consider the context in which Jesus spoke of these things. It is apparent that even in Jesus' time there were wars, famines, and plagues. It would be logical to assume he understood this. Jesus is simply saying that what will set these events apart from all those that have happened before is that they will be more severe than the world has ever experienced. It is not that famines have never happened before – but just prior to the end of the age there will be famine on a scale such as the world has never seen. It is not that wars have not occurred before – but just prior to the end of this age there will be wars and conflict on a level such as the world has never seen. It is not that the world has never confronted disaster and distress before – but just prior to the end of this age the world will endure a period of disaster and distress on a scale which has never been seen before. Jesus is very clear in his description of the enormity of these events. He said, "then shall be great tribulation such as was not since the beginning of the world to this time, no, nor ever shall be" (Matthew 24:21).

Daniel the prophet also confirmed that "there shall be a time of trouble; such as never was since there was a nation…" (Daniel 12:1). The crises of which Jesus and the prophets spoke of were significant because of the severity and scale on which they would occur – not because they would be unique in occurrence. Jesus warned that the severity of the crises would be such that "men's hearts (would) fail them for fear, and for looking after those things which are coming on the earth" (Luke 21:26).

Never before in the history of mankind has humanity confronted crises such as climate change with its potential of causing drought, food shortages, and natural disasters. This crisis alone is such that experts warn of its potential for wrecking havoc on human civilization and causing devastation all over the world. According to leading experts, the impending plagues that are now emerging are predicted to have the potential to be on a scale that human civilization has never experienced. The drastic increase in a global population which cannot be sustained by earth's resources is a crisis unique to this generation. Our entire world for the first time in history is dependent upon a declining and finite resource in the form of petroleum. The depletion of this unique resource is predicted by experts to have the potential of ending industrial civilization as we know it and precipitating global conflict, famine, and economic collapse. One cannot deny that the global crises, and the devastating consequences of the crises which confront our generation, are strikingly similar to what the prophets foretold would confront the world just prior to the end of the age. Simply thumb through the pages of Revelation and judge for yourself.

Although experts, writers, and men of science and secular persuasion have not approached their particular subjects from a spiritual perspective – their message clearly echoes the end-time apocalyptic message of Jesus and the prophets. Yet as Planet Earth enters the most perilous uncharted waters of human history, most of its inhabitants are not even aware of the significance of current events and the perils that await them. Author James Kunstler solemnly indicates that our generation is literally "sleepwalking into the future."[6] In spite of all the evidence and signs, he indicates that our world is oblivious to what is happening around them and the crises that are unfolding. Once again the warnings of Jesus are echoed. After his momentous message concerning the unmistakable signs that would herald the end of the age, Jesus made an amazing statement in comparing our generation to that of Noah's day. He said that in the last days it would be just as it was in the days of Noah, and they "knew not until the flood came, and took them away" (Matthew 24:39).

How can this be? How can a world that is standing upon the precipice of wars and international conflict of unprecedented magnitude, of pestilence (epidemics), and natural disasters on a scale never before imagined, be oblivious to the unmistakable warnings concerning these emerging crises? How can they be oblivious to the ominous implications of these events? Yet as astounding as it may seem – this is exactly the case in our world today. In spite of unmistakable warnings and signs, a sin-intoxicated world sleeps on in a spiritual stupor as it speeds toward eternity just as it did in the days of Noah!

According to the Apostle Paul (who apparently felt the same urgency) this spiritual stupor is equated to a "drunkenness" which impairs one's senses and perception of reality. He declares in his first epistle to the church at Thessalonica that everyone should be well aware that the "day of the Lord cometh as a thief in the night." But he continues by warning that there will be those that will sleep and be "drunken in the night" (I Thessalonians 5:1-7). They are in a spiritual slumber and their spiritual senses are dulled by a worldly intoxication induced by the cares of this life and the things of this world (Luke 21:34). In spite of all the indisputable signs of the approaching crises, they will scoff at the very thought of "the end." Walking in a drunken intoxication of their own "lusts," they will mockingly ask, "Where is the promise of his coming?" In spite of the overwhelming evidence that human civilization is entering into a period of crisis such as it has never known, they will say, "for since the fathers fell asleep, all things continue as they were" (II Peter 3:4).

The Bible specifically teaches that although the world will enter into a period of crisis such as it has never known – there will be a prevalent spirit of unconcern, apathy, and disbelief. People will be overcome with a spiritual intoxication that will dull their spiritual perception and foster a belief that "all things (will) continue as they were…" (II Peter 3:4). They will be thoroughly convinced that tomorrow will be much the same as today (Isaiah 56:12). But the prophetic word of God plainly declares that there is coming a day when tomorrow will not be anywhere near the same as today. There is coming a day when every life, every plan, and every future will be interrupted by a divine appointment. It is past time for our world to shake itself from its spiritual slumber. It is time to sound the trumpet! As the scripture says, "Cry aloud and spare not!" We are entering into an era of human history through which we have never traveled! We are about to confront numerous crises which will alter the course of human history and will transform civilization as we know it today! Things are about to change forever!

CONNECTING THE PROPHETIC DOTS

Even now we are farther along and moving more swiftly down the path to prophetic fulfillment than most people realize. The end-time prophetic scenario is already well underway. Israel has become a nation just as the prophets foretold would happen in the last days (Ezekiel 34:13, 36:24 and 37:21-22). The city of Jerusalem has been taken and is now in control of the Jewish people signifying the beginning of the end of the "times of the Gentiles" (Luke 21:24 and Romans 11:25-26). As we have seen in chapter two, this is of the utmost importance to the church and gentile nations. This momentous event signifies the nearing of the end of the church-age, the coming of Christ, the judgment of gentile nations, and the consummation of God's plan for the nation of Israel. In other words – this event rivals the rebirth of the nation of Israel in importance as it signifies that the world is entering into the final stages of prophetic fulfillment.

Other prophetic events have occurred (and are occurring) even as these events have taken place. The prophetic scriptures of the Bible indicate that in conjunction with the resurrection of the nation of Israel in the last days, that there would also be a resurrection or reunion of the people or nations which comprised the ancient Roman Empire as it existed in Christ's day (Daniel 2:36-44 and 7:1-28). We have watched as this prophetic event has emerged during our lifetime. In fact it is still in its prophetic development as it slowly progresses toward complete fulfillment. We have watched as the European Common Market rose from the ruins of World War II. We have watched as it slowly unified and became the European Union. It is not by coincidence that the nations which comprise this great union are the same nations (or peoples) which comprised the ancient Roman Empire. Never since the Roman Empire, have this people ever been unified as they are today.

T.R. Reid, in his classic book entitled *The United States of Europe*, describes this miraculous unification in this manner:

> At the dawn of the twenty-first century, a geopolitical revolution of historic dimensions is under way across the Atlantic: the unification of Europe... The new United States of Europe – to use Winston Churchill's phrase – as more people, more wealth, and more trade than the United States of America... The EU (European Union), with a population of nearly half a billion people stretching from Ireland to Estonia, has a president, a parliament, a constitution, a cabinet, a central bank, a bill of rights, a unified patent office, and a court system with the power to overrule the highest courts of every member nation. It has a 60,000-member army (or "European Rapid Reaction Force," to be precise)... It has its own space

agency with 200 satellites in orbit and a project under way to send a European to Mars before Americans get there. It has a 22,000 person bureaucracy and an 80,000-page legal code governing everything from criminal trials and corporate taxation to peanut butter labels and lawn mower safety... At the end of the twentieth century, the strong U.S. dollar reigned supreme. Four years into the new century, the young upstart, the euro, ranks as the world's strongest currency.[7]

Reid continues by stating that "while this historic transformation has been taking place, Americans have been asleep."[8] Most people have not even been aware how comprehensive this unification of Europe has been, much less aware of its prophetic implications. It would amaze many people to learn that the prophet Daniel foretold this momentous event nearly 2,500 years ago. But this is a transition that is still occurring. The European Union must still experience many significant changes as it emerges completely into the unified kingdom that Daniel saw. These changes are taking place even now, and these changes will have a significant impact upon the future of the United States of America.

The Bible emphatically indicates through numerous scriptures that the European Union will become the leading economic and political force in the world just prior to the end of the age. The United States of course is in a very precarious position as this prophetic fulfillment requires an economic and political shift in world power. Since the end of World War II the United States has been the leading economic and political power in the world. Up until this time there has been no rival, and a decline in the power and influence of the United States was almost unimaginable. But now with the economic malaise confronting the United States, and the growing influence and strength of Europe, this scenario is not only imaginable – but to many it has become very likely. Once again we turn to Reid for an explanation as to how this transition in world power and influence is taking place:

The threat facing the United States is that the euro, a strong currency backed up by some of the world's strongest economies, is beginning to look like a reliable alternative to the dollar... The members of OPEC, the cartel of oil-exporting countries, are already moving toward selling their product in euros... The explosive increase in euro-based international transactions suggests the worrisome possibility that foreign investors may have found a place other than the United States where they can safely store their money... there are indications that central banks, like the Peoples Bank of China, began putting significant portions of their reserves into euro bonds rather than dollar bonds beginning around 2003. If this trend continues – and most economists say that it will – it will be much harder for America to continue its import-and-borrow pattern of consumption... To put it simply, the success of Europe's common currency could bring America's financial house of cards tumbling down... If all that happened, Americans would wake up to the revolution in Europe in the most painful way.[9]

What is amazing is that what is happening at this time, and being forecast by economists and financial experts, was prophesied by Daniel some 2,500 years ago. In the last days, just prior to the end of the age, the European Union (or revived Roman Empire) will become the world's most dominating economic and political power. This of course means that there must of necessity be a transfer of power from the United States to the European Union. Of course this transition will not be by a willing acquiescence of the United States. This transition will not occur simply because the United States and Europe decide to make a transfer of power. There will be some geopolitical circumstance or some manner of economic crisis which will precipitate this transition. Some significant event will precipitate an economic or political upheaval that will bring about this transition. The current financial turmoil and the resulting instability in worldwide financial institutions, along with the tremendous trade and budget deficits of the United States, could be setting the stage for this economic transition.

Many financial and economic experts including Peter Schiff, Stephen Leeb, Addison Wiggin, David Wiedemer, Robert Wiedemer,

Cindy Spitzer and Eric Jansen, to name only a few, have predicted an economic collapse of the United States dollar and economy. While the experts cannot calculate with complete accuracy the degree and extent of the economic collapse, most predict that this collapse will be intense and possibly catastrophic. But these are the human experts.

What we know from the Bible is that the European Union (revived Roman Empire) is recorded to be the leading world power during the end-time. What we also know is that the United States of America – now the world's leading power – is not mentioned or even referenced in biblical prophecy. THE ABSENCE OF THE UNITED STATES IN THE UNFOLDING OF THE END-TIME SCENARIO OF GEOPOLITICAL EVENTS SPEAKS VOLUMES. This absence indicates that the United States is no longer a nation of influence or power on the geopolitical stage as the end-time scenario unfolds. It apparently has been reduced by some set events or circumstances to a non-involved party. No circumstance fits the bill more neatly than an economic collapse of the financial system in which the United States relinquishes its position to Europe by default.

The most likely nature of this economic transition is any one of the numerous scenarios already depicted in the previous chapters. This transition could be precipitated by the current economic meltdown, peak oil, a declining dollar, a loss of confidence in the economy of the United States by foreign investors, burgeoning trade and budget deficits, or a change of status in the world's reserve currency. Any one of these circumstances – or a combination of any of these – spells disaster for the United States economy. What is far more important for us to understand than the particular circumstances which will bring about this transition, is the fact that this transition MUST take place for prophetic fulfillment to occur.

Anyone can see that this transition in economic power will not be pleasant for the United States. As we have mentioned, it will not be a willing acquiescence. All of the evidence points to the fact that this transition will be comprised of a very painful economic meltdown that will drastically alter every facet of the American way of life. It will change this nation politically, socially, and economically. The United States will scarcely resemble the nation it was before this transition. Theologically there are numerous reasons why it is likely that the United States will suffer through an agonizing collapse and all that this disaster entails.

1. As mentioned already – at some point the United States must relinquish its position as the leading economic power to Europe. The European Union (or revived Roman Empire) is to be the dominant economic and military power in the end-time scenario as set forth in the prophecies of Daniel and the Apostle John in the Revelation.

2. The United States is not mentioned in the end-time prophetic scenario indicating that it has been reduced to a non-influential position. For this situation to occur, the United States must have suffered some event of catastrophic proportions. This conclusion is apparent as the United States will not even be in a position to resist a Russian and Islamic invasion into the Middle East against Israel (see Ezekiel chapters 38 and 39). This invasion will undoubtedly be initiated on the part of Russia to control vital petroleum resources that will become crucial as the effects of Peak Oil assert themselves. This invasion and control of vital energy resources would never be allowed under the current geopolitical alignment. The United States, as the world's strongest military and economic power, is totally committed to defending the petroleum resources of the Middle East as well as Israel. The United States must suffer some manner of catastrophe which effectively removes it from a position of power and influence. Israel will essentially be alone in resisting this invasion.

3. The Scriptures warn that all nations that have once known the blessings of God and reject him will be judged. The United States is a nation with a rich Christian heritage. Its founding fathers were Christians and the laws of this nation were predicated upon scriptural principles. During the latter part of the twentieth century the culture of the United States was transformed from a theistic orientation to one that is dominated by secular humanism. God has been removed from our schools and institutions along with prayer and the reading of the

Bible. The creation account of origins is not only ridiculed but completely rejected from being taught in public schools. All manner of immorality, including homosexual practices, have been legally sanctioned and publicly promoted throughout the new American culture. Promiscuity, obscenity, vulgarity, and violence dominate American culture through our entertainment, television, and other sources. Over 40 million unborn children have been murdered through abortion pursuant to the legal sanction of a perverted court system which has turned good into evil and evil into good. The list could go on, but essentially the word of God pronounces judgment upon nations that forget God. (see Psalm 9:17, Jeremiah 12:17 and 18:7-10)

4. The justice of God requires judgment. Should God not judge the United States for its abundance of sin he would have to apologize to Sodom and Gomorrah, Nineveh, Old Testament Israel, and every other nation and people that he has judged throughout history. As evangelist Leonard Ravenhill so eloquently puts it in his book, *Sodom Had No Bible*, "What obligation has God to people like us whose aggregate sin as a nation in one day is more than the sin of Sodom and her sister city, Gomorrah, in one year?"[10] He continues by asserting that "Sodom had no preachers – we have thousands. Sodom had no Bible – we have millions. Sodom had no histories of God's judgment to warn it of danger – we have volumes of them." He then summarizes his argument by saying, "Sodom perished in spite of all these disadvantages. America today is living only by the mercy of God. The only reason we are not smoking in the fire-wrath of a holy God is mercy – m-e-r-c-y, prolonged mercy!"[11]

5. If God did not spare Old Testament Israel from judgment when they were the "apple of his eye," why should the United states presumptuously assume that he will spare her from the same manner of divine judgment (Romans 11:21-22).

The overwhelming theological evidence indicates that the United States is moving swiftly toward divine judgment. The only escape from this judgment would be a sweeping national revival which would turn the nation back to God. It would need to be a society shaking, culture changing revival which would restore righteousness and a Christian heritage that has been forsaken. Barring this, only judgment awaits this country and time is running out. No longer is it simply the prophets who can see this coming judgment. Now economists, intelligence experts, and scientists have all joined ranks. Although they have preferred to call it an economic collapse, or an unraveling of industrial civilization along with other colorful terms, the message is still the same – the United States has an appointment with destiny and she will no longer be the country that she once was when this appointment takes place.

Chapter 11

THE NATION THAT FORGOT GOD

There is no doubt that we have entered into perilous waters and grave dangers lie ahead for the United States. We have already examined numerous global crises which have consequences that are growing increasingly severe every year. These consequences are not only affecting other nations but will increasingly manifest themselves in our country. We have examined the potential impacts of our planet's unsustainable population growth, resource depletion, diminishing energy resources, the escalating effects of climate change, and the ever growing global economic malaise. All of these crises are progressively escalating in severity and even now the tremors are being felt in nations throughout the world. Institutional and political foundations are being shaken and the United States has not been exempt. But sadly, this is just the beginning. There would not be enough time or pages in this book to examine in detail every crisis which threatens our nation today.

Even now we are confronting the dangers of an over extended military and hostile threats from numerous fronts. There is the mounting danger of nuclear weapons falling into terrorist hands or coming into possession of nations with hostile intentions. The persistent threat of terrorist attacks and the rising tensions in the Middle East continue to escalate holding the foreboding potential of global conflict. In fact, the potential for any number of geopolitical events to explode into an international incident which could have tremendous military and economic repercussions to our nation is enormous.

But all of these things simply scratch the surface of the dangers which confront us. In fact crises situations have become so endemic that we have grown accustomed to living in a world of tension, conflict, and crises. We have almost become numb to the persistent barrage of threatening situations. We see them presented daily on television. We hear them on the radio, and we read of them in the newspapers. We are bombarded daily with news of terrorist threats, rising international conflict, the dangers of new and developing diseases, increasingly severe and frequent natural disasters, and collapsing financial institutions along with an economy on the verge of collapse. Nevertheless, all of these are simply "the beginning of sorrows" just as Jesus predicted (Matthew 24:6-8).

But as severe as these crises are – there is a far more dangerous crisis confronting the United States of America. There is a spiritual crisis which has been escalating exponentially for some time. It is a crisis constituted by the unique spiritual and political position which the United States finds itself in as the world speeds toward its prophetic appointment with destiny. If we truly believe we are living in the "last days," and this is the generation which shall see the fulfillment of all things as Jesus prophesied – then the United States is in a very precarious position indeed. If these things are true, then in the very near future we will experience the climax of a spiritual and political crisis that will have enormous implications for this nation both spiritually and naturally.

Biblical prophecy seems to clearly indicate that the world stage is now being set for the climactic act in prophetic fulfillment. Circumstances and nations appear to be aligning themselves in preparation for the culmination of end-time events. Over the space of one generation we have seen the resurrection of the nation of Israel and the rise of the revived Roman Empire in the form of the European Union. Any student of prophecy will recognize the fact that these two entities are the leading characters in end-time events. But we are also witnessing the emergence of other nations and alliances which will play significant roles in these momentous events.

Even now we are witnessing the emerging alliance between Russia and other leading Islamic nations which are hostile to Israel. Treaties and agreements are being made between Russia, Iran, Libya, Egypt, Syria, and other Middle Eastern nations as we write. These momentously significant prophetic alliances are occurring with breathtaking speed and it seems as if the world is preparing itself for the raising of the curtain for the final act in prophetic revelation.

Events transpiring in the world today could be setting the stage for the fulfillment of prophecies written thousands of years ago by Hebrew prophets. The AIA (Axis Information and Analysis) newsletter, *Global Challenges and Research*, reported in its May, 2005, issue that "no one could have predicted such a succession of events (the alignment of these nations) five years ago." The article continued by indicating that due to Moscow's increased "interests in the Middle East," and Russia's "desperate efforts to return to Middle Eastern politics as a superpower," she has become the key player in a "quadrilateral alliance" consisting of "Russia, Turkey, Iran, and Syria." The nations of this alliance have pledged mutual cooperation, economic trade and assistance, along with military aid, mutual training, and military assistance commitments.[1] This alliance could be setting the stage for one of the most momentous prophetic events to date.

If this alignment is not frightening enough, consider the fact that Russia has extended its alliance even further to include Libya and Egypt. The *Daily News – Egypt*, in an article released on October 11, 2006, reported that Mohamed Rachid, the foreign Trade Minister of Egypt made a three day visit to Moscow with the mission of "creating new trade and investment opportunities." Rachid returned from his visit stating that "the time is now right to take the Egypt-Russia relationship onto a much stronger footing." He continued by acknowledging that Egypt could be "Russia's gateway into the Middle East and North Africa."[2] The alliances of course did not stop with Egypt. The *Eurasia Daily Monitor* reported in their May 9, 2007, publication that "Russian arms traders have been negotiating to resume trade with Libya." The article continued by indicating that Russia has offered a "hefty… write-off of all Libyan debt" of some

$4.7 billion "in exchange for a commitment to buy at least some quantity of Russian weapons."[3]

These events should be like a fire alarm in the night to students of prophecy. As the end-time scenario comes together, one of the more significant pieces is the alliance of the nations which we have just mentioned. These are the very nations that the prophet Ezekiel calls by name in the thirty-eighth chapter of his book. He predicted that these very nations would form an alliance in the "last days" and ultimately invade the Middle East in a war aimed at taking a "spoil" and the destruction of Israel. (Ezekiel 38:11-12)

Ezekiel prophesied concerning this alliance and invasion almost 2,500 years ago. He prophesied of this alliance when such an event would have been unimaginable. Consider the fact that 2,500 years ago most of these nations, including Russia, were backward tribes of nomadic peoples separated by enormous geographical distances and cultural differences. This alliance which would have been impossible at the time of Ezekiel's prophecy is now occurring even as you read this book. Today, with the intense Islamic hatred of Israel, as indicated by Ahmadinejad's public threat to "wipe Israel off the map," and Russia's ravenous hunger for the vast energy resources of the Middle East, the scenario which Ezekiel prophesied appears to be preparing itself for fulfillment.

All of this is of immense importance to the United States. As we have mentioned previously – all of the nations which are to play a significant role in the end-time prophetic scenario are mentioned in some manner in prophetic scripture. What is significant for the United States is that it is conspicuous by its absence. It is not mentioned in any prophetic scripture or in any end-time scenario. This is a significant in that the United States has been one of the key players in world politics and events for the past one hundred years. In fact, this nation has been the most influential economic and military power in the world for the past sixty to seventy years. To even consider that there could be a major conflict – much less a multinational invasion of the Middle East – without U.S. involvement or intervention is unthinkable.

Yet this is exactly the scenario presented by the prophet. The United States is not mentioned directly, indirectly, or even symbolically. All of the other key players are specifically listed in Ezekiel's prophecy. Russia is referred to by its Hebrew name of "Rosh," or as translated in English, "Chief Prince."[4] The Caucasus Mountain region between the Black and Caspian seas undoubtedly refers to the "land of Magog." This area of southern Russia, and the land now occupied by the former Soviet republics of Kazakhstan, Kyrgyzstan, Uzbekistan, Turkmenistan, and Tajikistan make up the ancient land of the Scythian, which were called Magogites by ancient scholars such as Josephus.[5] Meschek and Tubal were the grandsons of Noah who settled in the land which is now known as Russia. According to many bible expositors, Moscow is the linguistic derivative of Meschek, while the eastern capitol of Russia, Tobolsk, seems to have been derived from Tubal.[6] Iran which was just recently changed from Persia in the last century is easily identified. Togarmah, refers to the Armenian people who inhabit eastern Turkey.[7] Egypt, Libya, and Syria are much the same as they have been throughout history. Even the European Union is mentioned in bible prophesy although not in this particular scenario. The kings of the east – indicating China and perhaps other eastern nations are mentioned – but there is no mention of the United States anywhere in bible prophecy.

It is this conspicuous absence of any mention of the United States in this scenario that is of the utmost importance. The absence of the United States in this end-time prophecy speaks volumes. As the world exists today, a scenario in which there is a major military conflict in the Middle East which threatens the security of the world's largest reserves of petroleum which would not involve the United States does not exist. This scenario is completely unthinkable – unless. Unless some serious event has drastically altered the geopolitical landscape as it stands today. Unless some circumstance has occurred that is so devastating in its consequences it has prevented the United States from being an involved party.

This is exactly the scenario which confronts the United States at this time. For bible prophecy to be fulfilled – and the end-time scenario as predicted by Daniel, Ezekiel, and John in the Revelation to occur – there MUST be a transfer of power to the European Union as the world enters the period prophetically referred to as the "Tribulation."[8] The European Union (or the revived Roman Empire) is the leading economic and military power during this end-time period. It is this revived Roman Empire which dominates the end-time prophetic stage. It is this governmental entity from which the Antichrist arises. It is most likely through this governmental agency that the Antichrist will bring peace to the Middle East for a very short period of time. It is through the economic power of this entity that the economy of the world will be controlled during the Tribulation. It will be through the invigorated military power of the European Union that the Antichrist will attempt to maintain world "peace" and "control" during the Tribulation.[9]

During this "tribulation" period, the European Union will find itself not only performing in a very similar manner as the United States currently does – but will actually attempt to assume much more authority and influence in world affairs than the United States ever did. For this scenario to occur there must obviously be some type of significant geopolitical or economic event which removes the United States from its current position of world leadership. As the end-time scenario unfolds as predicted by the prophets, the European Union must suddenly move forward at some point and fill the void left by the fall, collapse, demise, or removal of the United States from the world scene. Whatever the event or scenario is – the effect will be that the United States will be relegated to an uninvolved party during this time. This once great nation will become a nonentity with little or no influence in critical world events. It is entirely possible that the event which has taken place to remove the United States from its position as world power will have left the country in political and economic chaos. In a condition such as this, survival rather than influencing world events would have priority.

What is important for us to understand is that this momentous political and economic power shift must occur prior to what we call the "Tribulation" period. This point is significant in that this event could occur prior to the rapture of the church. This significant fact must be given consideration no matter what prophetic persuasion one adheres to concerning the timing of our Lord's return. Even pre-tribulationists[10] must give consideration to the fact that whatever momentous event ultimately triggers the transfer of power from the United States to the European Union, it could occur prior to the rapture of the church. There is no special guarantee that the "saints" in the United States are destined to escape persecution, suffering, trial, or tribulation.[11] There is no special status given to the "saints" of any nation or time period that exempts them from suffering just as the saints of other ages have throughout history. There is no special security blanket or scriptural reason for the saints of this nation to assume that they will not endure hardship, persecution, and suffering just as their fellow brothers and sisters in Christ in many other nations are now doing.

The fact is that the United States is on a collision course with divine destiny, and we are all passengers aboard this spiritual Titanic. There is a spiritual crisis in this country which is swiftly coming to a climax. Whether one wishes to accept it or not – we are about to enter into a period of shaking such as we have never seen. This country is going to be shaken to its foundation and it will never again be the nation it once was. Every individual is going to be affected in some manner and to some degree by this shaking.

Every aspect of our modern industrial system is going to be shaken. Every manmade institution which has provided us with such unprecedented security and prosperity is going to be shaken to its foundation. Every enterprise which has provided us with entertainment, diversion, and pleasure is going to be severely disrupted. All facets of our humanly constructed civilization and culture are going to suffer serious dislocation. The pressures of a growing, unsustainable population, serious upheavals in nature, an ever increasing depletion of natural resources (especially energy), international strife and resource wars, not to mention the ever increasing economic instability and turmoil, are going to take a drastic toll on all human enterprises. The threat is real. The spiritual and scriptural evidence indicates that this country is about to arrive at its divine appointment with destiny. Secular experts in all fields of expertise predict that numerous crises are converging upon us and these crises are expected to climax within the first half of this century – and this country is totally unprepared spiritually and naturally.

THE DEIFICATION OF HUMAN WISDOM – MODERN IDOLATRY

The nature of this country's spiritual crisis and the implications of this "shaking" period should be made perfectly clear. Over the past one hundred years man's accumulative knowledge has increased exponentially and beyond comprehension. The scientific discoveries and wonders of man's wisdom almost stagger the imagination. As has been observed by numerous writers, America went from horse and buggies and kerosene lamps to space travel and cyber technology in just one hundred years. More progress was made in this nation over the course of one century than in all the other years of human civilization combined. But a tremendously negative spiritual aspect of all this enormous progress was the deification of human wisdom. This deification of human wisdom and accomplishments resulted in the gradual but persistent banishment of God from the public sector right along with the marginalization of Christian traditions.

One can draw their own conclusions, but the fact remains that as knowledge, technology, and progress increased in the United States, dependence upon God decreased right along with a reverence for spiritual and eternal values. As the focus upon physical and temporal well-being increased, there was a corresponding loss of interest in spiritual and eternal values. By all accounts it appears that sometime after the middle of the twentieth century there was a spiritual and cultural turning point in American history. Most historians agree that during this time the American society made a significant transition away from its traditional theistic foundation toward a more secular and humanistic one. The older Bible-based world-view which most Americans had embraced for generations was essentially replaced by one that was primarily dominated by humanism. This humanistic philosophy of course was propelled by the ever increasing accumulation of knowledge and the accelerating rate of progress which was occurring. Older traditional values which were embraced by the theistic world-view were swept aside by a rising new culture which materialized as a result of the overwhelming tide of human progress.

Over the course of one generation an entire value system was altered. The theistic bible based foundation which had been the directing philosophy of our nation since its beginning was violently removed and replaced with a new more progressive humanistic one. Patrick Buchanan describes this stunning cultural transition in the introduction of his provocative book, *The Death of the West.*

> Millions have begun to feel like strangers in their own land. They recoil from a popular culture that is saturated with raw sex and trumpets hedonistic values. They see old holidays disappear and old heroes degraded. They see art and artifacts of a glorious past removed from their museums and replaced by the depressing, the ugly, the abstract, the anti-American. They watch as books they cherished disappear from the schools they attended, to be replaced by authors and titles they never heard of. The moral code that they were raised to live by has been overthrown. The culture they grew up with is dying in the country they grew up in... In half a lifetime, many Americans have seen their God dethroned, their heroes defiled, their culture polluted, their values assaulted, their country invaded, and themselves demonized as extremists and bigots for holding on to beliefs Americans held for generations.[12]

This deterioration in spiritual values and drastic change in cultural values was vividly manifest during the 1960's when prayer, the Bible, and the creation account of beginnings were banned from public schools. This was an era in which the basic character of American society was transformed. Traditional Christian values were replaced as the directing philosophy by the exaltation of human reasoning and wisdom via humanism. This transition has not been peaceful. It has been marked by an ever increasing antagonism between the two philosophies as they have battled for dominance in the American culture. As humanism has gained control, this antagonism has steadily increased. Historian Paul Johnson, in his work on the *History of the American People,* notes this steadily increasing hostility. He observes that an environment of legal hostility toward traditional and Christian values was cultivated by the "secular-ization" of the "judiciary" and the established institutions of the country. He indicates that for "the first time in American history" an environment of "hostility" appeared toward these historically tradi-tional American values.

> For the first time in American history there was a widespread tendency, especially among intellectuals, to present religious people as enemies of freedom and democratic choice... This hostile adjectival inflation marked the changed perspec-tive of many Americans, the new conviction that religious beliefs as such, especially insofar as they underpinned moral certitudes, constituted a threat to freedom. Its appearance (hostility) was reflected in the extreme secularization of the judiciary, and the academy, and the attempt to drive any form of religious activity, however nominal or merely symbolic, right out of the public sector.[13]

It has been this unconditional rejection of God and the complete disregard for spiritual principles that has placed the industrial world – and especially the United States – in such a precarious position today. Our technology, human ingenuity, progress, and all that it has produced has brought with it the tendency to deify human wisdom and reject God as a relic of the superstitious past. Humanism and all of its accompanying principles and values now rule and direct the cultural values and ideas of the American industrial society. Human wisdom, technology, and industrialism have created a civi-lization over the past century such as the world has never seen. It is a civilization whose very foundation rests upon human wisdom and ingenuity. Our governments, our great cities, our towers of finance, our institutions of wealth, our commerce, our military might, are all established upon technology and mechanized industry. There is hardly a facet of our civilization that is not completely depen-dent upon these things. Essentially, human wisdom as demonstrated through all of these things has become the source of our security, prosperity, comfort, and pleasure.

In the final analysis, the modern industrial society of the United States rests upon the foundation of the principles of the Enlightenment. These philosophical principles, in conjunction with the scientific revolution, have provided the ideological basis for all of our modern institutions and societal structure. The core of these philosophies finds its roots in a firm belief that human intellect alone can provide mankind with the certainty it seeks. It is an arrogant confidence that asserts the true perception of reality, the true measure of values, and the complete understanding of truth can only be realized through human reasoning and wisdom. It is an absolute confidence in the possibilities of human wisdom to provide all the fullness of life that man will ever need.

These core values find their origin in the "Age of Reason" and have matured over the past three hundred years until they have gained preeminence as the guiding societal principles of this country. These fundamental philosophies of the Enlightenment have been reworked, modified, and reproduced until they have taken shape in the current form of secular humanism that we know today. But the basic principles and values are the same. It is a philosophy whose core value asserts that "the end of all being is the happiness of man." It is the absolute deification of human desires, human wisdom, and human accomplishments. And it is precisely this blatant deification of human wisdom and desires that places the United States in such a precarious spiritual position as it enters this period of "shaking." This humanistic foundation of greed, materialism, and pleasure is destined to be subjected to a storm in which everything that is not anchored upon the "rock" of God's word will be swept away (Matthew 7:24-27).

A FOUNDATION OF SAND OR A FOUNDATION OF ROCK

As we have previously noted, the United States has struggled with this conflict of foundational philosophies for some time. The struggle between the core principles of the Enlightenment and those of Christian theism for control of the philosophical foundation of our country has persisted since before its birth. The First and Second Great Awakenings were a major part of this ideological conflict.

Historians such as Paul Johnson and Karen Armstrong document that these great religious revivals were a direct result of a populous rejection of the rising humanistic values promoted through the Enlightenment. As Armstrong notes in her examination of the subject in her book, *The Battle for God*, the Great Awakenings were "a grassroots rebellion against the rational establishment" which had been instituted as a result of the Enlightenment. She noted in particular that "the Second Great Awakening mounted a rebellion against the learned rationalism of the ruling class and insisted upon a more religious identity" for the country.[14]

Alan Brinkley, in his college level text, *The Unfinished Nation*, also notes that many of the nineteenth century religious leaders had become "particularly alarmed" over the "emergence of new rational" ideas that had "originated among the Enlightenment philosophers in France." It was this concern which essentially led to the Second Great Awakening. Brinkley summarizes the message and purpose of the awakening in this manner:

> The basic message of the Second Great Awakening was that individuals must readmit God and Christ into their daily lives; must embrace a fervent, active piety; and must reject the skeptical rationalism that threatened traditional beliefs.[15]

As a result of these revivals in the early part of the eighteenth and nineteenth centuries, the principles and values of Christian theology retained their preeminence in the United States and would become inculcated into the very core of American social life and institutions. There is no argument concerning the great influence these revivals had on the social life of Americans. The populace overwhelmingly embraced the ideas maintained by the Christian world-view. As a result there was nearly a universal agreement that the Bible and Judeo-Christian concepts provided the basis by which reality and life were to be viewed in America. In fact, so dominating was the Christian influence that Benjamin Franklin, in his pamphlet encouraging immigration, would explain to the astonished French that atheism and infidelity were virtually unknown in America.

Bad examples to youth are more rare in America, which must be comfortable consideration to parents. To this may be added, that serious religion, under all denominations, is not only tolerated, but respected and practiced. Atheism is unknown there; infidelity rare and secret; so that persons may live to a great age in that country, without having their piety shocked by meeting either an atheist or infidel.[16]

This great Christian influence would also be confirmed by numerous other writers during the eighteenth and nineteenth centuries. One of the most notable among them would be Alexis de Tocqueville, a French writer who traveled extensively throughout the United States during the early 1800's. Tocqueville would make an exhaustive examination of all aspects of American life including its government and culture. He would provide this astounding assessment of the influence of religion on American life:

There is no country in the world where the Christian religion retains greater influence over the souls of men than in America; and there can be no greater proof of its utility, and of its conformity to human nature, than that its influence is most powerfully felt over the most enlightened and free nation on earth.[17]

Another European visitor who also traversed America during the 1830's was Harriet Martineau of England. She also examined the American social life and published her observations in a book entitled *Society in America*. Ms. Martineau confirmed Tocqueville's observations in this manner:

The institutions of America are, as I have said, planted deep down in Christianity. Its spirit must make an effectual pilgrimage through a society of which it may call a native; and no mistrust of its influences can forever intercept that spirit in its mission of denouncing anomalies, exposing hypocrisy, rebuking faithlessness, raising and communing with the outcast, and driving out sordidness from the circuit of this, most glorious temple of society that has ever yet been reared.[18]

The observations of these writers confirm the sweeping results of the great religious revivals which had swept through the United States in the early part of the eighteenth and nineteenth centuries. These great revivals had inspired a general rejection of the encroaching Enlightenment philosophies which were gaining favor in the Western World. The American people as a whole had rejected these philosophies along with their fundamental preference for human wisdom over that of God and the Bible. They had mounted a grassroots rebellion against the unbridled pursuit of material wealth, eroding values, and vanishing traditions.

Ministers such as Charles Wesley, George Whitefield, John Brown, Jonathan Edwards, Charles Finney, and many others had recognized the spiritual poverty which accompanied the ideas of the Enlightenment and had uncompromisingly addressed them. Brown provided a vivid description of the spiritual depravity which was perceived to have invaded the American society as it embraced these humanistic philosophies. In his book, *An Estimate of the Manners and Principles of the Times*, he provides an assessment of the spiritual condition of American social life prior to the revivals:

The sexes have now little other apparent distinction beyond that of persons and dress... the one sex having advanced into boldness, as the other having sunk into effeminacy... in their conduct. They curb not, but promote and encourage the trifling manners of the times... The sublime truths, the pure and simple morals of the Gospel, are despised and trod under foot.[19]

Samuel Wigglesworth had also condemned the hypocrisy and spiritual contradictions which had occurred as the churches slowly embraced the spirit of the age and Enlightenment philosophies. He had become tremendously concerned in that professing Christians were manifesting no fruit of their spiritual conversion. He described the unregenerate form of Christianity which was becoming ever more prevalent in this manner:

> We have a goodly exterior form of religion...(yet) we find ourselves stained with so much odious vices, especially Uncleanness, Drunkenness, Theft, Covetousness, Violence, Malice, Strife, and others... (though) looked upon with dishonor, yet multitudes are found who are not ashamed to commit them.[20]

Recognizing that the enemy had come in like a flood, these ministers, along with many others, rose to the spiritual challenge of their day. They began to proclaim "the terrors of the law to sinners, (along with) the unmerited favor of God, and the new birth."[21] They brought a blistering indictment against the sterile practices and the unregenerating message of traditional religions. They preached a gospel that required a moral change and brought about a visible transformation in the lives of converts. The passion of their spirit and the fervency of their message demanded action and transformation. There was no room for the timid of spirit or lukewarm of heart. Theirs was a message of "change or perish." It was a general revolt against every philosophy and idea which had exalted itself against the principles of God. It was a fervent spiritual endeavor to demonstrate the power of the kingdom of God in this world. It was an exerted effort to firmly establish the principles and values of bible Christianity into their society and culture.

Although the effects of the two great awakenings had begun to wan by the 1840's, it was apparent that they had transformed American Protestantism and the American society. To say that the revivals were merely a success would be a gross understatement. Dr. Karen Armstrong describes the tremendous effect of these spiritual awakenings in this manner:

> The prophets of the Second Great Awakening mounted a spiritual rebellion against the learned rationalism of the ruling classes and insisted on a more religious identity... They were not content with individual conversions... but wanted

to change society... they built from the ground up and led what amounted to a grassroots rebellion against the rational establishment.[22] (The "rational establishment" is a reference to the new emerging system founded upon the principles of the Age of Reason and Enlightenment philosophies – this author's parenthetical note.)

The impact of these revivals was unprecedented in American history and has been unequaled to this date. The number of conversions was so great that new converts and church congregations statistically grew faster than the rate of population growth. Dr. Armstrong describes the vitality and unprecedented growth of Christian churches during this period in her book:

> Between 1780 and 1860, there was a spectacular rise in the number of Christian congregations in the United States, which far outstripped the national rate of population growth. In 1780, there were only about 2,500 congregations... and by 1860 a phenomenal 52,000 – an almost 21-fold increase... In comparison, the population of the United States rose from about 4 million in 1780 to ... 31 million in 1860 – a less than 8 fold increase... By the 1850's, Christianity in America was vibrant, and seemed poised for future triumphs.[23]

It is apparent that evangelical revivalism had turned the tide against worldliness, human philosophies, and moral depravity during this period. Churches and congregations were "vibrant." Morality and respect for Christian principles and traditions were universal throughout the country. Institutions, laws, and social customs reflected biblical values and principles. As a whole, the philosophical foundation of the United States was undeniably established firmly upon the "rock" of Christian theology. God and the Bible had become a systemic part of the American culture.

But major political and economic changes were to occur in the American society after the middle of the nineteenth century. These political and economic changes would precipitate great social changes right along with them. While there were many factors which were at work in the reshaping of the American social landscape, primarily it was industrialization, urbanization, and the persistent advance of new philosophies which were the driving forces. All of these factors were working simultaneously and had an enormous impact on the lives of everyday Americans. While the "robber barons" and philanthropists dominated the historical and political stage, it was the common American family that was the most affected during this time. Their world changed at a pace never before seen in history. John Gordon would describe this massive transition in the American society in his book, *An Empire of Wealth*:

> In the half century between the end of the Civil War and the beginning of World War I in Europe, the American economy (and society) changed more profoundly, grew more quickly, and became more diversified than at any earlier period in nation's history. In 1865 the country... was still basically an agricultural one. Not a single industrial concern was listed on the New York Stock Exchange. By the turn of the twentieth century, a mere generation later, the United States had the largest and most modern industrial economy on earth, one characterized by giant corporations undreamed of in 1865.[24]

Historian Paul Johnson would also note that this era would become marked as "the takeoff period" for the phenomenal growth in manufacturing and industrialization in the United States. He pointed out that "in 1840, the United Sates ranked fifth in output among the world's manufacturing countries." But he notes that "by 1860 it was fourth (and) by 1894, it had taken the first place. There was a 79.6 percent increase in the number of companies engaged in manufacturing, with a 56.6 percent increase in the number of workers they employed."[25] This growth in manufacturing went hand in hand with the growth of urban areas and the migration of people from the rural areas to the city.

Social historian Carl Degler, along with numerous other historians, recognized that the vast social changes which were transpiring in America during this era were primarily due to mechanized industry which was swiftly replacing local craftsmen and artisans.

The new industrialized economy also brought about the rapid population shift from the rural areas to the cities. Cities were where the
new jobs were being created and the populous quickly followed. He
describes the changes in this manner:

> In the years between 1880 and 1915, industrialization and
> urbanization, like two gigantic hands touching the spin-
> ning clay on the potter's wheel, refashioned the contours of
> American society; institutions with long lineage and stability
> like the Church and home were shaken and altered. To an
> American who was alive in 1870, the world of forty years
> later lost many of its familiar benchmarks.[26]

This giant social earthquake was drastically reshaping American
institutions. Three of the most fundamental institutions of course
were the family, home, and church. While all of the devastating
effects of this transition would not manifest themselves in their fullness for another generation or so, the beginning of the assault upon
the home, family, and church had begun. Most scholars, along with
Degler, attribute the leading factor in the drastic change in American
values to industrialization and the transition from the simplistic rural
agrarian lifestyle to the more complex mechanized urban lifestyle.

Degler points out that there is a "considerable difference"
between the urban and rural lifestyles. He notes that "the man of the
land and the man of the city are different in essences." Their habits,
work, values, and thinking are totally different. Degler observes that
"the rural man lives a relatively simple, outdoor life in contrast with
the competitive, indoor, anxious search for prestige and position
which the highly mobile and social environment forces upon the city
dweller." He continues by emphasizing that "it is the rural community which holds fast to the old morality, to the traditional ways,"
whereas "it is the city which is so used to change that it accepts
it with equanimity."[27] He indicates that superficiality in manners
becomes the custom in the city as opposed to the basic morality one
finds in rural areas:

...the environment of the city loosens the hold of religion, the family, and traditional morality; to the extent it undermines the social forces which sometimes are all that keep men steady in times of stress.[28]

Perhaps it is more than just a coincidence that the population shift from the rural areas to the ever increasing urban areas seems to march hand in hand with the spiritual decline of America. All studies seem to confirm that as time has progressed and technology, industrialization, and urbanization have increased, so have secularization, modernization, and materialism. As the rural lifestyle and population have decreased, so have the basic morality, traditions, and fundamental Christian values which were once predominant in American culture. These differences in values are still noted in the "red" and "blue" demographics of the United States today. The more traditional rural areas and the modern urban areas tend to hold to an entirely different set of values, lifestyles, and philosophical perspectives.

It truly seems to be as Degler has pointed out, "the man of the land and the man of the city are different essences... The rural man lives a relatively simple outdoor life" where he is surrounded by nature and the handiwork of God. He sees the wonder of life and magnificence of creation in his everyday activities. The land itself provides his livelihood and sustains him. The seed that is planted in the earth bears fruit for harvest and food. He sees the miracle of life in the birth of a newborn calf, and waits patiently for the spring rain and warm summer sunshine to cause his crops to grow. His life and work is in partnership with God and nature. He is surrounded by mountains, meadows, forests, and springs. Everywhere he looks he sees the majestic handiwork of God and the magnificence of his creation. Life, reality, and the world as he knows it is inextricably connected to God and his creation. It is this one fundamental fact that provides the foundation of his philosophy of life.

The urban man on the other hand derives his livelihood from a wage based job and a weekly paycheck. Generally he works indoors, and quickly learns that his survival and comfort are directly dependent upon the amount of money he makes. He is surrounded by large buildings, bright lights, shopping centers, and every apparatus of manmade innovation and technology imaginable. His time is spent either in an effort to make more money or enjoying the pleasures and innovations of modern urban life. Everywhere he looks he is confronted with the marvels of manmade inventions, ingenuity, and innovation. He is immersed in an artificially manmade environment which controls and sustains all that he knows as life. His food comes from a supermarket with no thought as to how it got there. His clothing comes from the mall where the only consideration given is to what brand it is and if it is in style. He generally lives and works in technologically controlled environments where the comforts of air-conditioning and central heating are taken for granted. In short, he is surrounded and constantly bombarded with the wonders of manmade inventions and technological progress. His life is totally submersed in, and dependent upon, these manmade things. This is the world and reality as he knows it. It is an artificial, synthetic, manmade environment. His philosophy of life inevitably begins to reflect the human based values of the manmade environment in which he lives.

Indisputably these two individuals are different in essence and world perspectives. One is surrounded by nature and the handiwork of God and views life from this perspective. The other is surrounded by technology and the products of man's genius and views life from this perspective. The rural life is grounded in tradition and values, and the urban industrial life in modernism and progress. But for whatever reason, the spiritual decline in America has marched hand in hand with the decrease of rural America and the growth of urbanization and progress. As Degler notes, as far as Christianity is concerned, after the late 1800's, "among the cities of the nation a retreat from the old-time religion was in full swing".[29]

Nevertheless, the older theistic values and traditions which had been established by the great revivals of the early eighteenth and nineteenth centuries would come under extreme pressure as the Industrial and Scientific Revolution picked up momentum. The older values and traditions would slowly and consistently give way to the more "progressive" humanistic values until they would essentially be replaced by the latter part of the twentieth century. The culture of an entire nation would be almost completely transformed over the course of a little more than two generations. This is the reason our grandparents and parents shake their head in amazement as they see the swift and sweeping changes which have occurred during their lifetime. This is why a cultural gap, which came to be referred to as the "generation gap," appeared. It was the swift and sweeping cultural changes which were occurring in our country. Never before in the history of mankind has such a drastic cultural transition occurred so rapidly and in such a manner. It has been a complete change that has manifested itself not only in the newer more modern infrastructure, but also in traditions, values, and the basic philosophy of life.

Though we still see remnants of this struggle – for all intents and purposes the philosophies of the Enlightenment via secular humanism have effectively replaced the older theistic culture which existed at the end of the Second Great Awakening. Secular humanism, along with its fundamental deification of human wisdom, became thoroughly established as the prevailing philosophy of our nation by the latter part of the twentieth century. Today, our nation as a whole has embraced this world-view and life perspective. Secular humanism and the values it promotes control our legal philosophy (laws), our institutions, our educational system, our courts, and even our economic philosophies. Our nation is completely dominated from top to bottom by this anti-God, human exalting, and self-gratifying philosophy of life. If we look at the foundation upon which our nation is standing today – it is secular humanism. It is the deification of man. It is the exaltation of man, his wisdom, his accomplishments, and his desires above God and his divinely inspired word.

It is apparent to any observer that greed, envy, ambition, and the pursuit of material gain and pleasure have become the characteristic features of our modern industrial culture. Vices which had been unconditionally rejected by previous generations are now being enthusiastically embraced. Values that had been established for centuries have quickly become outdated and even found to be detrimental to success and advancement in a progressive society. It has been an astounding transformation of values. Those moral practices that had once been considered virtues are now detrimental and abandoned. Those practices that were once abhorred and rejected in society as a whole are now embraced and promoted as beneficial. It is a value system that has been turned upside down by the elevation of human self-interest and a complete obsession with technological progress.

It is the "good of mankind" that is now the only rule by which values and moral practices are to be determined. If any new innovation, gadget, discovery, or practice is thought to be beneficial to mankind in any way it is not to be questioned. If it increases wealth, brings comfort, provides some convenience, or promotes human freedom and expression, it is deemed to be beyond reproach. As social critic Neil Postman observes in his book, *Building a Bridge to the 18th Century*, it is a firm belief that mankind is "moving inexorably toward a more peaceful, intelligent, and commodious life" and is not to be impeded by any institution or outmoded value. It is a conviction that nothing should stand in the way of progress and human comfort. Postman noted that the philosophers of the Enlightenment laid this foundation by presenting the argument that certain human vices such as envy, pride, and greed could become "human virtues" in that they stimulate industry and innovation. He would point out that Hume would go so far as to contend that the "pleasure of luxury and the profit of commerce roused men from their indolence."[30]

It has been this mindless pursuit of human self-interest and progress that has firmly established an environment in which traditional vices have become virtues, and values held for generations have become vices. Anything thought to be beneficial to humanity, increase prosperity, or promote progress has become "good" no matter what residual moral effects it may have.

Anything that resists progress or questions the moral value of the new order is to be considered backward, archaic, superstitious, or simply downright wrong or evil. This presumption is simply an adaptation of the Enlightenment philosophies from their very inception. It has been an unabated attack on the orthodox and traditional while promoting "change" without consideration of the consequences. Once again, Postman critically examines the effects of progress via technology:

Technology does not invite a close examination of its own consequences. It is the kind of friend that asks for trust and obedience, which most people are inclined to give because its gifts are truly bountiful. But, of course, there is a dark side to this friend. Its gifts are not without a heavy cost... the uncontrolled growth of technology destroys the vital sources of our humanity. It creates a culture without moral foundation. It undermines certain mental processes and social relations that make human life worth living... technology (has) become a particularly dangerous enemy.[31]

Two opposing world-views – the progressive and the traditional – are even now in the final throes of a major cultural conflict. By nature, technology and industrialism with their promotion of consumerism, materialism, self-indulgence, and self-interest, must eliminate all alternatives to itself. Progress insists that all forms of culture must submit to the sovereignty of technology and industrialism along with the values it promotes. It virtually leaves no alternative. By its very nature it must eliminate all competing and obstructing perspectives and values. This of course has been the very basis of the virulent hostility between Christianity and the Enlightenment philosophies. One has human self-interest as it highest priority and the other holds God's interest as supreme. Progress holds that the reason for all existence is human happiness, while true Christianity holds that the reason for all existence is for the glory of God. Progress holds that man can find fulfillment through human endeavors, while Christianity maintains that true human fulfillment is to be found only in God and the principles set forth in his word.

It has been this fundamental philosophical conflict that has caused the great "disconnect," not only between God and man, but between man and all of God's creation. It is apparent to all that human "progress" has brought about a great disconnect between the natural world and the technological synthetic world man has created. Climate change, ecological collapse, endangered species, pollution, resource depletion, and a myriad of other nature related crises are all evidence of the "disconnect" between modern man and his natural environment. Dr. David Suzuki, respected geneticist and former professor at the University of British Columbia in Vancouver, thoroughly examines this great disconnect between man and nature in his book, *The Scared Balance*. He summarizes the conflict in this manner:

> ...human numbers, technology, consumption and a globalized economy have made us a new kind of force on the planet... With explosive speed, we have transmogrified from a species like most others that live in balance with our surrounding into an unprecedented force, a super species. Like a foreign species that flourishes in a new environment, we have expanded beyond the capacity of our surroundings to support us. It is clear from the history of the past two centuries that the path we embarked on after the Industrial Revolution is leading us increasingly into conflict with the natural world... As we distance ourselves further from the natural world, we are increasingly surrounded by and dependent on our own inventions. We become enslaved by the constant demands of technology created to serve us... (and) we have lost our connection to the rest of the living planet.[32]

As we have indicated, this great disconnect between man and the natural creation is also manifest in a parallel disconnect between man and his creator. As man's wisdom increased through science and technology, the apparent need for God decreased proportionally. Medical science was discovering new cures almost daily. Technology was providing comfort and conveniences that were unimaginable a century before. The new industrial economy was providing wealth and raising the standard of living to a level which would make kings of an earlier age envious. It seemed that a deity was no longer needed to provide the basic needs of security, comfort, and provision. Man had effectively created a culture and civilization in which technology appeared to have given him the ability to supply all of these things without the aid of God.

With the advent of industrial technology the God that had been depended upon for generations for the basics of life was no longer

needed. Over the course of two generations he was essentially relegated to the archives of history as a crutch of an earlier superstitious
era. He was displaced by the "Age of Reason" and the march of
progress via the scientific and Industrial Revolution. Man had intel-
lectually progressed to the point where he could now control his
own destiny. The *Humanist Manifesto* clearly articulates the new
culture's ideological position concerning this altogether new relationship between God and man:

…we can discover no divine purpose or providence for the
human species. While there is much that we do not know,
humans are responsible for themselves and for what we
are or will become. No deity will save us; we must save
ourselves.

The time has come for widespread recognition of the radical
changes in religious beliefs throughout the modern world.
The time is past for mere revision of traditional attitudes.
Science and economic change have disrupted the old beliefs.
Religions the world over are under the necessity of coming
to terms with new conditions created by a vastly increased
knowledge and experience. Traditional, dogmatic, or author-
itarian religions that place revelation, God, ritual, or creed
above human needs and experience do a disservice to the
human species.[33]

Postman critically examines this new "state of mind" in his
book, *Technolpoly*. He confirms that along with the scientific revolution of the twentieth century came a transformation in thinking
which created a new "culture." He explained that this transformation of thought and culture basically consisted "in the deification
of technology" and an inherent misguided belief "that technical
progress is humanity's supreme achievement and the instrument by
which our most profound dilemmas may be solved." He continued
by explaining that the new technological culture had effectively
provided a "replacement" for every "Old World" belief and tradition.
He succinctly observed that "there is (now) a technological alterna-

tive" for most everything. "To prayer," he states that "the alternative is penicillin; to family roots, the alternative is mobility; to reading, the alternative is television; to restraint, the alternative is immediate gratification; to sin, the alternative is psychotherapy…" His somber conclusion is that all forms of our previous culture must ultimately surrender to the seduction and "sovereignty of technology."[34]

Postman continues by explaining that the modern technological society actually "requires the development of a new social order." This new social order is so inherently antithetical and incompatible with the older order that it "of necessity leads to the rapid dissolution of much that is associated with traditional beliefs."[35] The very foundation of modern human based progress requires the dissolution or removal of the older traditional deity based foundation. There can be no compromise between a philosophy whose foundation focuses upon humanity and one which focuses upon God.

Postman's critique is well-founded. As man's wisdom increased, his dependence upon God diminished and his foundation of spiritual values eroded. Man, via human wisdom, effectively deified technology and human progress. Through this veneration of human wisdom and achievement, cultural values have been transformed and human security, prosperity, and happiness, have become totally dependent upon modern technology. To most progressive and enlightened minds of the twenty-first century, God and religion have been effectively replaced. In essence, man has effectively deified his own wisdom and the work of his own hands. The creations of man's hand, via scientific and technological innovation, have become his idols. He has become convinced that human wisdom holds the answer to all life's problems, and he no longer has any need of God.

THE GREAT SHAKING

But God has given clear warning to societies that reject his principles and build upon human centered foundations. The prophet Isaiah bears witness from his book:

Therefore hear now this, thou that art given to pleasures, that dwellest carelessly, that sayest in thine heart, I am and none

248

else beside me... thou hast trusted in thy wickedness: thou has said, None seeth me. Thy wisdom and thy knowledge, it hath perverted thee; and thou hast said in thine heart, I am, and none else beside me... Therefore shall evil come upon thee; thou shalt not know from whence it riseth... desolation shall come upon thee suddenly, which thou shalt now know. (Isaiah 47:8 and 10-11)

And the loftiness (pride) of man shall be bowed down, and the haughtiness (arrogance) of men shall be made low: and the Lord alone shall be exalted in that day... when he ariseth to shake terribly the earth. (Isaiah 2:17 and 19)

The scriptures are very clear in their description of the "day" when God will "shake" the earth. This "day" is depicted numerous times in Old Testament prophecies including Haggai chapter two and verses six and seven. Here the prophet clearly states that God will "shake all nations" just prior to the establishment of his Messianic kingdom. According to most biblical scholars this "day" when the great "shaking" of nations occurs is during "the final upheaval of nations in the last days," and in conjunction with the second coming of Christ.[36] As MacArthur notes in his bible commentary, this shaking "goes far beyond the historical removal of kingdoms and the establishment of others." This particular shaking is a universal "cataclysm" which signifies the "subjugation of the nations by the Messiah (Christ)" just prior to the establishment of his kingdom at his coming.[37]

This day of course is exactly the time that the disciples had inquired of Jesus about. As you recall they had asked, "What shall be the sign of thy coming (the second coming of Christ), and the end of the world (age)" (Matthew 24:3). According to Jesus, one of the great signs which would indicate the approach of this time was to be great "distress of nations" as the "times of the Gentiles" comes to a close (Luke 21:24-25). As we have seen in chapters one and two, according to the scriptures we are living in that generation. We have seen the resurrection of the nation of Israel in 1948 and the recapture of Jerusalem in 1967. We understand that even now we are experiencing the beginning of the end of that time known as the "times of the Gentiles." We have entered into that perilous period in which all the nations of the earth are going to be shaken as the world prepares itself for the second coming of Christ.

This period of "distress" or "shaking" will be significant for all nations on the earth. But we will focus our attention in particular on the United States of America. This great nation which was established upon Christian principles and has been blessed with numerous spiritual visitations will have much to answer for during this period. This nation which has forsaken its spiritual heritage and established itself upon another foundation of manmade philosophies is going to be subjected to a severe "shaking." It will be tried according to Matthew chapter seven as a house in a storm. The "floods" of crises and the "winds" of distress will beat against it revealing the foundation upon which it is built. And as Jesus said, "the floods came, and the winds blew, and beat upon that house; and it fell: and great was the fall of it" (Matthew 7:26-27).

> Therefore whosoever heareth these sayings of mine, and doeth them, I will liken him to a wise man, which built his house upon a rock: And the rain descended, and the floods came, and the winds blew, and beat upon that house; and it fell not: for it was founded upon a rock. (Matthew 7:24-25)

> And every one that heareth these sayings of mine, and doeth them not, shall be likened unto a foolish man, which built his house upon the sand: And the floods came, and the winds blew, and beat upon that house; and it fell: and great was the fall of it. (Matthew 7:26-27)

It will be a perilous time marked by grievous spiritual storms and severe testing in which everything that is not established by God or upon his word will be shaken to its foundation. All great nations and governments will be shaken. All of the great financial institutions and industrial establishments will be rocked to their core. Human technology, wisdom, and innovation will be confounded and brought to nothing. Everything in which man has placed his trust, confidence, and hope will be destroyed. All of the great inventions and accomplishments of science and technology that have instilled such a sense of omnipotence and pride in human ingenuity will be shaken. There will be nothing left but that which has been established by God and built upon his word (Revelation 6:12-17):

> Whose voice then shook the earth: but now he hath promised, saying, Yet once more I shake not the earth only, but also heaven. And this word, Yet once more, signifieth <u>the removing of those things that are shaken</u>, as of things that are made, <u>that those things which cannot be shaken may remain</u>. Wherefore we receiving a kingdom which cannot be moved, let us have grace, whereby we may serve God acceptably with reverence and godly fear. (Hebrews 12:26-28).

In these scriptures the Apostle Paul emphatically confirms what the prophets Isaiah and Haggai had written years earlier. He too provides us with a warning concerning this unique period in which God is going to shake the heavens and the earth. He states that this momentous event is established by the authority of the word of God. It is as sure to happen as the rising of the sun. He then proceeds even further and tells us that this same "word" has ordained a time of testing in which there will be "the removing" of those "things that are made..." That is a time of shaking in which those things which have been built, manufactured, or fabricated upon human foundations will be removed, so "that those things which cannot be shaken may remain."

We can clearly see from the context of the scripture that this is a comparison between "those things that are made," as opposed to the "kingdom which cannot be moved" or shaken. It is a comparison between all things which man has made and those things established by God. The message is clear. There is coming a time when everything that is not established by God is going to be shaken to its foundation. The only thing that will remain after this shaking will be the kingdom of God that cannot be moved. All kingdoms, powers, institutions, and human endeavors are going to be shattered and broken (Matthew 21:42-44).

THE CHOICE – REVIVAL OR JUDGMENT

The prophecies which we have examined are extremely significant to the United States. There are only two future alternatives for this great nation. The first alternative is one of hope. It is the hope that this nation which has been so blessed of God in the past will receive one more blessing in the form of a national revival on the scale of the First and Second Great Awakenings. It is the hope that a spirit of repentance will sweep across this nation from one ocean to the other and we will see a culture transforming revival as in the days of Charles Finney and Jonathan Edwards. If there was ever a nation that stands in need of a spiritual awakening it is this nation. We are a nation that is now standing upon the precipice of divine judgment and our only hope is revival. We are in desperate need of a culture transforming nation changing revival!

We are a nation that stands as Old Testament Israel stood in the days of Isaiah and Jeremiah. We are a nation that stands before God on the precipice of judgment with an overwhelming burden of sin and iniquity. We are a nation that has given itself to materialism, immorality, pleasure, and greed. We are a nation that is staggering under the burden of more than 46 million unborn children who have been murdered through legalized abortion since 1973. We are a nation in which one half of all our marriages will end in divorce. We are a nation in which 50 to 60 percent of married men will engage in an extra marital affair sometime during their marriage. We are a nation in which pre-marital sex has become an acceptable practice. We are a nation which has become saturated with crudeness and sexuality. We are a nation in which over 90 percent of children between the ages of 8 and 16 view some type of pornography. We are a nation in which the pornographic business revenues exceed the combined revenues of ABC, NBC, and CBS. We are a nation in which homosexual relationships have become accepted as an alternative lifestyle. The list could go on endlessly. Our sins have reached up unto the heavens and yet there is no spiritual concern whatsoever.

We are a nation that has lost our moral and spiritual compass. Right has become wrong and wrong has become right. That which was once considered evil is now "cool" and good. It is fashionable to be considered "bad" or naughty. To push the limits of moral acceptance in our world is now "neat" and "hip." Our generation respects those that show no respect, and idolizes those who idolize themselves. It is a narcissistic, hedonistic, and self-focused generation which has made vices virtues and virtues vices. Those things which were once good are now considered as evil, bigoted, or prejudicial. To be "good" is boring, square, and definitely not "cool." We are living in a nation whose value system has been completely turned upside down.

It has only been since the middle of the twentieth century that bible quoting has become hate speech and objections to homosexual and lesbian acts considered to be bigoted. The recent inversion of values regards the condemning of immorality as prudishness, and speaking out against immodest apparel, materialism, and worldly entertainment as legalism. Ours is a generation that glories in blatant sensuality, excessive materialism, constant pleasure, and perverse values. As David Kupelian, the author of *The Marketing of Evil*, so clearly points out, "As Americans, we've come to embrace, and even champion many things that would have horrified our parents' generation." He continues by stating that we glorify "dysfunctionality and corruption" and "there is no societal consciousness of sin." He then plunges the sword of truth right to the heart of the matter by pointing out that we have become beguiled "by our scientific and technological advances into believing we are enlightened" while "we move farther and farther away from our Judeo-Christian spiritual roots."[38]

Kupelian elaborates further by pointing out that "within the space of our lifetimes, much of what Americans once universally abhorred has been packaged, perfumed, gift-wrapped, and sold to us as though it had great value."[39] Hollywood and MTV have dictated (and destroyed) the standards of family values, desensitized our senses to what is right and wrong, designed our fashions of dress and apparel, and ridiculed anything having to do with traditional value. "In fifty years we've gone from a nation unified by traditional Judeo-Christian values to one in which those same values are increasingly scorned, rejected, and demonized."[40] It is a generation whose values have been completely transformed by the powers of an industrialized technological system which hates Christianity, the Bible, and the very mention of God. It is a generation that has given itself completely over to unbridled lasciviousness and self-indulgence and hates anyone that would dare condemn it. It is a generation where violence is rampant, immorality unchecked, and wickedness encouraged or tolerated.

That the American society is one of excess and extravagance is beyond debate. As a nation we comprise only about 4.5 percent of the world's population, yet we consume almost 30 percent of the earth's resources[41] and 25 percent of the earth's energy supplies.[42] We thrive off this obvious imbalance in order to sustain a life-style that is unimaginable in most countries. We spend more on make-up, hair products, clothing, jewelry, fitness, and other non-basic commodities than many nations have as a Gross National Product. As one college text so bluntly puts it; "one American consumes hundreds of times the resources of a single African."[43] Scientist Peter Raven notes that "if everyone lived like Americans, you'd need three planet earths... to sustain that level of consumption," and John de Graaf adds that "since 1950, we Americans have used up more resources than everyone who ever lived on earth before then."[44]

Excess, self-indulgence, and overindulgence are the rule of the day in modern America. We Americans, by our own admission, are overweight, over extended, and over indulged. We are so out of touch with reality that we consider luxuries and commodities that were not even dreamed of one hundred years ago (and not even possessed by most people on the planet) as necessities of life. We have constructed a manufacturing and consumer oriented social framework from which we cannot extricate ourselves. We cannot imagine life without cell phones, television, video games, microwaves, dishwashers, and computers. We cannot conceive of living without a change of clothing for every occasion, and less than three pair of shoes would be an atrocity that could not be described. Our diet is so varied and sumptuous that kings of generations past would be envious.

How could one argue that the general population of the United States does not live in excess when our homes are full of non-essential items? We are not satisfied with simply having the necessities of life – we want all the toys and the very best and latest of everything. We must have boats, four wheel drives, quads, jet skies, and countless other lavish toys – along with a three car garage to put them in. While one may argue that this is accepted as normal in the United States – that is exactly my point. What is accepted as normal in the United States is overindulgence and extravagance. What is normal here and now – is the abnormal.

Paraphrasing the words of the Apostle Paul in Romans chapter one, and Jesus in Matthew chapter twenty-four: This is a generation that has known God, but has refused to honor him as God or even give him thanks or recognition. This is a generation that has endeavored to remove God from its schools, courts, and every public institution. It is a time of increasing wisdom and technological expansion as never before. But in the name of this worldly wisdom, wrong has become right, and right has become wrong. The foolishness of evolution and the nonsense of alternative values are enthroned in the courts and schools of the land. Tolerance has become the exalted virtue through which every evil practice and custom has been sanctioned and accepted. It is a generation in which the love of God has grown desperately cold and iniquity predominates. It is a generation that has broken past the barricades of Godly restraint and is even now plummeting over the precipice toward divine judgment. There can be no doubt that this is a generation of crises! It is a generation desperately in need of a spiritual awakening! Yet hear the pleadings of merciful God to a nation standing on the verge of judgment:

> Ah, sinful nation, a people with iniquity, a seed of evildoers, children that are corrupters: they have forsaken the Lord, they have provoked the Holy One of Israel unto anger, they are gone away backward... they declare their sin as Sodom, they hide it not... (Isaiah 1:4 and Isaiah 3:9)

This is a nation that has forsaken God – and yet God extends his mercy and calls us to return and find mercy. Listen to his plea:

> Wash you, make you clean; put away the evil of your doings from before mine eyes; cease to do evil... Come now, let

us reason together, saith the Lord: though your sins be as scarlet, they shall be white as snow; though they be red like crimson, they shall be as wool. If ye be willing and obedient, ye shall eat of the good of the land. (Isaiah 1:16-19)

At what instant I shall speak concerning a nation, and concerning a kingdom, to pluck up, and to pull down, and to destroy it; If that nation, against whom I have pronounced, turn from their evil, I will repent of the evil I thought to do unto them. (Jeremiah 18:7-8)

This is the alternative of hope and national revival. The second – and only other alternative is that of divine judgment. The only alternative outside of revival is to prepare ourselves to endure a time of turmoil, crises, and distress such as we have never experienced as a nation. The alternative to a national revival is to be subjected to a spiritual hurricane from which there will be no refuge for those who do not know God. At the risk of being redundant – this storm will consist of political, economic, and natural crises which will rock this nation. The crises examined in previous chapters are not figments of the imagination. They are not delusions of some ranting doomsday prophet. They are crises which are even now in the making. They are crises in which secular experts from all fields are warning of dire, momentous, and cataclysmic consequences. They are crises which Jesus and the prophets have foretold will come upon this generation. Only the truly arrogant or foolish would ignore the darkening clouds that are gathering on the horizon.

I cannot help but feel that we are a nation standing upon the very precipice of destiny. It is our choice. It is either to have revival and enter into the coming storm under the protection of the Almighty God – or continue our present course of sin and rejection of God thus entering into this storm trusting in our own might and wisdom. This last is complete and utter folly. Just as sure as God has promised mercy to the nations that return to him – he has promised judgment upon those that reject him. This is not harsh or unmerciful. In fact, one cannot help but feel the urgency of the hour in which we live. God is extending his hand in mercy even now to his country. I cannot help but feel that he is imploring, begging, entreating, this nation to return to its Godly heritage and foundation. It is only after mercy has been rejected that judgment comes. In fact, when mercy is rejected it leaves a merciful but righteous God no alternative – Judgment must follow the rejection of mercy. REVIVAL IS NOT AN OPTION FOR A DYING NATION – IT IS A VITAL NECESSITY!

At what instant I shall speak concerning a nation and concerning a kingdom, to pluck up and to pull down, and to destroy it; if that nation, against whom I have pronounced, turn from their evil, I will repent of the evil that I thought to do unto them. (Jeremiah 18:7-8)

And at what instant I shall speak concerning a nation, and concerning a kingdom, to build and to plant it; If it do evil in my sight, that it obey not my voice, then I will repent of the good, wherewith I said I would benefit them. (Jeremiah 18:9-10)

But if they will not obey, I will utterly pluck up and destroy that nation, saith the Lord. (Jeremiah 12:17)

With the understanding that our nation has placed itself in a very precarious spiritual position – the questions we should be asking ourselves are these – upon what philosophy of life are our values and morals based? Which philosophy of life directs our everyday activities? How much do we indulge in the very activities which are eroding the foundations of our nation? Into what are most of our time, efforts, and fortunes directed? How much of our time is consumed by pleasure, sports, leisure, and self-indulgent activities? How much – and to what extent have we invested ourselves into God and his kingdom? If we were to fully comprehend that this world is about to enter into a time of crisis where institutions, government, and things which have been around for years were going to crumble and fall – would our priorities be changed? If we could actually grasp that civilization as we have known it for the past one hundred years is going to drastically change in the very near future – would it change how we live?

Chapter 12

PREPARING FOR THE STORM

"At the approach of danger there are always two voices that speak with equal force in the heart of man: one very reasonably tells the man to consider the nature of the danger and the means of avoiding it; the other even more reasonably says that it is too painful and harassing to think of the danger, since it is not in man's power to provide for everything and escape from the general march of events; and that it is therefore better to turn aside from the painful subject till it has come, and to think of what is pleasant."[1] (Leo Tolstoy – *War and Peace*)

There is no doubt that a storm is coming. And not just any storm. All of the evidence indicates that the storm that is even now building upon the horizon will be a tremendous civilization shaking hurricane. Even now we can see the darkening sky and the storm clouds gathering. If you listen closely you can hear the rolling of the thunder in the distance, and every now and then a few spatters of rain falls upon the ground warning us of the deluge to come. We see something on the evening news about economic distress. We hear rumors of natural disasters, turmoil, and conflict in distant lands. Our daily news warns of spreading economic distress that could be "worse than the great depression." All of the warning signs are here.

All of the signs indicate that our nation is swiftly moving toward a tremendous economic, environmental, and political shaking.

Anyone – and everyone – should be able to clearly see that humankind is entering into critically perilous times. It has been my objective throughout the pages of this book to clearly present the nature of the crises which are converging upon this generation. It has also been my objective to demonstrate that the circumstances with which we are confronted are not coincidental. These converging crises are not flukes of nature nor are they merely the evolving conditions of progress. I have attempted to show that these crises clearly conform to the prophetic conditions that will exist as we near the end of the age. We have seen through both scriptural and secular evidence that these converging crises have the potential of inflicting consequences that are almost unimaginable in their magnitude. Without any stretch of the imagination – these crises hold the potential of fulfilling the exact circumstances as described by the prophets concerning the end-time.

But even as I present this evidence I realize that I am confronting an enormous impediment. Jesus himself earnestly gave warning of this obstacle to awareness. He repeatedly emphasized that the generation of people upon whom these crises came would generally be unaware of the approaching danger. He indicated they would be so overcome by an attitude of indifference and denial that they would fail to recognize the urgency of the time in which they lived. As the storm approaches, and the evidence materializes around them, they would fall into the same mental quandary as do all humans when confronted with imminent disaster. As Leo Tolstoy points out, they would be forced to choose between confronting the issues relevant to the oncoming danger, or choosing to thrust it aside and continue with the pleasantries of everyday life. Unfortunately, as Tolstoy so pointedly states, most people will "turn aside from the painful subject... and think of what is pleasant."

As people in Jesus' day could not sense the urgency of the times nor make the connection between the natural signs and their spiritual implications – so also are many in this generation insensible to both the urgency of the hour and the implications of the signs. The signs are clear for all to see – but somehow the spiritual significance of these signs has eluded most people. Even now they are pursuing their lives with an arrogant assurance that all things will continue just as they always have. They refuse to alter or adjust their life-styles in spite of the ever building evidence. Most people today are continuing their daily existence with no real thought concerning the drastic changes that lie ahead. They have refused to even acknowl-edge or consider the fact that Planet Earth is swiftly approaching a divine appointment with destiny.

Sadly this complacent attitude, reinforced by denial and unbelief, will be the leading factor which will cause most of this generation to be unprepared for the coming crises. No wonder Jesus compared this generation to that of Noah's day. We would do well to give very special heed to his warning in Matthew chapter twenty-four:

> But as the days of Noe (Noah) were, so shall also the coming of the Son of Man be. For as in the days that were before the flood they were eating and drinking, marrying and giving in marriage, until the day that Noe (Noah) entered into the ark. **And (they) knew not until the flood came, and took them all away**; so shall the coming of the Son of Man be. (Matthew 24:37-39)

The world in Noah's day continued their complacent absorption in everyday affairs right up until the very end. This persistence in the continuation of normal everyday activities while living upon the very precipice of an unprecedented global disaster was due to one thing – denial. They refused to believe not only the preaching of Noah, but even as they neared the end they undoubtedly even refused to accept the natural signs that must have heralded such an enor-mous geological catastrophe as a worldwide flood. The only ones to escape this global cataclysm were Noah and his family because they had prepared themselves according to the warning they had received from God.

> By faith Noah, being warned of God of things not seen as yet, moved with fear, **prepared** an ark to the saving of his house. (Hebrews 11:7)

The Bible is filled with warning after warning concerning the danger of being caught unprepared for the day of visitation. The five wise and the five foolish virgins (Matthew 25:1-13), and the "evil servant" who "said in his heart, my Lord delayeth his coming" (Matthew 24:42-51), are just a few of many examples. The sad fact remains however, that in spite of the warnings and countless signs, most people in the United States (and the world) are going to be caught totally unprepared for the crises that are coming.

> And **take heed to yourselves**, lest at any time your hearts be overcharged with surfeiting (excess and lack of self restraint), drunkenness, and the cares of this life, **so that day come upon you unawares**. For as a snare shall it come on all them that dwell on the face of the whole earth. (Luke 21:34-35)

Jesus himself had wept over the city of Jerusalem as he prophetically saw the destruction of that city in 70 A.D. He wept because he had attempted to warn the Jews of the dangers which lay only a few years ahead – but they could not comprehend. When those days of crises came, some of the only ones saved were the Jewish Christians who recalled Jesus' warning and had fled from the city as they saw the predicted signs manifesting themselves:[2]

> And when he was come near, he beheld the city, and wept over it, Saying, If thou hadst known, even thou, at least in this thy day, the things which belong unto thy peace! But now they are hid from thine eyes. For the days shall come upon thee, that thine enemies shall cast a trench about thee, and compass thee round, and keep thee in on every side, And shall lay thee even with the ground, and thy children within thee; and they shall not leave in thee one stone upon another; **because thou knewest not the time of thy visitation**. (Luke 19:41-44)

This complete state of ignorance and un-preparedness should not be. In view of all the signs and evidence, there is absolutely no reason why these things should come upon any society "unawares." Preparation begins with a state of mind. It begins with faith (believing), and then works into every other facet of our lives. If we truly believe and understand the magnitude of the crises which are converging upon our generation there is no reason why we should be caught unprepared.

The children of Israel believed Moses and prepared themselves for the Passover night with the sacrifice of a lamb and the spreading of its blood upon the doorposts of their houses. They packed their belongings and ate the Passover meal with their shoes on while awaiting the Lord's pass-over and judgment upon the land of Egypt. (Exodus 12:3-14)

Many years earlier Joseph had instructed all of the land of Egypt to prepare for seven years of severe famine which God had revealed was to come upon the land. They prepared themselves by storing food during the seven good years that God had revealed would precede the famine (Genesis 41:25-36). Joseph had told Pharaoh, "what God is about to do he has revealed..." (verse 28). Preparation was an essential part of their deliverance. They understood what was to come and had believed that it was going to happen. Based upon their faith they prepared themselves accordingly. If we truly believe the spiritual implications and understand the magnitude of the crises which are swiftly coming upon this world – it would be the height of either arrogance or ignorance to fail to prepare ourselves!

THE FATAL DANGER OF DENIAL

Mental preparation for any significant life changing event is extremely difficult. The greater the change or more bizarre the event the more difficult it is to prepare oneself mentally. The mind does not readily accept change. Under normal circumstance it does not quickly adapt to circumstances to which it cannot relate. This, however, is exactly the situation to which we must adapt. The converging environmental, economical, political, and energy crises all have the potential of drastically altering life as we know it. Granted these changes will begin slowly and the initial signs may seem almost trivial, but as the crises deepen, the changes will come faster and the consequences will become ever more significant. In fact, the consequences will be such that every facet of modern civilization will be affected in some manner. The effects will definitely seem bizarre and drastic as compared to life as we now know it. The potential for human suffering will be enormous as the earth enters the deepest phases of these crises.

Because of the nature of these materializing crises, mental preparation is extremely difficult. By difficult – I mean the ability of the mind to grasp the significance of what is taking place. The difficulty is presented by the fact that these crises are emerging slowly and the consequences seem to be insignificant or are even altogether invisible at first. We have a tendency to grow immune to the warnings concerning these events because we do not observe any significant manifestations or danger in the initial stages. The subtle danger of denial has already manifested itself in that the general population has failed to correctly assess the extent of the threat these crises hold. But as we have noted, as these crises continue to escalate, the changes will come more and more quickly and will become ever more significant. The problem is that the power of denial is very strong – once denial has asserted itself it becomes increasingly difficult to escape from its grasp.

Author Saul Friedlander presents an exhaustive study in reference to the thoughts, rationalization, and actions of the European Jews prior to, and during World War II. His study presents an exceptional illustration of the power and influence of denial. In his book, *Nazi Germany and the Jews: 1939-1945, the Years of Extermination*, he reveals that the great loss of life and the high casualty rate of the Jews during the time of the Holocaust was primarily due to the "inability of most European Jews to assess the seriousness of the threat they faced." He noted that "during the first five years of Hitler's regime, barely one-third of the German Jewry emigrated, even with the persecution and the indignities that descended upon them month after month, year after year, starting as early as January 1933."[3]

Friedlander notes that "notwithstanding" the mounting accumulation of evidence manifest by "furious anti-Jewish threats and the steep rise in hostility," the majorities of the Jewish people refused to accept the reality of the threat and were unable to comprehend the dire nature of the growing menace. He states that "this apparent passivity in the face of mounting danger seems hard to understand in retrospect." He notes that in spite of "ominous rumors" which were circulating everywhere, "most of the Jews refused to believe them."[4]

The tendency to cling to the misguided belief that life will always continue as it has in the past is very difficult to overcome. This is the subtle danger of denial. Denial feeds upon uncertainty and the lack of knowledge. How could anyone in modern civilized Europe of the 1930's imagine the horrors of the Holocaust that were to descend upon the continent in just a few years? The horrors of the Holocaust are almost unbelievable in retrospect, how much more difficult would they have been to grasp prior to their manifestation?

But what is striking is the fact that even as the horrors began to materialize, denial continued to maintain control of the Jewish mind-set. Friedlander records an incident in which "two young political prisoners who had witnessed the earliest gassing in Auschwitz were released from the camp." He describes in great detail how they returned to Holland and attempted to warn Jewish and church leaders of what they saw. He states that all of their warnings were "to no avail." Their warnings were simply too horrific to believe.[5] The things that were transpiring were plainly beyond the ability of the cultured mind to grasp. In spite of the accumulating evidence, the implications of what they were hearing was beyond comprehension. It did not conform to the realities of life as the Jews knew it, and therefore it could not be accepted. The details and warnings were far too fantastic and bizarre to accept as reality in the world as they understood it.

Friedlander sadly notes that by the time the Jews realized the seriousness of the situation and experienced their "moment of real awakening," the "means of departure had become impossible." They had waited in an unbelieving state of denial until escape was impossible. There was now seemingly nothing left to do but be swept along with the tide of unfolding events.

Once the crisis had asserted itself, confusion and indecision reigned. There was no consensus on how to react or what to do. All pillars of stability which had formerly anchored the Jewish life had been removed. Within the parameters of their mental understanding there was no rational explanation for what was happening. All the stabilizing factors of their lives had slowly been removed. With nothing left to guide them, and having no plan or direction, panic and hysteria overwhelmed many. The Jews simply did not understand what was happening, nor could they comprehend the nature of the malignant forces which had gained control of their lives. As Friedlander somberly notes, "an atmosphere of total uncertainty" prevailed.

Laurence Rees, in his book, *Auschwitz, A New History*, also observed the prevailing attitude of denial among the European Jews. He detailed the onset of denial by explaining that it was "the sudden shocking change that was taking place in their life." It was a complete inability to accept circumstances that were unfolding. With each phase of the downward spiral of events, there would be a prevalent attitude that "nothing can be as bad as this…" But the circumstances continued to deteriorate, and as the circumstances deteriorated, denial and disbelief grew. After a while they "closed" their minds to what was happening around them, adamantly refusing to accept the reality of the situation. They became "numb" to where "nothing bothers you."[6] This was their mental escape and the only way they could maintain their sanity in a world turned upside down.

Amanda Ripley examined this phenomenon in her book, *Unthinkable: Who Survives When Disaster Strikes – and Why*. Hundreds of individuals who had been involved in life and death crises situations were interviewed. Research studies from psychologists and experts in the field of stress management and disaster situations were also examined. Her research surprisingly revealed that "the human mind has extreme difficulty in coming to terms with catastrophic situations." She pointed out that people have a tendency to want to believe that everything is "okay" simply because it almost always has been in the past. This tendency is what psychologists refer to as the "normalcy bias," or denial.[7]

The brain uses information from the past as it attempts to understand what is happening in the present, and to anticipate the future. When things are occurring to which the mind has no reference, training, or knowledge, it has difficulty recognizing and responding to these exceptions. It responds according to preset patterns and impulses so that "we error on the side of under-reacting," or not acting at all.[8] This under-reaction, or inaction, is directly attributable to denial. This condition prevails because we have never experienced anything on the scale or in the manner as the circumstances which are now materializing. This seemingly bizarre and surreal situation is so far outside the parameters of normality as we know it that our mind refuses to accept it as reality.

According to psychologists and disaster experts, denial can have a remarkably powerful influence on the mind. It can cause people to refuse to accept indisputable evidence or obvious circumstance even as they transpire. In many cases it will continue to rationalize, ignore, and deny right to the very end. This was manifest time and again in the death of millions of Jews during the Holocaust. Most refused to accept the awful reality of what was happening to them even as they entered the gas chambers.

Rees confirms this in *Auschwitz*. His research showed that "even the sound of screams of those dying in the improvised gas chambers in front was not enough to incite a spirit of resistance or opposition. The Jews felt they were being swept away by circumstances that were too overwhelming to resist. It was a river of human events in which the current was too great to defy." He states that the peculiar horror of the circumstances was such that the Jews "were extremely shocked, utterly frightened and petrified, and you could do what you wanted with them. They resigned themselves to their fate."[9] They followed any direction and tended to follow the crowd (group think) no matter how spurious the direction. They followed the crowd like "sheep to the slaughter" never fully comprehending what was happening to them right to the end.

The pattern we see manifest in the European Jewish population just prior to, and during the Holocaust strongly reflects the mental attitude of the world as described by Jesus in Matthew chapters twenty-four and twenty-five. Just as the Jews of the 1930's were unable to correctly assess the seriousness of the threat they faced, so our world today does not understand the nature of the threat it faces. In spite of mounting evidence and witnesses that are providing ample warning of the dangers confronting our world, most people will continue their lives without any consideration of the drastic changes that lie just ahead. They refuse to accept the reality of the threat and are unable to comprehend the dire nature of the growing menace. I fear that in retrospect it will be very difficult to understand this passivity and inaction. I truly fear that when the full fury of these crises asserts itself, the horrors of the Holocaust may pale in comparison.

Our nation is on the precipice of divine judgment and the world is speeding toward Armageddon. The swift current of unfolding events is carrying us rapidly toward the fulfillment of all things. Warnings such as this seem too outlandish for many people to accept. Even though the signs are becoming ever clearer and nations and kingdoms are aligning themselves just as the prophets have said – most people will still refuse to accept the reality of the situation. Prosperity and pleasure have blinded their minds to the point that they cannot see nor comprehend the nature of the malignant forces that are arrayed against this world and the devastation that is looming upon the horizon. For this world there is no great optimistic message of hope outside of Jesus Christ. At some point things in this world will never become better again. They will continue to deteriorate until redemption shines forth at the second coming of Christ. This will be the dawning of a new day. This is the day the church awaits with great anticipation. This is the blessed hope of the church and of a dying world.

FOREWARNED IS FOREARMED

There are many details concerning future events that we do not know. We may not know the exact timing of certain events and we may not understand every specific detail as to how these events will unfold or manifest themselves. But most assuredly, as these crises materialize and the nature of their consequences become clearer, we can make reasonable forecasts as to what some of the effects may be. And what we can know for sure by looking into the prophetic scripture is the overall picture of future events – and it is not pretty. Simply thumb through the pages of the Revelation of John and you will see the culmination of many of the crises which have been examined throughout the pages of this book. You will see the result of world-wide famine, disease, and conflict which will ultimately cause the death of over one quarter of the population of the earth (Revelation 6:8). You will see natural disasters on a scale never before seen; you will see social chaos, nations in worldwide conflict, and suffering on a scale that is almost unimaginable. All of the events set forth in The Revelation could very well be the culmination of crises that are in the making and gathering momentum at this time.

But being forewarned is being forearmed. As pointed out at the very beginning of our examination – one reason that God provides prophetic insight is for a warning. It is insight into the future so that preparation can be made for what is to come. It is a revelation of divine insight so that people may prepare themselves spiritually and physically for critical life changing events. In our case, we have been given valuable insight into one of the most crucial periods of human history. We have been provided a divine roadmap through the word of God to guide us through some of the most perilous and dangerous times in history. Though we may not know or understand all the specific details, we can see the overall results of the culmination of these events – and they are not good. In view of the gravity of the circumstances which will likely culminate in our lifetimes we cannot afford to ignore this insight.

We understand that all of these converging crises will be global in nature. Population growth, epidemics, famine, climate change, diminishing resources, and international conflicts will affect the entire planet. But we have intentionally focused much of our attention upon how these crises will affect the United States. Certain factors which have been examined in previous chapters lead me to believe it is very likely that this great nation could be subjected to very critical and devastating circumstances even before the culmination of these crises as recorded in The Revelation. I cannot help but feel that God is attempting to give this nation a divine wake-up call. There are too many great men of God who are feeling this same spiritual foreboding and are even now sounding the alarm.

The late Dr. John Walvoord, along with John Hitchcock, clearly states that "the question is no longer whether America deserves judgment, but rather why divine judgment has been so long withheld from a wasteful nation that has been blessed so abundantly." They continue by explaining that as the end-time scenario unfolds and the world marches toward Armageddon, it is perfectly clear that "something will have happened to the United States' role as the world policeman. It will simply drop out as a superpower. The end-time events do not include America as the great international superpower it was at the beginning of the twenty-first century."[10] They catalogue a list of events which may occur which would remove the United States from its role in world leadership. They agree with this author in stating that a vicious terrorist attack, energy depletion, and an unprecedented economic crisis lead the list of probable events which could precipitate the collapse of the United States.

Whatever the cause, Walvoord and Hitchcock agree that "the scriptural evidence is sufficient to conclude that America in that day will not be a superpower and apparently will not figure in either political, economic, or religious leadership of the world," and the "the balance of power will shift quickly to Europe and the Middle East."[11]

Ron Rhodes also notes the conspicuous absence of the United States in end-time prophecy in his book, *Northern Storm Rising*. In this book he also vividly describes numerous catastrophic scenarios which could bring about the demise of America and remove her from a position of prophetic influence.[12] Steve Farrar joins the list along with David Wilkerson and Dr. Henry Blackaby. Dr. Blackaby points out that "if you put the United States up against the scriptures, we're in trouble. I think we're very close to the judgment of God."[13] Wilkerson supports this conclusion by emphatically stating in his monthly *World Challenge Pulpit Series* that "a great disaster is coming upon us soon and suddenly. It will be so devastating, the world will shudder. Things will never be the same."[14] Then in another issue he gives us further warning, "darkness is certainly coming and judgment is at our very door."[15]

These are only a few of the ministers today who are sounding the alarm. The United States is nearing judgment. Most seem to agree that some catastrophic event must occur shortly in the United States. This event – or series of events—must occur to set the stage for the final prophecies of the end-time to be fulfilled. They must also occur to fulfill the righteousness of a holy God against a nation who has abused his blessing and rejected his mercy. The overwhelming feeling is that we are even now standing upon the doorsteps of judgment. The United States is entering into perilous times and there is no guarantee that the lukewarm Laodacian church in America will escape these events.

With this understanding our pulpits should be aflame with this message. Christians in this country should be preparing both spiritually and physically for the greatest prophetic event since the crucifixion, resurrection, and ascension of Jesus. This day should not catch the church unawares. As the Apostle Paul wrote to the church in his day, we should understand the "times and the seasons." He emphatically stated that "sudden destruction" would come upon the world because they are in spiritual "darkness" and cannot discern the signs of the times. But he said that the church was of the "day." We are the children of the light. We have spiritual insight and there is no reason why this "day should overtake you as a thief" (I Thessalonians 5:1-4).

If anyone should understand what is about to happen in this world – it should be the church. If anyone should have a sense of urgency concerning the hour in which we live – it should be the church. If anyone should have a sense of impending judgment because of the overwhelming wickedness of our nation – it is the church. WE SHOULD BE ALIVE WITH THIS MESSAGE AND IN FULL-SCALE PREPARATION FOR THE FULFILLMENT OF THE THINGS WHICH GOD HAS REVEALED TO US.

RIGHT CHOICES AND RIGHT ACTIONS

As he stood on the desert hillside overlooking the prosperous cities of the valley with his uncle Abraham, Lot could not have known that he was about to make one of the most important decisions of his life. Their herds and flocks had become so great that "the land was not able to bear them." They were about to separate and each would go their own way. Abraham, or Abram as he was known at this time, turned to Lot and allowed him to make the first choice.

He could have picked anywhere in the land. The choice was his, and little did he realize that the choice he was about to make would affect everything about his future.

Before him was the whole land and he could go anywhere he wanted. There were the seemingly barren wilderness and desert areas where he and his uncle had traveled for years. True, God had provided for them and miraculously prospered them even in the wilderness areas – but now before them were the well watered plains of Jordan. They were green, they were flourishing, there was plenty of water, and most of all there were bustling cities where prosperity and luxury abounded. The choice between the dry barren wilderness and the well watered valley with thriving cities seemed to be a "no-brainer" for Lot. When presented with the choice, he chose the prosperity and security of the thriving world system of his day.

The Bible indicates that while Abraham continued his journey of faith trusting God to sustain and provide for him in the wilderness, Lot looked toward the cities of Sodom and Gomorrah. He looked at these cities and the scripture records they appeared to him to be "even as the garden of the Lord." He looked at the depraved cities of Sodom and Gomorrah, and somehow convinced himself that this was the place and the system to which he would commit himself. He committed his prosperity, his possessions, and most importantly the lives of his family to this system. For a while everything went well. He prospered and fared sumptuously. He purchased or built a new home, his wealth increased, his daughters married and life could not have seemed better.

But when "the day of visitation" came, and the cities of the plain along with their decadent system was subjected to the great shaking – Lot literally lost everything he had. He lost his home, his property, his wealth, his wife, and his sons-in-law. When the Bible closes its narrative account concerning the life of Lot – he is living in a cave with two morally degenerate daughters. Though his life was spared in the end, his choice to trust in, and entangle himself in the world system of his day cost him greatly.

Abraham, on the other hand, continued to prosper even as the cities, cultures, and systems around him were shaken and destroyed. He had chosen to live outside of the world system of his day. He had chosen to live in the wilderness area and trust God for his sustenance. His faith in God preserved not only him and his family – but established Abraham as the father of faith to whom the scriptures point to as an example for all to live by.

Much of our spiritual and physical preparation is going to depend upon the choices we make. Part of these choices will hinge upon just how much we choose to be entangled in the system of our world today. The more entangled we are in this system the more painful it will be in the "day of visitation," or the great shaking that is upon us. The more areas of our lives that are involved within the web of the social and economic structure of this system the more we are going to suffer and the greater our loss will be. Although Lot was saved in the end, his losses were tremendous. He lost all of his possessions, his home, his sons-in-law, and his wife.

The entanglement and addiction of this system was so great that his sons-in-law refused to consider separating themselves from it even as danger approached. His wife was so fascinated by the allurements of the city that she could not help looking back even as it was crumbling in destruction. His daughters were so influenced by the moral depravity of this system that their conscience and moral inhibitions were destroyed. The lesson should be clear. We cannot afford to become so attached or attracted to this system that we cannot make the crucial separation. Just as Sodom and Gomorrah were overthrown in their day of visitation, so also shall our world system be overthrown. As this morally depraved anti-god system begins to crumble and fall during the imminent shaking period, we cannot afford to be entangled within it. Many of us have a number of critical decisions to make in the very near future that will have a tremendous impact upon our families and their future.

The pain that will be involved in the collapse of this world system cannot be fully comprehended. What we do know is that different parts of our country and the world will be affected differently. Some areas will feel the effects of societal and economic collapse more severely than others. Industrial, commercial, and urban areas will suffer to a much greater extent than rural and small towns that are less dependent upon technology and mechanized industry. The areas of the country that are more self-sufficient and independent of this system will suffer the least.

As Stephen Leeb has noted, "...the most technologically complex systems will be the ones most subject to dysfunction and collapse..." He continues by explaining that "a decline in complexity would mean shortages of food and other items, a breakdown of law and order and a corresponding reign of terror. Malnutrition and starvation... could be widespread, resulting in a much lower population. Diseases would be harder to prevent and control. Cities and towns across the continent might come to look like New Orleans after Katrina. Civilization could truly collapse."[16]

The more dependent upon this world's industrial and technological infrastructure an area is, the more susceptible it will be to the contraction or collapse of this system. Our goal should be to become as spiritually and physically separated from this system as possible. God is going to shake this man-made system and the only place of safety will be under his blood and in the shelter of his Spirit. **Our spiritual goal should be to become as dependent upon God as is humanly possible. Our physical goal should be to become as self-sufficient and independent of this world system as possible**. A complete trust in God and an utter rejection of man-made confidences should be the rule of the day.

> It is better to trust in the Lord than to put confidence in man. (Psalm 117:8)

> Thus saith the Lord; Cursed be the man that trusteth in man, and maketh flesh his arm, and whose heart departeth from the Lord. For he shall be like the heath in the desert, and shall not see when good cometh; but shall inhabit the parched places in the wilderness, in a salt land and not inhabited. (Jeremiah 17:5-6)

> Blessed is the man that trusteth in the Lord, and whose hope the Lord is. For he shall be as a tree planted by the waters, and that spreadeth out her roots by the river, and shall not see when the heat cometh, but her leaf shall be green; and shall

not be careful in the year of drought, neither shall cease from yielding fruit. (Jeremiah 17:7-8)

REFUGE IN THE STORM

Come, my people, enter thou into thy chambers, and shut thy doors about thee: hide thyself as it were for a little moment, until the indignation be overpast. (Isaiah 26:20)

A prudent man foreseeth the evil, and hideth himself: but the simple pass on, and are punished. (Proverbs 22:3)

Our first priority must be our spiritual preparation. The first thing one must do in any time of crisis or calamity is to flee to the sheltering wings of God. He is our refuge and fortress. He is our very present help in the time of need. It is He who will sustain any and all that put their trust and confidence in him. During the shaking time that is to come, only those who have learned to put their entire confidence and trust in God will last. Only those that have committed their sustenance, their well being, and their very lives to God will prosper. Our first priority in preparation for any critical circumstance is to insure that our relationship with God is sure. Half-hearted, lukewarm, doubtful, and carnal Christians will be shaken along with everything else. It is crucial that we make our calling and election sure. Being right with God and having all things under the blood is the only sure refuge in the coming storm. **There is no substitute for spiritual preparation!**

We will find, however, that our natural preparation will be directly connected to our spiritual priorities. Our spiritual perception of the circumstances will dictate our natural inclinations and decisions. The first natural priority which we should attend to as we see the approaching storm should be to get out of debt. I mean completely if at all possible. Many homes were lost during the Great Depression not only because mortgages could not be paid, but also because many people could not pay their taxes. Get completely out of debt. It is not insignificant that the Bible teaches that "the rich ruleth over the poor, and the borrower is servant to the lender" (proverbs 22:7). To be indebted to this world system during this time of spiritual and natural shaking is to risk severe loss. A person in debt becomes a servant or slave to those who control the debt. It would not be wise to be indebted to this world system during the shaking period. What little money there may be will be needed for the basic things such as taxes and essential commodities that cannot be bartered for or made.

One should strive to own his home and property free and clear. I feel that it is even preferable to own at least five acres of good land if not more. By good land I am speaking agriculturally. This means land that is fertile, well watered, and cultivatable. In other words, it should be able to grow things and sustain life. It should either be in a place where rainfall is abundant or have a well or live water of some kind. Live water or a well are preferable as the effects of climate change may bring severe or extended drought into areas that normally do not experience such things. It is true that God will provide, but he expects us to respond to his warning concerning future events and take a prudent course of action (Proverbs 22:3).

While this undoubtedly may seem extreme to some people, consider the fact that during the Great Depression people were fleeing from the great urban areas and going by the droves into the rural areas where they could squat on vacant land and find shelter in abandoned houses. In these abandoned homes and on vacant parcels of land they found the basics of survival in that they had a place to live and could grow a garden for food. Thousands more abandoned their homes in semi-arid areas of the country during the dust bowl when drought came and their land became worthless. They moved on in great migrations to other parts of the country in search of "good land." This is a fact of history and not conjecture. This happened in the past and there is no reason to believe that it could not happen again.

Cities will be the hardest hit as the economy contracts and the modern infrastructure begins to falter. It is here that unemployment will be the greatest as wage earning jobs begin to disappear. Energy will become more expensive and in short supply causing essential services to fail or be reduced. Factories will close. Government services including financial support will be curtailed. Basic utility services will be disrupted and infrastructure maintenance will deteriorate. The social integrity of urban areas will deteriorate very quickly. We observed how rapidly this occurred in New Orleans during Katrina. When the infrastructure began to fail, everything else quickly went with it.

The second area which will feel the pain will be the desert and semi-arid places where water is already in short supply. Consider that all food supplies and basic commodities are shipped into these places. Just as in urban areas, these places are completely dependent upon outside sources and the modern transportation system for even the most basic of essentials. They neither make nor provide anything of sustenance for themselves. As supplies become scarce and the transportation system contracts, these non-sustainable areas will suffer greatly.

Simplicity and self-sufficiency will be principal values during this time. Farming and agriculture will quickly become the most important industry as food production becomes essential. The days of luxury and convenience will be over. Survival and necessity will be the reigning motivators of the day. Craftsmen, handymen, and artisans will become invaluable. Community and family will once again become the center of life and essential for survival. People will need one another. What one person is unable to do, another will be able to do. What one family does not have, another in the community will be there to supply. There will be an essential dependence upon one another for survival.

This communal and cooperative working together toward common goals has always been a basic characteristic of rural living. Rural people have historically worked together and shared hardship, labor, and sustenance. These values were what formed the strong familial and community bonds of early America. Thankfully these values are still found in many areas of rural America today. Although suffering and hardship will be universal during this time, these areas will suffer the least. The areas that tend to be more independent of technology and industrialism, while at the same time being more self-sufficient and communal in nature, already have the basic foundation that will be so necessary for survival in trying days ahead.

The values and social structure that made America the great country it once was will be revived out of necessity. Community, family, and dependence upon God will provide the basics of survival and life during this time. An environment that promotes people working together in harmony as a community and family, while maintaining a great faith in the providence and protection of God is the only thing that will bring people through this time of trial. While many will be looking to man's wisdom and technology to save them, there will be those who understand the nature of the "shaking" and will return to the basic values which God instituted from the beginning. Love, benevolence, and generosity will become not only leading virtues, but the basic essentials of survival. Trust and faith in God will be fundamental. God will be the only true source for health, food, shelter, and protection. Prayer, piety, and devotion to God will not be optional for those who choose to live outside of the world system.

God will become the centerpiece of life for these people during this time. Those that know their God will become strong and do exploits (Daniel 11:32). The common brotherhood and faith that infused the church in the Book of Acts will be restored. Believers will have all things in common and return to a basic faith and trust in God for all things (Acts 2:44-47 and Acts 4:32-35).

The church as we know it in modern America will endure a great transformation. Gone will be the days of the mega-churches and theatrical church services. With cities and urban areas in chaos, and people unable to travel very far, church gatherings will become smaller and local in nature. Meetings will undoubtedly primarily be held in homes or small meeting houses just as in the Book of Acts. Large church buildings with their environmentally controlled heating and cooling systems will become obsolete at some point. They will become impractical and far too inefficient and costly to maintain as the crises deepens. Instead of people and congregations traveling great distances (over a few miles) to these now impractical and useless buildings, ministers will travel from community to community, home to home, and gathering to gathering to minister, distribute to those in need, and provide news and fellowship. Once again, simplicity and practicality will dictate human actions during this time.

Church giving will be focused upon helping the unfortunate and providing basic necessities for those members who have lost their jobs or homes. Christians will find it common to share their homes with the more unfortunate brothers and sisters. Brotherly love will not be in word, but will become a practical reality. Churches will return to "having all things common" just as in the Book of Acts. All of this will undoubtedly have a tremendous impact on the spirituality of the church. Prayer, faith, commitment, dedication, and the outpouring of brotherly love will bring a great revival. God will manifest his glory in a manner not witnessed since the Book of Acts.

Many of the unsaved that recognize the nature of the crises will flee to the only refuge during this time of calamity – the Church. Conversions, relationships, and experiences with God will become much closer and much more real than we can imagine. People will know God in a way that has not been seen in generations. It will be a time of miracles, wonders, deliverance, and revival. God will show himself strong in the midst of his people.

While the coming time of crises will be a time of darkness and gloom for the world – it will be a time of glory and revival for the church. It will be a time when God will be exalted above all else and will reveal himself in a manner not seen for generations and generations.

> For behold, the darkness shall cover the earth, and gross darkness the people: but the Lord shall arise upon thee, and his glory shall be seen upon thee. (Isaiah 60:2)

> **And what will ye do in the day of visitation**, and in the desolation which shall come from far? To whom will ye flee for help? And where will ye leave your glory? (Isaiah 10:3)

The ultimate question is simply this: are you prepared for the "day of visitation?" Have you made a proper assessment of the dangers which are confronting our world? Are you one who has decided to ignore all of the signs and continue life as it always has been, or are you preparing for the changes that are coming? Have you committed your life and providence to Jesus Christ? That is the ultimate question. That is primarily the reason for this book. It has been written with the hope that a compilation of the accumulating evidence which confronts us will motivate some to make the right decisions and prepare for what is to come. It has been written with the objective of pointing the way to the only true refuge from the coming storm – Jesus Christ.

> He that dwelleth in the secret place of the most High shall abide under the shadow of the Almighty. I will say of the Lord, He is my refuge and my fortress: my God; in him I will trust. Surely he shall deliver thee from the snare of the fowler, and from the noisome pestilence. He shall cover thee with his feathers, and under his wings shalt thou trust: his truth shall be thy buckler. Thou shalt not be afraid for the terror by night; nor for the arrow that flieth by day; Nor for the pestilence that walketh in darkness; nor for the destruction that wasteth at noonday. A thousand shall fall at thy side, and ten thousand at thy right hand; but it shall not come nigh thee. Only with thine eyes shalt thou behold and see the reward of the wicked. Because thou hast made the Lord, which is my refuge, even the most High, thy habitation. There shall no evil befall thee, neither shall any plague come nigh thy dwelling. (Psalm 91:1-10)

NOTES

Chapter 1 – A WORLD ON THE THRESHOLD

[1] James Howard Kunstler, *The Long Emergency* (Atlantic Monthly Press: New York)

[2] Jared Diamond, *Collapse: How Societies Choose to Fail or Succeed* (Viking, Published by the Penguin Group, New York)

[3] James Howard Kunstler, *The Long Emergency* (Atlantic Monthly Press: New York)

Chapter 2 – FIRST AND LAST DAYS

[1] James Strong, *Strong's Exhaustive Concordance of the Bible* (Zondervan, Grand Rapids, MI; See reference 5048 under Greek Dictionary Index)

[2] Some of the prophecies are found in the following scriptures; Isaiah 43:1 and 5-6; Jeremiah 31:4 and 8; Ezekiel 11:17 and 19; Ezekiel 37:1-15, 21 and 22 and Psalms 126:1 and 2

[3] Flavius Josephus: Translated by William Whiston, *The Works of Josephus* (Hendrickson Publishers)

[4] *Ibid.*

[5] *Ibid.*

[6] Dore Gold, *The Fight for Jerusalem* (Regnery Publishing Company)

[7] Gedaliah Alon, *The Jews in Their Land in the Talmudic Age* (Jerusalem: The Magnes Press, The Hebrew University, 1984)

[8] Dore Gold, *The Fight for Jerusalem* (Regnery Press)

[9] The only prophetic marker needed to completely fulfill the prophecies concerning the "times of the Gentiles" is the rebuilding of the Temple of Solomon. Events to fulfill this objective are occurring almost every day. On July 30, 1980, the nation of Israel passed the "Jerusalem Law" which established the city of Jerusalem as their official capitol. In 1987 the Temple Institute was founded for the sole purpose of orchestrating the rebuilding of the temple. Even now they are collecting funds, artifacts, and furnishings in anticipation for this great event.

Chapter 3 – THE GROWING POPULATION CRISIS

[1] William A. Haviland, *Cultural Anthropology;* 9th edition (Harcourt and Brace College Publishers)

[2] *Ibid.*

[3] *Scientific American* (September 2005, Vol. 293, No. 3)

[4] *The Little Green Handbook* (Picador: New York)

[5] Ron Nielson, *The Little Green Handbook* (Picador: New York)

[6] Statistics from: *World Population Perspectives: The 2000 Revision* (Population Division, Department of Economics and Social Affairs, United Nations)

[7] Robert H. Dott Jr. and Donald R. Prothero, *Evolution of the Earth;* 5th edition (McGraw Hill Inc.)

[8] *Ibid.*

[9] Joel E. Cohen, *Scientific American: Human Population Grows Up* (September, 2005, Vol. 293, No. 3)

[10] United Nations, *World Population Prospects:* The 2002 Revision New York: 2003

[11] Edward Goldsmith, "Global Trade and the Environment" (from: *The Case Against the Global Economy;* Sierra Club Books, San Francisco)

[12] Donella Meadows, Jorgen Randers, and Dennis Meadows, *Limits to Growth: The Thirty Year Update* (Chelsea Green Publishing Company, White River Junction, VT)

[13] Tim Flannery, *The Weathermakers* (Atlantic Monthly Press: New York)

[14] Ron Nielsen, *The little Green Handbook* (Pecador: New York)

[15] Bryjak Soroka, *Sociology;* 2nd edition (Allyan and Bacon, A Division of Simon and Schuster, Inc.)

[16] Lester R. Brown, *Plan B 2.0: Rescuing a Planet Under Stress and a Civilization in Trouble* (W. W. Norton and Company)

[17] Mathis Wackernagel et.al., *Tracking the Ecological Overshoot of the Human Economy* (Proceedings from the National Academy of Sciences, July 2002, Vol. 99, No. 14)

[18] David Pimentel, et al., *Will Limits of the Earth's Resources Control Human Numbers* (College of Agriculture and Life Sciences, Cornell University)

[19] James Howard Kunstler, *The Long Emergency* (Atlantic Monthly Press: New York)

[20] Walter Youngquist, From: *Population and Environment: A Journal of Interdisciplinary Studies* (Vol. 20, No. 4, March 1999 "The Post-Petroleum Paradigm – and Population")

[21] Lester R. Brown, *Outgrowing the Earth* (W. W. Norton and Company)

[22] L. Grant, *Jaggernaut* (Seven Locks Press: Minneapolis MN, 1996)

[23] James Kunstler, *The Long Emergency* (Atlantic Monthly Press: New York)

[24] Karl Schwenke, *Successful Small-Scale Farming* (Storey Publishing)

[25] Walter Youngquist, From: *Population and Environment: A Journal of Interdisciplinary Studies* (Vol. 20, No. 4, March 1999 "The Post-Petroleum Paradigm – and Population")

[26] Ron Nielsen, *The Little Green Handbook* (Picador: New York)

[27] Sandra Postel, *Water and Sustainability: Dimensions of the Global Challenge* (Global Water Policy Project, World Watch Institute, Amherst, MA)

[28] Lester R. Brown, *Plan B 2.0: Rescuing a Planet Under Stress and a Civilization in Trouble* (W. W. Norton and Company)

[29] Ron Nielsen, *The Little Green Handbook* (Picador: New York)

[30] Al Fry, Lead Author, *Facts and Trends: Water* (WBCSD, August 2005. Reprint March 2006)

[31] *Ibid.*

[32] Lester R. Brown, *Plan B 2.0: Rescuing a Planet Under Stress and a Civilization in Trouble* (W. W. Norton and Company)

[33] U.S. Department of the Interior / U.S. Geological Survey, "Groundwater Depletion" (URL: http://ga.water.usgs.gov/edu/gwdepletion.html / August 31, 2005)

[34] P. Beaumont, 1985, *Environmental Conservation* "Irrigated agriculture and groundwater mining on the high plains of Texas"

[35] David Pementel, et al., *Will Limits of the Earth's Resources Control Human Numbers* (College of Agriculture and Life Sciences, Cornell University)

[36] Fred Pearce, *When the Rivers Run Dry: Water – The Defining Crisis of the 21st Century* (Beacon Press: Boston)

[37] *Ibid.*

[38] *Ibid.*

[39] LeRoy W. Hooten, Jr., "Colorado River Users Face potential Shortages" (www.slcgov.com.utilities/)

[40] Tim Flannery, *The Weather Makers* (Atlantic Monthly Press: New York)

[41] Greg Bluestein, "Tennessee Town Out of Water: Worst-case Scenario in the South" (Associated Press October 2007)

[42] Brain Skoloff, "Much of U.S. Could See a Water Shortage: Crisis Feared in Nation's Freshwater Supplies" (Associated Press; as reported by ABC News October 26, 2007)

[43] Ron Nielsen, *The Little Green Handbook* (Picador: New York)

[44] Sandra Postel, *Water and Sustainability: Dimensions of the Global Challenge* (Global Water Policy Project, World Watch Institute: Amherst, MA)

Chapter 4 – PAMDEMICS AND MUTATING DISEASES

[1] Laurie Garrett, *The Coming Plague: Newly Emerging Diseases in a World out of Balance* (Farrar, Straus and Giroux: New York)

[2] *Ibid.*

[3] *Ibid.*

[4] *Ibid.*

[5] J. A. Najera, "Malaria and the Work of WHO" (Bulletin of the World Health Organization, 67; 1989)

[6] Elinor Levy and Mark Fischetti, *The New Killer Diseases* (Crown Publishers: New York)

[7] *Ibid.*

[8] *Ibid.*

[9] *Ibid.*

[10] Jeremy Farrar: As quoted in: "The Next Killer Flu, Can We Stop It?" an article by Tim Appenzeller (National Geographic; October 2005)

[11] R. M. Krause, *The Restless Tide: The Persistent Challenge of the Microbial World* (The National Foundation for Infectious Diseases: Washington D.C.)

[12] S. S. Morse, from the Forward by, R. M. Krause, *Emerging Viruses* (Oxford University Press, 1993)

[13] Laurie Garret: from the Preface by: Jonathan M. Mann, M.D., M.P.H, *The Coming Plague* (Farrar, Straus and Giroux, New York)

[14] Tim Appenzeller, *The Next Killer Flu* (National Geographic; October 2005)

[15] Elinor Levy and Mark Fischetti, *The New Killer Diseases* (Crown Publishers: New York)

[16] *Ibid.*

Chapter 5 – CLIMATE CHANGE AND THE ENVIRONMENTAL CRISIS

[1] The International Panel on Climate Change (IPCC), *Climate Change 2007: The Physical Science Basis*

[2] Joseph Romm, *Hell and High Water* (HarperCollins Publishers: New York)

[3] *Ibid.*

[4] The International Panel on Climate Change (IPCC), *Climate Change 2007: The Physical science Basis*

[5] Jeffrey Kluger, Article: "What Now?" (Time Magazine; The Global Warming Survival Guide; April 9, 2007)

[6] Tim Appenzeller and Dennis R. Dimick, "Signs From Earth" (National Geographic; September, 2004)

[7] *Ibid.*

[8] Joseph Romm, *Hell and High Water* (HarperCollins Publishers: New York)

[9] Jeffery Kluger, *Time: Global Warming – When a Planet Fights a Fever* (Time Books, Time Incorporated: New York)

[10] Joseph Romm, *Hell and High Water* (HarperCollins Publisher: New York)

[11] Robert Henson, *The Rough Guide to Climate Change* (Penguin Putnam Inc.: New York)

[12] S. J. Hassol, *Impacts of a Warming Arctic: Arctic Climate Impact Assessment* (Cambridge University Press, 2004: Cambridge)

[13] Tim Flannery, *The Weather Makers* (Atlantic Monthly Press: New York)

[14] Robert Henson, *The Rough Guide to Climate Change* (Penguin Putnam Inc.: New York)

[15] Gary Braasch, Information and Data from: *Earth Under Fire* (University of California Press)

[16] Joseph Romm, *Hell and High Water* (HarperCollins Publishers: New York)

[17] Gray Braasch, Information and Data from: *Earth Under Fire* (University of California Press)

[18] *Ibid.*

[19] Joseph Romm, *Hell and High Water* (HarperCollins Publishers: New York)

[20] Daniel Glick, "The Heat is On: GeoSigns" (National Geographic; September, 2004)

[21] *Ibid.* (National Geographic; September, 2004)

[22] *Ibid.* (National Geographic; September, 2004)

[23] *Ibid.* (National Geographic; September, 2004)

[24] Tim Flannery, *The Weather Makers* (Atlantic Monthly Press: New York)

[25] *Ibid.*

[26] Gary Braasch, Information and Data from: *Earth Under Fire* (University of California Press)

[27] *Ibid.*

[28] Daniel Glick, *The Big Thaw: GeoSigns* (National Geographic; September, 2004)

[29] *Ibid.*

[30] *Ibid.*

[31] Gary Braasch, Information and Data from: *Earth Under Fire* (University of California Press)

[32] Joseph Romm, *Hell and High Water* (HarperCollins Publishers: New York)

[33] Lester R. Brown, *Plan B 2.0: Rescuing a Planet Under Stress and a Civilization in Trouble* (W. W. Norton and Company)

[34] Tim Flannery, *The Weather Makers* (Atlantic Monthly Press: New York)

[35] Robert Henson, *The Rough Guide to Climate Change* (Penguin Books Limited: London)

[36] *Ibid.*

[37] Al Gore, Statistics from: *An Inconvenient Truth* (Rodale Publishers: New York)

[38] Juliet Eilperin, Article: "More Frequent Heat Waves Linked to Global Warming " (Washington Post; August 4, 2006)

[39] Robert Henson, *The Rough Guide to Climate Change* (Penguin Putnam Inc.: New York)

[40] Geoffrey B. Holland and James J. Provenazano, *The Hydrogen Age* (Gibbs Smith Publisher)

[41] Evan Thomas, Article from: "Special Report: After Katrina – The Lost City" (Newsweek; September 12, 2005)

[42] Nancy Gibbs, Article from: "An American Tragedy" (Time Magazine; September 12, 2005)

[43] Kerry Emanuel, Article from; "Nature" (Time Magazine; Summer Edition, September 12, 2005)

[44] *List of Extreme Weather Events* (www.answers.com)

[45] "Bizarre Weather Ravages Africa Crops" (The Washington Post; January 7, 2003)

[46] Contact: NEIC Web Team, *U.S. Department of the Interior/U.S. Geological Survey* (http://neic.usgs.gov/neis/eqlists/eqstats.hml)

[47] Michael Elliot, Article from: "Sea of Sorrow" (Time Magazine; January 10, 2005)

[48] www.theage.com.au, "Tsunami Quake Wobbled Earth's Axis" (The Age Company Ltd.)

[49] Robert Henson, *The Rough Guide to Climate Change* (Penguin Books Limited: London)

[50] *Ibid.*

[51] *Ibid.*

[52] *Ibid.*

[53] www.arlingtoncardinal.net/fireblog, *California Wildfire Summary Statistics for October 2007 Fires* (The Cardinal)

[54] www.earth-policy.org/Updates/2006/Update58_data.htm, *Hurricane Damage Soars to New Levels* (Earth Policy Institute; June 22, 2006)

[55] Lester R. Brown, *Plan B 2.0: Rescuing a Planet Under Stress and a Civilization in Trouble* (W. W. Norton and Company)

[56] *Ibid.*

[57] *Ibid.*

[58] Tim Flannery, *The Weather Makers* (Atlantic Monthly Press: New York)

[59] *Ibid.*

[60] *Ibid.*

[61] www.unep.org:UNEP News Release 01/11, *Impact of Climate Change to Cost the World $300 Billion a Year* (United Nations Environment Program)

[62] *Ibid.*

[63] Ruth Rosen, Article from: *Imagine the Unthinkable* (The San Francisco Chronicle; April 1, 2004)

[64] Peter Schwartz and Doug Randall, *An Abrupt Climate Change Scenario and Its Implications for United States National Security*: October 2003

[65] Information and Data from: Peter Schwartz and Doug Randall, *An Abrupt Climate Change Scenario and Its Implications for United States National Security*:

October 2003, Ruth Rosen, Article from: "Imagine the Unthinkable" (The San Francisco Chronicle; April 1, 2004), David Stipp, Article: "The Pentagon's Weather Nightmare" (Fortune Magazine; February 9, 2004)

[66] http://lwf.ncdc.noaa.gov/oa/reports/mitch.html, (National Climatic Data Center)

[67] *Ibid.*

[68] Lester R. Brown, *Plan B 2.0: Rescuing a Planet Under Stress and a Civilization in Trouble* (W. W. Norton and Company)

[69] Press Release: Commodity Information Systems Inc., February 8, 2007, "Global Grain Shortage of Historic Proportions Ahead" (Mass Media Distribution LLC)

[70] Lester Brown, "World Grain Stocks Fall to 57 Days of Consumption… " (Earth Policy Institute: June 15, 2006)

[71] *Ibid.*

[72] *Ibid.*

[73] Marcia Merry Baker, "Globalizations Policy of Famine: Wheat Supplies Plunge" (Executive Intelligence Review; October 20, 2006)

[74] Michael Byrnes, "Australian Farmers Face Bankruptcy from Drought" (Reuters News Service; October 25, 2007)

[75] Article: "EU Acts on World Grain Shortage" (British Broadcasting Company (BBC News); September 26, 2007)

[76] http://www.ncdc.noaa.gov/oa/climate/research/2007/aug/aug-heat-event.php, *August 2007 Heat Wave Summary* (National Climatic Data Center; August 31, 2007)

[77] *Ibid.*

Chapter 6 – THE COMING ENERGY CRISIS – PEAK OIL

[1] Richard Heinberg, Quote by Paul Ehrlich, *The Party's Over* (New Society Publishers)

[2] *Ibid.*

[3] Paul Roberts, *The End of Oil* (The Houghton Mifflin Company: New York)

[4] *Ibid.*

[5] Michael C. Ruppert, *Crossing the Rubicon* (New Society Publishers)

[6] Paul Roberts, *The End of Oil* (The Houghton Mifflin Company: New York)

[7] *Ibid.*

[8] Peter Maass, Article: *The Breaking Point* (New York Times Magazine; August 21, 2005)

[9] Peter Tertzakian, *A Thousand Barrels A Second* (McGraw Hill)

[10] *Ibid.*

[11] James Howard Kunstler, *The Long Emergency* (Atlantic Monthly Press: New York)

[12] C. J. Campbell, *The Coming Oil Crisis* (Multi-Science Publishing Company & Petroconsultants S.A.)

[13] Paul Roberts, *The End of Oil* (Houghton Mifflin Company)

[14] Peter Tertzakian, *A Thousand Barrels A Second* (McGraw Hill)

[15] Peter Tertzakian, *Basic Petroleum Statistics* (Statistics from: U.S. Energy Information Administration, Data from 2006, and last updated on July, 2007)

[16] Richard Heinberg, Quote by Paul Ehrlich, *The Party's Over* (New Society Publishers)

[17] U.S. Department of Energy, March 2004, Source: *Strategic Significance of America's Shale Oil Resource* (Vol. I, Assessment of Strategic Issues, Office of Deputy Assistant Secretary for Petroleum Reserves, Office of Naval Petroleum and Oil Shale Reserves, U. S. Department of Energy, March 2004; www.fe.doe. gov/programs/reserves/publications/Pub-NPR/npr_strategic_significancev1.pdf)

[18] *Ibid.*

[19] Russell Gold and Ann Davis, Article: *Oil Officials See Limit Looming on Production* (The Wall Street Journal; November 19, 2007)

[20] *Ibid.*

[21] Stephen Leeb, PhD, From: *The Coming Economic Collapse* (Warner Business Books)

[22] Richard Heinberg, *The Party's Over* (New Society Publishers)

[23] Paul Roberts, *The End of Oil* (Houghton Mifflin Company)

[24] Stephen Leeb, PhD, From: *The Coming Economic Collapse* (Warner Business Books)

[25] www.odac-info.org/, Oil Depletion Analysis Centre; News Release February 9. 2004

[26] Richard Heinberg, *Powerdown* (New Society Publishers)

[27] Richard Heinberg, *The Party's Over* (New Society Publishers)

[28] *Ibid.*

[29] Michael T. Klare, *Blood and Oil* (Metropolitan Books, Henry Holt and Company: New York)

[30] Matthew R. Simmons, *Twilight in the Desert* (John Wiley and Sons Inc.)

[31] *Ibid.*

[32] *Ibid.*

[33] *Ibid.*

[34] *Ibid.*

[35] Statistics from: *OPEC Monthly Market Report: October 2004, October 2005, October 2006, and October 2007 (Obere Donaustrasse 93, A-1020 Vienna, Austria: www.opec.org)*

[36] *Ibid.*

[37] Lananh Nguyen and Spencer Swartz, Article: *OPEC Pulls Oil Away From $100 mark: Relief May Be Brief As Saudi Arabia Pumps Up Output* (Wall Street Journal, November 26, 2007)

[38] Chip Cummins, Article: *OPEC's Freeze Keeps Pressure on Prices* (Wall Street Journal, December 6, 2007)

[39] Stephen Leeb, PhD, *The Coming Economic Collapse* (Warner Business Books: New York)

[40] Richard Heinberg, *The Party's Over* (New Society Publishers)

[41] Paul Roberts, *The End of Oil* (Houghton Mifflin Company)

[42] James Howard Kunstler, *The Long Emergency* (Atlantic Monthly Press: New York)

[43] *Ibid.*

[44] C. J. Campbell, *The Coming Oil Crisis* (Multi-science Publishing Company and Petroconsultants S.A.)

[45] Jeremy Leggett, *The Empty Tank* (Random House: New York)

[46] Kenneth S. Deffeyes, *Hubbert's Peak: The Impending World Oil Shortage* (Princeton University Press)

[47] Robert L. Hirsch, SAIC, Project Leader, *Peaking of World Oil Production: Impacts, Mitigation, & Risk Management* (Commissioned by the United States Department of Energy)

[48] James Howard Kunstler, *The Long Emergency* (Atlantic Monthly Press: New York)

[49] Stephen Leeb, PhD, *The Coming Economic Collapse* (Warner Business Books: New York)

[50] *Ibid.*

[51] *Ibid.*

[52] Richard Heinberg, *The Party's Over* (New Society Publishers)

Chapter 7 – CONSEQUENCES AND CRISIS

[1] James Howard Kunstler, *The Long Emergency* (Atlantic Monthly Press: New York)

[2] Michael T. Klare, *Blood and Oil* (Metropolitan Books, Henry Holt and Company: New York)

[3] U.S. Department of Energy, Energy Information Administration, *Annual Energy Outlook, 2004* (As quoted from: *Blood and Oil*, Metropolitan Books, Henry Holt and company)

[4] Michael T. Klare, *Blood and Oil* (Metropolitan Books, Henry Holt and Company: New York)

[5] Spencer Abrahm, as quoted by Michael T. Klare, *Blood and Oil* (Metropolitan Books, Henry Holt and Company: New York)

[6] Michael T. Klare, *Blood and Oil* (Metropolitan Books, Henry Holt and Company: New York)

[7] President Jimmy Carter, *State of the Union Address; January 1980*

[8] United States Department of Energy, *Annual Energy Outlook, 2004*

[9] Thomas L. Friedman, *The World is Flat* (Farrara, Straus and Giroux: New York)

[10] James Howard Kunstler, *The Long Emergency* (Atlantic Monthly Press: New York)

[11] Kenneth S. Deffeyes, *Beyond Oil* (Hill and Wang, A division of Farrar, Straus and Giroux)

[12] *Ibid.*

[13] James Howard Kunstler, *The Long Emergency* (Atlantic Monthly Press: New York)

[14] Michael T. Klare, *Resource Wars* (A Metropolitan/Owl Book: Henry Holt and Company: New York)

[15] *Ibid.*

[16] Michael T. Klare, *Blood and Oil* (Metropolitan Books, Henry Holt and Company: New York)

[17] Asim Oku, AIA Turkish Section, "Russia and Turkey in the Middle East" (Global Challenges Research; May 3, 2005)

[18] Asim Oku, AIA Turkish Section, "Russian-Turkish Economic Relations in the Post-soviet Era" (Global Challenges Research; April 19, 2005)

[19] Richard Heinberg, *The Party's Over* (New Society Publishers)

[20] James Howard Kunstler, *The Long Emergency* (Atlantic Monthly Press: New York)

[21] Tim Flannery, *The Weathermakers* (Atlantic Monthly Press: New York) and Mathis Wackernagel et al., *Tracking the Ecological Overshoot of the Human Economy* (Proceeding from the National Academy of Sciences; July 2002, Vol. 99, No. 14)

[22] Bryjak Soroka, *Sociology; 2nd Edition* (Allyn and Bacon, A Division of Simon and Schuster, Inc.)

[23] James Howard Kunstler, *The Long Emergency* (Atlantic Monthly Press: New York)

[24] Walter Youngquist, Quoted from: *Population and Environment: A Journal of Interdisciplinary Studies*; March 1999, Vol. 20, No. 4 "The Post-Petroleum Paradigm – and Population"

[25] Gwynne Dyer, "How Long Can the World Feed Itself?" (From; The Energy Bulletin, October 10, 2006)

[26] *Ibid.*

[27] Richard Heinberg, *The Party's Over* (New Society Publishers)

[28] Allen DeBlasio, Terrance Regan, Margaret Zirker, Kristen Lovejoy, and Kate Fichter, Statistics from: *Public Roads* (U.S. Department of Transportation, Federal Hwy. Admn. September/October, 2004 Vol. 68, No. 2)

[29] "Effects of the August 2003 Blackout on the New York City healthcare delivery system", *Critical Care Medicine*, January 2005 (Published by: Lippincott Williams & Wilkens)

[30] Mark Beatty, Scott Phelps, Chris Rohner, and Isaac Weifuse, *Blackout of 2003: Public Health Effects and Emergency Response* (Association of Schools of Public Health, Public Health Reports: January – February 2006, Vol. 121)

[31] *Ibid.*

[32] Bill Parks, *Transforming the Grid to Revolutionize Electric Power in North America* (U.S. Department of Energy, Edison Electric Institute's Fall 2003 Transmission, Distribution and Metering Conference, October 13, 2003)

[33] Mark Beatty, Scott Phelps, Chris Rohner, and Isaac Weifuse, *Blackout of 2003: Public Health Effects and Emergency Response* (Association of Schools of Public Health, Public Health Reports: January – February 2006, Vol. 121)

[34] Richard Heinberg, *The Party's Over* (New Society Publishers)

[35] Elinor Levy and Mark Fischetti, *The New Killer Diseases* (Crown Publishers: New York)

[36] Richard Heinberg, *The Party's Over* (New Society Publishers)

[37] S.S. Morse (Forward by: R. M. Krause), *Emerging Viruses* (Oxford University Press, 1993)

[38] Stephen Leeb, PhD, *The Coming Economic Collapse* (Warner Business Books: New York)

[39] *Ibid.*

Chapter 8– AN ECONOMY IN CRISIS

[1] Peter D. Schiff and Lynn Sonberg, *Crash Proof: How to Profit From the Coming Economic Collapse* (John Wiley and Sons, Inc.: Hoboken, New Jersey)

[2] Senator Byron L. Dorgan, *Take This Job and Ship It* (Thomas Dunne Books / St. Martin's Press: New York)

[3] *Ibid.*

[4] Duane Elgin, *Voluntary Simplicity* (William Morrow: New York)

[5] Gary B. Nash and Julie Roy Jeffrey, *The American People*; Fifth Edition (Addison-Wesley Educational Publishers)

[6] John Steele Gordon, *An Empire of Wealth* (Harper Collins Publishers)

[7] David C. Korten, *When Corporations Rule the World* (A Co-Publication of Kumarian Press Inc. and Berrett-Koehler Publishers, Inc.)

[8] William Leach, *Land of Desire* (Vintage Books, a Division of Random House, Inc.: New York)

[9] Lou Dobbs, *Exporting America* (Warner Books: New York and Boston)

[10] Senator Byron L. Dorgan, *Take This Job and Ship It* (Thomas Dunne Books / St. Martin's Press: New York)

[11] Donald L. Barlett and James B. Steel, *America: Who Stole the Dream?* (Andrews and McMeel, A Universal Press Syndicate Company: Kansas City)

[12] Senator Byron L. Dorgan, *Take This Job and Ship It* (Thomas Dunne Books / St. Martin's Press: New York)

[13] *Ibid.*

[14] Lou Dobbs, *Exporting America* (Warner Books: New York and Boston)

[15] [1] Peter D. Schiff and Lynn Sonberg, *Crash Proof: How to Profit From the Coming Economic Collapse* (John Wiley and Sons, Inc.: Hoboken, New Jersey)

[16] Released by the Associated Press, Article; "Stocks Fall Sharply as Dollar Sinks" (Mohave Valley Daily News: November 8, 2007)

[17] Riva Froymovich, Article: "Dollar Retreats Against Rivals" (The Wall Street Journal: November 27, 2007)

[18] David Enrich, Randall Smith and Damian Paletta, Article: "Citigroup, Merrill Seek More Foreign Capital" (The Wall Street Journal; January 10, 2008)

[19] Peter D. Schiff and Lynn Sonberg, *Crash Proof: How to Profit From the Coming Economic Collapse* (John Wiley and Sons, Inc.: Hoboken, New Jersey)

[20] Neil King Jr., Chip Cummins and Russell Gold, Article: "Oil Hits $100, Jolting Markets" (The Wall Street Journal; January 3, 2008)

[21] Timothy Aeppel and Sudeep Reddy, Article: "Factory Slowdown Sets Off Alarm" (The Wall Street Journal; January 3, 2008)

[22] Damian Paletta, Valerie Bauerlein and James Haggerty, Article: "Countrywide Seeks Rescue Deal" (The Wall Street Journal; January 11, 2008)

[23] John Wilen, Associated Press, Article; "$100 a Barrel, Milestone Unlikely to Shake Consumers – But Rising Prices Will Pinch Over Time" (Mohave Valley Daily News; January 3, 2008)

[24] Tom Lauricella, Liz Rappaport, and Annelena Lobb, Article: "Mounting Fears Shake World Markets As Banking Giants Rush to Raise Capital" (The Wall Street Journal; January 19-20, 2008)

[25] David Enrich, Robin Sidel and Susanne Craig, Article; "World Rides to Wall Street's Rescue" (The Wall Street Journal: January 16, 2008)

[26] *Ibid.*

[27] Nick Timiraos, Article: "Why Banks Pain Could Continue" (The Wall Street Journal; January 19-20, 2008)

[28] Susan Pulliam and Serena Ng, Article: "Default Fears Unnerve Markets" (The Wall Street Journal; January 18, 2008)

[29] Peter D. Schiff and Lynn Sonberg, *Crash Proof: How to Profit From the Coming Economic Collapse* (John Wiley and Sons, Inc.: Hoboken, New Jersey)

[30] *Ibid.*

[31] *Ibid.*

[32] William Leach, *Land of Desire: Merchants, Power, and the Rise of a New American Culture* (Vintage Books, A division of Random House Inc.: New York)

[33] *Ibid.*

[34] Christopher Lasch, *The Culture of Narcissism* (W.W. Norton and Company: New York)

[35] *Ibid.*

[36] *Ibid.*

[37] Brink Lindsey, *The Age of Abundance* (HarperCollins Publishers: New York)

[38] *Ibid.*

[39] William Leach, *Land of Desire: Merchants, Power, and the Rise of a New American Culture* (Vintage Books, A division of Random House Inc.: New York)

[40] *Ibid.*

[41] Brink Lindsey, *The Age of Abundance* (HarperCollins Publishers: New York)

[42] http://www.usatoday.com/money/perri/general/2004-03-17debtcover_x.htm

[43] John de Graff, David Wann and Thomas H. Naylor, Data from: *Affluenza: The All-Consuming Epidemic* (Berrett-Koehler Publishers, Inc.: San Francisco)

[44] http://calculatedrisk.blogspot.com/2005/03/mortgage-debt-and-trade-deficit.html

[45] Kim Kahn, "How Does Your Debt Compare?" (MSN Money: Editorial)

[46] Herb Greenburg, Article: "Americans Living Beyond Their Means" (MarketWatch)

[47] Stephen Leeb, PhD, *The Coming Economic Collapse* (Warner Business Books: New York)

[48] *Ibid.*

[49] *Ibid.*

[50] *Ibid.*

[51] Peter D. Schiff and Lynn Sonberg, *Crash Proof: How to Profit From the Coming Economic Collapse* (John Wiley and Sons, Inc.: Hoboken, New Jersey)

[52] *Ibid.*

[53] Kelly Evans and Kris Maher, Article: "Yearly Job Loss Worst Since 1945" (The Wall Street Journal; January 10-11, 2009)

[54] Justin Lahart and Kelly Evans, Article: "Consumer Woes Start to Damp U.S. Economy" (The Wall Street Journal; January 12-13, 2008)

[55] Jeannine Aversa, Associated Press, Article: "Confidence Fades as U.S. Consumers Sink to Gloomy" (The Arizona Republic: January 12, 2008)

[56] Max Jarman, Article: "Honeywell to Eliminate 240 Jobs in Phoenix" (The Arizona Republic; January 11, 2008)

[57] Max Jarman, Article: "Arizona's Semiconductor Slump" (The Arizona Republic; January 13, 2008)

[58] Justin Scheck and Ben Charny, Article: "Hewlett-Packard to Lay Off 24,600 Workers" (The Wall Street Journal; September 16, 2008)

[59] Peter D. Schiff and Lynn Sonberg, *Crash Proof: How to Profit From the Coming Economic Collapse* (John Wiley and Sons, Inc.: Hoboken, New Jersey)

Chapter 9 – THE COMING ECONOMIC POWER SHIFT

[1] William R. Clark, *Petrodollar Warfare: Oil, Iraq and the Future of the Dollar* (New Society Publishers)

[2] Peter D. Schiff and Lynn Sonberg, *Crash Proof: How to Profit From the Coming Economic Collapse* (John Wiley and Sons, Inc.: Hoboken, New Jersey)

[3] William R. Clark, *Petrodollar Warfare: Oil, Iraq and the Future of the Dollar* (New Society Publishers)

[4] *Ibid.*

[5] *Ibid:* This agreement is also documented by: David E. Spiro, *The Hidden Hand of American Hegemony: Petrodollar Recycling and International Markets* (Cornell University Press)

[6] William R. Clark, *Petrodollar Warfare: Oil, Iraq and the Future of the Dollar* (New Society Publishers)

[7] William A. Fleckenstein with Frederick Sheehan, *Greenspan's Bubbles: The Age of Ignorance at the Federal Reserve* (McGraw-Hill Books: New York)

[8] *Ibid.*

[9] *Ibid.*

[10] Peter D. Schiff and Lynn Sonberg, *Crash Proof: How to Profit From the Coming Economic Collapse* (John Wiley and Sons, Inc.: Hoboken, New Jersey)

[11] William Bonner and Addison Wiggin, *Empire of Debt* (John Wiley and Sons Inc.)

[12] Niall Ferguson, *Colossus: The Price of America's Empire* (The Penguin Press: New York)

[13] John D. McKinnon, Article: "Bush's Budget for 2009 Will Break $3 Trillion" (The Wall Street Journal; February 1, 2008)

[14] Michael M. Phillips and John D. McKinnon, Article: "Budget Hits $3 Trillion As Debt Marks Bush Legacy" (The Wall Street Journal; February 1, 2008)

[15] Joanna Slatter and Chip Cummins, Article: "Inflation Forces Gulf to Rethink Peg to Dollar" (The Wall Street Journal; November 20, 2007)

[16] Patrick Barta and Marcus Walker, Article: "Developing Economies Face Reckoning as U.S. Stumbles" (The Wall Street Journal; January 24, 2008)

[17] Peter D. Schiff and Lynn Sonberg, *Crash Proof: How to Profit From the Coming Economic Collapse* (John Wiley and Sons, Inc.: Hoboken, New Jersey)

[18] Edith M. Lederer, Article: "Economist: China Loses Faith in Dollar" (Associated Press; January 26, 2005)

[19] William Clark, Article: *Petrodollar Warfare: Dollars, Euros and the Upcoming Iranian Oil Bourse* (Media Monitors Network: August 8, 2005)

[20] *Ibid.*

[21] T.R. Reid, *The United States of Europe: The New Superpower and the End of American Supremacy* (The Penguin Press: New York)

[22] William Clark, Article: "Petrodollar Warfare: Dollars, Euros and the Upcoming Iranian Oil Bourse" (Media Monitors Network: August 8, 2005)

[23] Peter D. Schiff and Lynn Sonberg, *Crash Proof: How to Profit From the Coming Economic Collapse* (John Wiley and Sons, Inc.: Hoboken, New Jersey)

[24] Haviland, Prins, Walrath and McBride, *Cultural Anthropology: The Human Challenge*; 11th edition (Wadsworth/Thomson Learning)

Chapter 10 – THE DECLINE AND FALL OF AMERICA

[1] S.S. Morse (Forward by: R.M Krause), *Emerging Viruses* (Oxford University Press: 1993)

[2] James Howard Kunstler, *The Long Emergency* (Atlantic Monthly Press: New York)

[3] *Ibid.*

[4] *Ibid.*

[5] Judy Shelton, Article: "Security and the Falling Dollar" (The Wall Street Journal; February 15, 2008)

[6] James Howard Kunstler, *The Long Emergency* (Atlantic Monthly Press: New York)

[7] T.R. Reid, *The United States of Europe: The New Superpower and the End of American Supremacy* (The Penguin Press: New York)

[8] *Ibid.*

[9] *Ibid.*

[10] Leonard Ravenhill,, *Sodom Had No Bible* (Fires of Revival Publishing: Zachary, LA)

[11] *Ibid.*

Chapter 11 – THE NATION THAT FORGOT GOD

[1] Asim Oku, AIA Turkish Section, "Russia and Turkey in the Middle East" (Axis Information and Analysis – Global Challenges and Research; May 3, 2005)

[2] Ahmed A. Namatalla, Article: "Rachid After Closer Ties with Russia" (Daily News – Egypt; October 11, 2006)

[3] Pavel Felgenhaur, "Putin Makes Sweetheart Arms Deal to Benefit His Cronies" (Eurasia Daily Monitor; May 9, 2007)

[4] Jon Mark Ruthven, *The Prophecy That is Shaping History* (Xulon Press) and C.F. Keil and F. Delitzsch, *Keil and Delitzsch Commentary on the Old Testament*; Vol. 9, Ezekiel and Daniel (Erdmans: Grand Rapids)

[5] Flavius Josephus: translated by William Whiston, *Antiquities of the Jews*; Book 1, chapter 6 (Hendrickson Publishers)

[6] Jon Mark Ruthven, *The Prophecy That is Shaping History* (Xulon Press)

[7] Mark Hitchcock, *The Coming Islamic Invasion of Israel* (Multnomah: Sisters, OR)

[8] The Tribulation is a seven year period of severe crises and trouble at the end of the age and just prior to the second coming of Christ. It will be marked by numerous global crises and calamities including famine, economic chaos, war, and natural disasters. There will be great international distress which will usher in the rise and reign of the Antichrist. It is a period marked by global conflict and suffering as the Antichrist and his forces wage war against God and his kingdom.

[9] See Revelation chapter thirteen and Daniel chapter seven.

[10] Pre-tribulation is the belief that Jesus will return for the church at the "rapture" prior to the seven year tribulation. He will then return with the church after the Tribulation period for the 2nd coming at which time he will restore his earthly kingdom.

[11] See John 16:33, Romans 8:35-36, II Thessalonians 1:4 and II Timothy 2:12. These are just a few of the scriptures which indicate that these conditions are to be expected rather than avoided by the church.

[12] Patrick J. Buchanan, *The Death of the West* (Thomas Dunne Books, St. Martin's Press: New York)

[13] Paul Johnson, *A History of the American People* (Harper Perennial)

[14] Karen Armstrong, *The Battle for God: A History of Fundamentalism* (Alfred A. Knop: New York)

[15] Alan Brinkley, *The Unfinished Nation: A Concise History of the American People*, 4th edition (McGraw Hill" New York)

[16] Benjamin Franklin, Two Tracts: *Information to Those Who Would Remove to America* and *Remarks Concerning the Savages of North America* (Printed by John Stockdale, London – 1784)

[17] Alexis de Tocqueville, *Democracy in America* (Arlington House Press: New York)

[18] Harriet Martineau, *Society in America* (Saunders and Otley; 1873)

[19] John Brown, *An Estimate of the Manners and Principles of the Times* (London: 1757)

[20] Samuel Wigglesworth, *An Essay for Reviving Religion* (Boston: 1773)

[21] Encyclopedia Britannica, Inc., 15ᵗʰ edition — *The First Great Awakening* (The New Encyclopedia Britannica; Vol. 5)

[22] Karen Armstrong, *The Battle for God: A History of Fundamentalism* (Alfred A. Knop: New York)

[23] *Ibid.*

[24] John Steele Gordon, *An Empire of Wealth* (Harper Collins Publishers)

[25] Paul Johnson, *A History of the American People* (Harper Perennial)

[26] Carl N. Degler, *Out of Our Past: The Forces that Shaped Modern America*, 3ʳᵈ edition (Harper Perennial)

[27] *Ibid.*

[28] *Ibid.*

[29] *Ibid.*

[30] Neil Postman, *Building a Bridge to the 18ᵗʰ Century: How the Past Can Improve Our Future* (Vintage Books, a Division of Random House, Inc.: New York)

[31] Neil Postman, *Technopoly: The Surrender of Culture to Technology* (Vintage books, a Division of Random House, Inc.: New York)

[32] David Suzuki with Amanda McConnell, *The Sacred Balance: Rediscovering Our Place in Nature* (Greysone Books, The Douglas & McIntyre Publishing Group: Vancouver Toronto)

[33] *Humanist Manifesto I and II* (Prometheus Books, 1977: Buffalo, New York)

[34] Neil Postman, *Technopoly: The Surrender of Culture to Technology* (Vintage books, a Division of Random House, Inc.: New York)

[35] *Ibid.*

[36] *The Popular Bible Prophecy Commentary,* Edited by: Tim Lahaye and Ed Hindson (Harvest House Publishers" Eugene, OR)

[37] John MacArthur, *The MacArthur Bible Commentary* (Nelson Reference & Electronic, A division of Thomas Nelson Publishers)

[38] David Kupelian, *The Marketing of Evil* (WND Books, Published by Cumberland House Publishing, Inc.; Nashville, TN)

[39] *Ibid.*

[40] *Ibid.*

[41] Robert H. Dott Jr. and Donald Prothero, *Evolution of Earth*, 5th edition (McGraw Hill Inc.)

[42] Kenneth S. Deffeyes, *Beyond Oil: The View From Hubert's Peak* (Hill and Wang)

[43] William A. Haviland, Harald Prins, Dana Walrath, and Bunny McBride, *Cultural Anthropology: The Human Challenge*, 11th edition (Thomson Learning Inc.)

[44] John de Graaf, David Wann, and Thomas H. Naylor, *Affluenza: The All-consuming Epidemic* (Berrett-Koehler Publisher, Inc.)

Chapter 12 – PREPARING FOR THE STORM

[1] Leo Tolstoy, *War and Peace*

[2] Gedaliah Alon, *The Jews in Their land in the Talmudic Age* (The Magnes Press, The Hebrew University, 1984 Jerusalem)

[3] Saul Friedlander, *Nazi Germany and the Jews: 1939-1945, The Years of Extermination* (Harper Perennial)

[4] *Ibid.*

[5] *Ibid.*

[6] Laurence Rees, *Auschwitz, A New History* (Public Affairs: Perseus Book Group)

[7] Amanda Ripley, *Unthinkable, Who Survives When Disaster Strikes – and Why* (Crown Publishers)

[8] *Ibid.*

[9] Laurence Rees, *Auschwitz, A New History* (Public Affairs: Perseus Book Group)

[10] John F. Walvoord with Mark Hitchcock, *Armageddon, Oil, and Terror: What the Bible Says About the Future of America, the Middle East, and the End of Western Civilization* (Tyndale House Publishers, Inc.: Carol Stream, IL)

[11] *Ibid.*

[12] Ron Rhodes, *Northern Storm Rising* (Harvest House Publishers: Eugene OR)

[13] Steve Farrar, Dr. Blackaby is quoted by Steve Farrar in: *Get in the Ark – Finding Safety in the Coming Judgment* (Thomas Nelson Publishers: Nashville, TN)

[14] David Wilkerson, *World Challenge Pulpit Series: That Dreadful Day No One Wants to Talk About*; February 5, 2007 (World Challenge, Inc.,: Lindale, TX)

[15] David Wilkerson, *World Challenge Pulpit Series: Resting in Jesus in Perilous Times*; October 27, 2008 (World Challenge, Inc.,: Lindale, TX)

[16] Stephen Leeb, PhD, *The Coming Economic Collapse* (Warner Business Books: New York)